Studies in Literature and Religion

General Editor: **David Jasper**, Director, Centre for the Study of Literature and Theology, University of Glasgow

This is a series of interdisciplinary titles, both monographs and essays, concerned with matters of literature, art and textuality within religious traditions founded upon texts and textual study. In a variety of ways they are concerned with the fundamental issues of the imagination, literary perceptions and theory, and an understanding of poetics for theology and religious studies.

Titles include:

David Scott Arnold
LIMINAL READINGS
Forms of Otherness in Melville, Joyce and Murdoch

John D. Barbour
THE CONSCIENCE OF THE AUTOBIOGRAPHER
Ethical and Religious Dimensions of Autobiography

Tibor Fabiny
THE LION AND THE LAMB
Figuralism and Fulfilment in the Bible, Art and Literature

Max Harris
THEATRE AND INCARNATION

David Jasper (*editor*)
POSTMODERNISM, LITERATURE AND THE FUTURE OF THEOLOGY
READINGS IN THE CANON OF SCRIPTURE
Written for Our Learning
TRANSLATING RELIGIOUS TEXTS

Ann Loades and Michael McLain (*editors*)
HERMENEUTICS, THE BIBLE AND LITERARY CRITICISM

Irena S. M. Makarushka
RELIGIOUS IMAGINATION AND
LANGUAGE IN EMERSON AND NIETZSCHE

Linda Munk
THE TRIVIAL SUBLIME

George Pattison
KIERKEGAARD: THE AESTHETIC AND THE RELIGIOUS

Kiyoshi Tsuchiya
DISSENT AND MARGINALITY
Essays on the Borders of Literature and Religion

Graham Ward
THEOLOGY AND CONTEMPORARY CRITICAL THEORY

Studies in Literature and Religion
Series Standing Order ISBN 0–333–71497–0
(*outside North America only*)

You can receive future titles in this series as they are published by placing a standing order. Please contact your bookseller or, in case of difficulty, write to us at the address below with your name and address, the title of the series and the ISBN quoted above.

Customer Services Department, Macmillan Distribution Ltd, Houndmills, Basingstoke, Hampshire RG21 6XS, England

Theology and Contemporary Critical Theory

Graham Ward

Second Edition

Published in Great Britain by
MACMILLAN PRESS LTD
Houndmills, Basingstoke, Hampshire RG21 6XS and London
Companies and representatives throughout the world

A catalogue record for this book is available from the British Library.

ISBN 0–333–79031–6 hardcover
ISBN 0–333–79032–4 paperback

Published in the United States of America by
ST. MARTIN'S PRESS, INC.,
Scholarly and Reference Division,
175 Fifth Avenue, New York, N.Y. 10010

ISBN 0–312–22766–3

Library of Congress Cataloging-in-Publication Data
Ward, Graham.
Theology and contemporary critical theory / Graham Ward. — 2nd
ed.
p. cm. — (Studies in literature and religion)
Includes bibliographical references and index.
ISBN 0–312–22766–3 (pbk.)
1. Theology, Doctrinal—History—20th century. 2. Critical
theory. 3. Philosophy and religion. I. Title. II. Series.
BT85.W37 1999
230'.01—dc21   99–33805
                                                     CIP

© Graham Ward 1996, 2000

First edition 1996
Second edition 2000

This book is printed on paper suitable for recycling and made from fully managed and sustained
forest sources.

10   9   8   7   6   5   4   3   2   1
09 08 07 06 05 04 03 02 01 00

Printed and bound in Great Britain by
Antony Rowe Ltd, Chippenham, Wiltshire

Contents

Preface to the Second Edition

In the three years since the first publication of this book theological conversation has undergone something of a sea-change. Certain geographies are emerging as the Christian evangelical position is becoming distinct from the older Liberal tradition and a younger critical liberalism is staking out territory with respect to Catholic orthodoxy and Radical orthodoxy. In this regrouping the impact of critical theory has been pronounced – particularly among those critical liberals and radically orthodox theologians. More divinity schools and departments of religion and theology are developing courses in postmodern theology to reflect an increasing interest among undergraduates and postgraduates in the way critical theory is shaping the way we examine and reflect upon cultures in a digital age. Interdisciplinary work is now being encouraged in these schools and departments. In part, this is an expression of the new engagement of theological discourse with the discourses of other disciplines. In part, this is an expression of the changing economic situation in universities – the external funding of faculty-based projects, the internal encouragement for departments to work closely with each other.

These changes, and the way this book has been adopted by several teachers of Christian studies to assist in introducing students of theology to critical theory and its implications for interdisciplinary study, have made this second edition in paperback timely. Furthermore, within critical theory itself there have been new emphases. In particular, there has been an increasing interest in postcolonial and gender studies, and new demands upon poststructural thinkers to engage with the political implications of their thinking. To reflect these new emphases – and the theorists responsible for initiating them – I have added new sections. To the chapter on 'Theology and Representation' I have added an account of the work done by Judith Butler, who is at the forefront of the development in gender studies known as *queer theory*. To the chapter 'Theology and History' I have added an account of the work done by the New Historicists on the movement of social energies, particularly by Stephen Greenblatt. To the chapter 'Theology and Ethics' I have added an account of the work done by Jean-Luc Nancy, who has taken poststructural modes of thinking into discussions of political concern – freedom and community. To the chapter on 'Theology and Aesthetics' I have added an account of the work of Michel de Certeau, who has explicitly examined notions of the sublime with respect to mysticism and analyzed what makes a belief believable in any given culture.

Finally, I have lengthened my conclusion. For it does seem even more evident to me today that theological investigation, whether that investigation is Christian, Jewish, Islamic, or non-Western in its focus, is embarking upon a new era. In my conclusion, then, I suggest, through an examination of the Lacanian social theorist, Slavoj Žižek, that what we are hearing today is the theological voice that modernity repressed. We are hearing this voice not from theologians – we theologians are following in the wake of wider cultural movements. But the onus is upon those of us working in theology to examine what is being said, employing our expertise to refine and assess what is being said in the light of the theological traditions to which we belong and about which we have knowledge. What is so fundamentally different today is that a cultural space has been opened up, a space for theological engagement with those people rethinking representation, gender, ethics, politics, the aesthetic, the historical, the ideological, the hermeneutical, the anthropological. Theologians need no longer simply speak to and write for other theologians. Modernity marginalized and ghettoised in a way which dramatically narrowed our horizons and channelled our energies into in-house debates. But we have to see a new opportunity has presented itself. There is an invitation to be part of a cross-cultural conversation; not where we are the key-players, but where we have a contribution to make and a contribution that, in my experience, is welcomed.

University of Manchester GRAHAM WARD

Introduction

Thresholds are academically fashionable. Projects discussing borders, frames, frontiers, margins and edges proliferate. Divisions are not only seen as divisive, but political, pragmatic, even arbitrary. Derrida, writing about 'all those boundaries that form the running border of what used to be called a text, of what we once thought this word could identify', points to 'a sort of overrun that spoils all these boundaries and divisions and forces us to extend the accredited concept, the dominant notion of a "text" ... a "text" that is henceforth no longer a finished corpus of writing, some content enclosed in a book or its margins, but a differential network, a fabric of traces referring endlessly to something other than itself'.[1] Foucault frequently employed the image of the tide along the shoreline to describe the transgressive action of language. But the complexities of boundaries (the extent to which they are natural or conventional) and their transgression is as old as sin itself. Discussions of beginnings and endings, of birth, of death, of the sacred, of the secular, of the profane – discussions about thresholds – are a venture into the ambivalent in the hope of reclaiming something of the otherness and the silence which waits in the margins, excluded, but for that very reason, omnipresent.

To venture beyond the thresholds of our own intellectual discipline (defined by university faculties and departmental divisions of labour) is to venture into interdisciplinary studies and to question the cultural politics which separate philosophy from literature, sociology from anthropology, theology from critical theory. Theology's business has always been the transgression of boundaries. It is a discourse which requires other discourses for its very possibility. In article five of the opening *quaestio* of the *Summa Theologiae*, Aquinas observes the way the science of theology has to make use of the other sciences: 'That it uses them is not due to its own defect or insufficiency, but to the defect of our intelligence, which is more easily led by what is known through natural reason (from which proceed the other sciences), to that which is above reason.'

Much can be learnt about the difficulties and experience of living in the border lines from that master poet of thresholds and their transgression, Dante. In the last 13 lines of *Inferno*, Virgil leads Dante down 'to the farthest part' of Satan's frozen kingdom, 'which is known not by sight, but by the sound of a stream that descends there'. Here the 'Leader and I entered on that hidden road to return into the bright world, and without caring to have any rest we climbed up'.[2] Between the movement down and the movement up runs the thread of an invisible stream, the 'hidden road' and the ambivalence of 'a gentle slope'. Is the slope going up or going down? The experience of crossing thresholds, especially when we are not quite sure at what point we have crossed, is the experience of vertigo, of discovery, of surprise, of danger and therefore risk. The anthropologist, Victor Turner, in discussing sacred rites of passage, draws attention to the 'liminal period'. Liminal conditions, he points out, are transformative. A subject is taken out of the familiar and stable state of affairs and placed into a transitional space. In this way the subject is rendered 'naked' – that is, stripped of the roles and offices normative to life outside – and vulnerable. In this state the impress of the other, the unfamiliar, can be felt and the subject challenged and transformed by the encounter.[3]

Intellectual vertigo and vulnerability are the characteristics of interdisciplinary encounter. Any attempt to create a place in which theology, literature, philosophy, social anthropology, politics and psychology (the main interests of contemporary critical theory) jostle and quip will have to suffer a certain amount of vertigo and vulnerability. Just when you thought you were thinking theologically you discover metaphysical assumptions and ethnographic assumptions all caught up within the textual strategies of discourse which you simply took as 'truth'. Where do we begin to think theologically? Where are the thresholds which mark the inception and stake out the various subdivisions composing theology, on the one hand and critical theory, on the other? What standpoint can be taken above discourse from which to survey and plot the lines of social force which relate intellectual *loci*? No such standpoint exists except a pragmatic one. That is, we have to write *as if* such a standpoint were possible, *as if* our own discourse belonged to none of the intellectual disciplines upon which it is commenting, *as if* its standpoint was neutral and its author omniscient.

It is the intention of this book to proceed *as if* – to attempt to map out this interdisciplinary realm. At a time when the interdisciplinary study of literature and theology, philosophy and literature, psychology and social anthropology, politics and theology is expanding, to draw a map (however rudimentary and heuristic) is a way of enabling the student to have access to, and *some* orientation within, the vast territories of the intratextual. This book is not intended, therefore, for the initiated. It is written for the interested enquirer; for those in the study of Christian theology interested in finding a place from which to survey, and appreciate, the relevance of contemporary critical theory to that study. The book is written from a standpoint from within the study of Christian theology itself. The intention, then, is not simply to outline the different forms that such theory takes – Derrida's understanding of *différance*, for example, or Fish's appeal to a community of readers. The intention is to outline these forms of critical theory within the purview of questions raised in the study of theology. Both the resource and the relevance of contemporary critical theory for the study of Christian theology will then become evident. Let us begin, then, with those elements which comprise the study of theology.

The study of theology

This book uses the term 'theology' in a broader sense than a concern with doctrine or the teachings of a major theologian. By 'theology' what is understood in this book is 'the principle disciplines of theology'.[4] We might define these disciplines in terms of the various courses, whether optional or compulsory modular units, which are on offer within faculties of theology, divinity or religious studies. So, for example, exegesis of canonical texts (like the Old Testament, the New Testament or the Dead Sea Scrolls) plays an important role in theology. So too does the philosophy of religion, the history and development of a religion, ethics, dogmatics and pastoral studies. Specific courses are expressions of these disciplines – patristics, feminist theology, comparative religion, the sociology of religion and so on. By a process of abstraction (and reduction) we can delineate the key concerns of the study of Christian theology as: textual, exegetical, historical, philosophical, ethical, doctrinal and anthropological. Some or all of these elements are involved in any theological assignment – the emphasis given to any one being dictated by a specific nature and handling of the material involved. These key concerns relate to larger questions concerning methodology itself (how any material is approached and appreciated, for what reasons and with what results). For example, when examining the Book of Isaiah, analysis might proceed via 'form criticism' which pays attention to the genres of discourse which compose a text (hymns, liturgies, letters, prophetic utterances) and the conventions or presuppositions by which these genres function (their poetics). Analysis might proceed via 'redaction criticism', identifying various editorial layers betrayed by breaks in the narrative or the syntax or the interests propounded which point to a history of textual transmission. Or the analysis might be literary, examining the narrative structure and technique, the use of *personae*, tone, voice, the employment of various styles. However, each approach to the examination of the text treats those key concerns of history, textuality and exegesis very differently.

Methods of handling texts function on the basis of presuppositions or prejudices – blindspots that enable any method to perform a reduction of the heterogeneity and complexity of the material and its contexts (past and present). Only through such a reduction is an interpretation possible. Only on the basis of an interpretation can a thesis or argument proceed. Methodology always operates within the horizon of much larger hermeneutical (and therefore philosophical, linguistic and anthropological) concerns. The choice of method (or methods) and the awareness of the presuppositions of that method are part of a politics of meaning and an ethics of reading. The politics and the ethics are indissociable. All acts of representation as acts of communication involve the making of meaning. This making is partial and prejudicial and, therefore, all acts of communication assert and assume a certain politics. The receiving and understanding of these meaningful acts involves an ethics, a responsibility for the integrity of our response. It is the intention of this book to clarify the points at which these underlying concerns in the study of theology are treated and transformed by contemporary critical theory.

Critical theory

Critical theory has its roots in *Kulturkritik*, in the development of analyses of culture and theories of culture which began to take place in the nineteenth century on the basis of earlier ethnographies. Although there is some question concerning the sophistication of Karl Marx's theory of culture and cultural production,[5] it would be agreed that his work, and the work of Friedrich Nietzsche, did most to facilitate a critique of social existence and to promote the role of the cultural sciences in that existence. It was on the basis of their work that the Frankfurt School of critical theory emerged in the 1920s. This school included Max Horkheimer and Theodor Adomo in particular and, with some qualification, Walter Benjamin. In 1937, Horkheimer published his highly influential essay 'Traditional and Critical Theory'[6] in which he distinguished between scientific theory and theory in the cultural sciences which must acknowledge its own social and historical context. Knowledge in the human sciences is sociologically conditioned and needs to reflect upon its own determinates. However, reasoning and ideas cannot be reduced to social conditions, Karl Mannheim's work on the sociology of knowledge seems to suggest.[7] Nevertheless, a tension arises for Horkheimer between the concepts and methods which critical theory presupposes (the appeal to the rational and the universal) and cultural embeddedness of all thinking which it proposes.

In 1947, following in the wake of the National Socialist barbarism that had overtaken Germany and the German language, following in the wake also of revelations concerning the genocide perpetrated on the Jews, Horkheimer (now in the United States), along with Adorno, published *The Dialectic of the Enlightenment*. In this book critical theory was attempting 'the negation of reification'.[8] 'Reification' is an important concept in Marx's critique of culture, where it describes what happens when the worker is alienated from the product of his labour. The product becomes a fetishized commodity, a desired thing, and the labour producing it an economical property of the thing's value. The Frankfurt School saw themselves as providing a critique of the social conditions generated by the consumer capitalism of their time. They observed and commented upon the mechanization serving the greedy desire of consumer capitalism pressing everything into objects whose value was fixed by the exchange economy of goods.

With *The Dialectic of the Enlightenment*, critical social theory turned to the myths of Enlightenment reasoning itself – the reasoning which lay behind the mechanization of reality. As one scholar of this period has recently argued, with *The Dialectic of the Enlightenment*, the 'scope of critical theory is thereby extended. What is to be criticized is not simply a rationalistic conception of science, but the rationalism of the entire modern era'.[9] The critique was negative, but the negativity was part of an attempt to wipe away the mists of illusion (particularly those conjured by what was termed the 'culture industry') and liberate society from the domination of certain cultural ideologies. The critique frequently focused upon, and developed its analyses out of, literature and music, and in this way fed a growing stream of Marxist literary criticism.

George Steiner sums up the main literary and aesthetic interests of these 'para-Marxists', as he terms them:

The belief that literature is centrally conditioned by historical, social and economic forces; the conviction that ideological content and the articulated world-view of the writer are crucially engaged in the act of literary judgement; a suspicion of any aesthetic doctrine which places major stress on the irrational elements of poetic creation and the demands of 'pure form'.[10]

The concerns of contemporary inheritors of the Frankfurt School legacy – Jürgen Habermas and communication, Jean Baudrillard and simulacrum, Pierre Bourdieu and fields of symbolic production – evidently develop critical social theory's interest in the cultural and aesthetic.

Critical theory itself began to broaden the horizons of its operation, but its work was paralleled by another tradition. Rather laconically and schematically, if we can say that the critical tradition emerges with Kant towards the end of the eighteenth century and gathers pace with the prevailing neo-Kantianism that reacted against Hegel and dominated German thinking throughout the second half of the nineteenth century, then the parallel tradition is the Romantic hermeneutical tradition emerging through the work of the theologian Friedrich Schleiermacher, the philologist Wilhelm von Humboldt and idealist philosophers from Johann Gottlieb Fichte and George Wilhelm Friedrich Hegel to Wilhelm Dilthey. This tradition continued into the twentieth century with the work of Edmund Husserl and Martin Heidegger. In brief, the hermeneutical tradition sought, in various ways, to define the methods and processes whereby what is meaningful is made meaningful *for us* (whether by 'meaningful' we refer to a text or our experience of the world). The critical tradition, on the other hand, sought to develop critiques of the methods, theories and politics of these appropriators of the meaningful. So we can appreciate why the history of the two traditions is littered with conflicts – Hamann *contra* Kant, Hegel *contra* Nietzsche, Heidegger *contra* Cassirer, Heidegger (and Husserl) *contra* Adorno, and, more recently, Gadamer *contra* Derrida. To sharpen the edges of that conflict we could say that, generally, the presupposition of the hermeneutical tradition is a holism which guarantees that meaning can be discovered. On the other hand, the presupposition of the critical tradition is that meaning is always historically embedded, is always caught up with the exercise of individual and institutional 'will-to-power'. The presupposition of hermeneutics is that universal meaning exists independent of, but is accessible through, all local expressions of meaning. The presupposition of the critical tradition is that meaning is constructed – by the way we perceive, conceive and think (Kant), and by our language (Derrida). Contrary to being discovered, meaning is created and invested with value within certain cultural matrices – the critical tradition seeks to unmask the processes of such investment and their implications.

We can see from this all too brief historical survey how the hermeneutical tradition will prioritize semantics, while the critical tradition will always concern itself with semiotics: meaning and expression on the one hand, rhetoric and signs on the other. The history is not so neat in its details. We would find Heidegger's name in the ranks of both traditions depending upon what part of his *oeuvre* is under discussion and how he is being read. Similarly, the Swiss linguist Ferdinand de Saussure builds his understanding of the relativity of languages, the arbitrary signifier, and the different forms of reality embedded within each language upon the ground prepared by Humboldt's work. Yet it is upon Saussure's shoulders that much of the blame has rested for the collapse of belief in a reality independent of language. Saussure is still seen as the father of the idea that there is no getting beyond the text of the world to the meaning of the world *in itself.* In fact, this position develops from the critical distiction made by Kant between the way we make sense of our experience of the world, through the categories of of our understanding, and the way the world is in and of itself, the *Ding an sich* of which we can know nothing at all directly. This is a philosophical position which goes back to late mediaeval nominalism, particularly the linguistic theories of William of Ockham.

Nevertheless, Saussure's work marks a convenient watershed for those attempting to give historical shape to the development of critical theory. In Saussure's remarks about the arbitrariness of the linguistic sign (where the word 'arbitrary' is understood technically as meaning that there is no natural correspondence between the sign and the object signified) and language as 'a semiological phenomenon',[11] the structures of language were understood to inscribe the structures of what *is.* The world is known through the representations of it.

If language constitutes our understanding of the real, then it seems logical to assume that the methodology and conclusions of structural linguistics could be transported and applied to other cultural studies or the study of culture itself. Hence in the mid-1950s Claude Lévi-Strauss related Saussure's work to the anthropology of myths and the analysis of social laws. In 1957, influenced by Lévi-Strauss, Jacques Lacan delivered his astonishing lecture at the Sorbonne entitled 'The Agency of the Letter in the Unconscious'. In that lecture he argued that 'what the psychoanalytic experience discovers in the unconscious is the whole structure of language'. The entry into the symbolic constitutes and constructs the subject's self-identity.[12]

In a scathing and intelligent attack on structuralism and deconstruction, Thomas Pavel mapped out three major types of structuralism – the moderate, scientistic and speculative forms.[13] Moderate structuralism attempts to take certain aspects of linguistic theory and relate them to stylistics and poetics. It was dominant through the 1960s and 1970s and led to attempts to systematize the determinative characteristics or poetics of a given genre. The work of Tzvetan Todorov (Julia Kristeva's first mentor) and Gerard Genette on narrative provide examples of moderate structuralism. A brief survey of Genette's classic account of narrative structure, *Narrative Discourse* (first published in 1972 and translated into English in 1982), may assist here. For in that book the role of time in a story (dependent upon verbal tenses), the role of view-point (or how the story is constructed by the relationship between pronouns, the implicit or explicit narratorial 'I' and the other *personae*), the role of mood (the various styles employed by the writer to create literary effects) and the role of the narratorial voice – are each examined and the 'results' charted. The work of New Criticism in the United States – where the organic relationship between stylistics and meaning in a text is investigated – would provide another example of moderate structuralism. Questions of biography, authorship and historical context are displaced here.

Scientistic structuralism is based more rigorously on the study of linguistics, as is particularly evident in the work of Louis Hjelmslev and Roman Jakobson. Practitioners of scientific structuralism applied linguistic method to anthropology, semiology and narratology. In this camp we can locate the work of Lévi-Strauss, A.J. Greimas and the early Roland Barthes. *Structural Anthropology*, for example, by Lévi-Strauss, opens with a section on methodology entitled 'Language and Kinship'. Here Lévi-Strauss discusses how structural linguistics seeks to discover general laws and basic operations within spoken language. He then asks whether 'the anthropologist, using a method analogous *in form* (if not in content to the method used by structural linguistics, [might not] achieve the same kind of progress in his own science'.[14] The scientism here surfaces in the explicit association drawn between 'method' and 'progress'.

Finally, there is speculative structuralism, which is more philosophical and iconoclastic. It sought to work out the implications for metaphysical thinking of the work of Saussure, Hjelmslev and Jakobson. Jacques Derrida's *Of Grammatology* (first published in 1967 and translated into English in 1976) would be a pertinent indicator of this trend. Here Derrida, on the basis of the arbitrary relation between the signifier and the idea signified, develops the philosophical implications of there being no single origin for language and therefore no stable meaning. He examines the way this has been forgotten through prioritizing the signified object presented by the signifier. He examines how the spoken word colludes with the transparency of the signifier in relation to the signified. He proposes an abandonment of the hierarchy which has exalted the spoken over the written, on the basis of the ineradicable nature of the *graphē*, the material body of the sign. In this way we arrive at his ambivalent and by now infamous statement that *'il n'y a pas de hors-texte* [there is no outside-text]' or *'il n'y a rien hors du texte* [there is nothing outside the text]'.[15] Anything proposed outside textuality has already become textuality. Therefore, there is a nothing, a null site, posited by the text as that which is outside it. The work of Michel Foucault, Jacques Lacan and the later Roland Barthes each exemplifies speculative structuralism and, in doing so, provides a reflective critique upon structuralism which initates poststructuralism and deconstruction.

Critical theory has drawn much of its philosophical and methodological strength and its analytical rigour from these three forms of structuralism (moderate, scientistic and speculative) and also from the phenomenological and existential projects of the hermeneutical tradition. The work of each of the theorists examined in this book will return us to this cultural development. In 1987 the Critical Theory Institute was established at the University of Califomia, Irvine. Here 'critical theory' is understood to describe a multifaceted and interdisciplinary investigation into forms of critical and interpretive practice, their methods, their presuppositions and their limitations. Several of the key texts written by theorists which we will examine later were delivered as lectures at the Institute (Jacques Derrida's *Mémoires for Paul de Man*, Jean-François Lyotard's *Peregrinations* and Hélène Cixous' *Three Steps on the Ladder of Writing*, for example). David Carroll, a Professor and, at one time, Director of the Program for Critical Theory at the Irvine Institute has written that

> these forms of theory attempt to confront unexamined aspects of the dominant critical strategies and analytical methods and to deal with the contradictions and complexities inherent in traditional

questions. They seek to ask different kinds of questions or to ask questions in a different way, to make possible other forms of critical practice.[16]

This is succinctly put, and admirably sets out the continuing challenge of critical theory after the Frankfurt School, its continuing attention to specific social and textual practices and the anti-theory questions which enable critical theory both to proceed and glimpse its own provisional nature. It is now a corpus of changing and even conflicting ideas that cannot consolidate into any one school of thought or around any one strategy for the negotiation of texts. For the study of theology, too, it poses new lines of questioning. It raises to the surface of theological texts and interpretive strategies those theoretical and methodological questions frequently concealed.

There is no conceivable limit to what critical theory cannot comment upon, nor what form that comment can take. Every discipline and cultural phenomenon is swept into its purview and all representation is viewed as both ideological and a form of commentary. Critical theory is just as much at home offering a critique of the methods and assumptions of scientific investigation or jurisprudence as analysing modes of allegory and irony in Romantic poets. It can express itself in architecture or painting, just as easily as in film or music. For all these forms of cultural expression are collections of organized signs; they are forms of 'discourse'. In fact, critical theory has deepened our understanding of textuality. A text is the composition and arrangement of signs, any signs: words, colours, fabrics, details in a photograph. A text is not simply 'the wording of anything printed' (*Oxford English Dictionary*) – it is a tissue, a network, a collection of material bodies made significant through a web of differences and relationalities. It is because critical theory issues from a general semiotics that it has far wider cultural implications and applications than literary theory. It embraces literary theory by locating and interrogating it in the context of the wider philosophical and sociological issues of rhetoric and representation, power and policing.

The distinction between critical theory and literary theory is important for understanding the nature of this book. For there are several guides now available on literary theory and books introducing literary analysis to students of Biblical interpretation.[17] Similarly, since the 1950s and the pioneering work at the University of Chicago under Nathan Scott and Amos Wilder, there has been a reawakening of interest in the association of literature and theology or religion which has spawned several works mapping out interdisciplinary connections.[18] However, the *rapprochement of* literature and religion is not the primary concern of this book. The intention of this book is to locate the axiomatics for the study of theology (and the literary approach of that study) within the much broader field of questions raised by contemporary *Kulturkritik* or critical theory.

We have already sketched the governing axiomatics for the study of theology. The main concerns of contemporary critical theory are related to questions not only of discourse, but time, ontology, phenomenology, freedom (from the domination of bad faith, and for the oppressed and marginalized), thresholds and therefore finitude. Four significant sets of questions in particular have attracted the attention of critical theorists – questions of representation, questions of history, questions of ethics (individual and social) and questions of aesthetics. As we examine the work of individual theorists we will become increasingly aware of how closely these different sets of questions follow from, overlap and map upon each other. The theorists concerned, for example, with representation (Jacques Derrida, Luce Irigaray, Gayatri Spivak and Judith Butler) could equally be said to be concerned with aesthetics (Derrida), ethics (Irigaray and Butler) and history (Spivak). But in the interests of pedagogy we will proceed *as if* these four emphases (and the work of the people who exemplify them) cannot only be identified but distinguished. As discussed at the beginning of this Introduction, the experience of working on several different thresholds is vertiginous. With critical theory's transgression of boundaries, all divisions (divisions necessarily made in order to proceed) are somewhat heuristic. Within an examination of these four emphases, the aim of this book is to discuss the work of four or five major thinkers who sometimes are in conflict with each other and sometimes modify each other's proposals. There are any number of possible theorists whose work could be drawn upon, but this study cannot be exhaustive and, because of that, tries to locate seminal figures in the field near which other figures (some no less seminal) stand. So, for example, this book chooses to examine the work of Stanley Fish on 'reading' rather than that of J. Hillis Miller, and chooses to examine the work of Jacques Derrida on mimesis rather than that of René Girard. The specific choice of critical theorists is also directed by the correlation between the questions arising in the study of theology and the four emphases of critical theory (representation, history, ethics and aesthetics).

Theology as 'God-talk' and 'God-reasoning' (*theo-logos*) is intimately associated with questions of representation; Jewish, Christian and Islamic theology, as religions based in foundational historic events, necessarily are engaged in questions of history; in so far as God has traditionally been understood as absolute Good and salvation as the coming to full well-being of the person and the community, then theology is indissociable from ethics and politics; and since theology roots itself anthropologically in the religious experience of a mediated transcendence, throughout its history it has always espoused or eschewed some relation to aesthetics. Each of the four chapters in the study that follows, therefore begins by examining in detail the critical theory questions as they arise in, and are important for, the various disciplines of the study of theology. When the importance of these questions has been established the book will proceed to examine the specific work of any series of relevant critical theorists. At the end of each of the four chapters, the book will then draw out the implications for the study of theology of the way in which the questions concerning representation, history, ethics and aesthetics have been treated by contemporary critical theory.

In the Conclusion the book will briefly highlight the new directions for theology as they are opened up by the work of the critical theorists we have examined. Modernity, the age which fostered the disenchantment of the world, will be viewed, following Slavoj Žižek, as a pathological condition. At the end of modernity, the suppressed voices of theology, the return of God-talk from the other side of Nietzsche, call forth a new re-enchantment. By orchestrating some of these voices, it is hoped that the overriding intention of this book will be achieved: to facilitate a greater understanding of the exciting relevance and challenges posed by contemporary critical theory and also to facilitate a transposition of the present study of theology into a new key.

University of Manchester   GRAHAM WARD

1
Theology and Representation

Introduction

In Thomas Pynchon's kaleidoscopic novel, *The Crying of Lot 49*, the heroine, one Oedipa Mass, experiences (possibly) self-transcendence. Standing above the city of San Narciso, she stares down at the ordered streets which suggested 'a hieroglyphic sense of concealed meaning ... an intent to communicate'. A revelation

> trembled just past the threshold of her understanding. Smog hung all round the horizon, the sun on the bright beige countryside was painful; she and the Chevy seemed parked at the centre of an odd, religious instant. As if, on some other frequency, out of the eye of some whirlwind rotating too slow for her heated skin even to feel the centrifugal coolness of, words were being spoken.[1]

If theology is not to dissolve simply into psychology or, more generally, anthropology, it must have its origin in revelation. The interpretation of, or models for, revelation can differ. We understand the nature of revelation as punctuating the world with its violent intervention, or as ever-present in the world despite our blindness, or as some dialectical mediation between the poles of transcendence and immanence.[2] The way we understand how God reveals Himself will have theological consequences – for the way we view creation and history, for example. Whatever the consequences the object of such an interpretation is revelation itself – what has been given to us and which, by faith, we receive as divine. But having made the distinction between revelation and its interpretation, and pointed to how the interpretation can have further consequences for our thinking, it is

1

necessary to say that the distinction is not so easily (if ever) available. For theology is an act of representing that revelation, examining it, relating it to other aspects of our lives and knowledge of the divine.

So, if the basis for the discipline of theology is revelation, its other, equally important basis, is language itself. There can be no theology without language. There may be religious experience in some microsecond when self-consciousness is silenced and the self dissolves into the transcendent; but theology arises with the return of reflection. Theology needs and employs concepts, names, ideas, metaphors, grammar – in short, rhetoric. It requires a discourse and all discourses are culturally embedded. For concepts, names, ideas and metaphors change within, disappear from and emerge into particular historical and social conditions. Theology arises, then, from both the recognition that we are being spoken to by that which is other and exterior to ourselves and the conscious appropriation of that event, or speech-act. The conscious appropriation is a response to what has been received or experienced in that 'phase transition'; that moment of suspension when the mind is hushed and the whole being hears. Theology is, then, a peculiar form of discourse: for its single thread of thinking is composed of two voices – the other's and our own, the word given and the word received.

We can see this clearly in the way two traditional theologians – Augustine and Anselm – approach the task of doing theology.

Augustine and Anselm

Towards the close of the fourth century, sitting isolated and defensive on the North African coast, having just been made a bishop by unorthodox and contentious means, St Augustine thrashes out the question of how we know God: 'Grant me Lord to know and understand which comes first – to call upon you or to praise you, and whether knowing you precedes calling upon you. But who calls upon you when he does not know you?'[3] The questions multiply, chasing each other in the search for a definitive starting point – knowing God or responding to Him in prayer and praise. The questions multiply within a prayer itself.

The whole narrative of the way Augustine was formed into a Christian, in the context of God's ongoing creativity in the world, beginning when out of nothing the world was created,[4] is examined in *The Confessions*, through an extended prayer. However, as prayer, it is not a monologue. God too speaks throughout: bringing to mind things hidden in the recesses of Augustine's memory; revealing His hand in the pattern of Augustine's life, in the connections Augustine is allowed to see; announcing His presence in moments of mystical experience; allowing Scripture to voice in 'time-conditioned language' His eternal Word. Augustine's theology, issuing from his reflections upon the question of knowing God, is inseparable from this ongoing liturgical dialogue in prayer. It is in the circulation of this dialogue that theology takes place: in and through this weaving of two voices into one discourse. It is impossible to distinguish what is being received and what is being given. The eternal exchange between God and human beings, motivated by the desire of later finding its true satisfaction in the circulating, trinitarian desire of the other, is the main focus of Augustine's attention. Without the use of language, without the dialogue found and pursued in language which incarnates the twofold desiring, this unending doxology, there can be no theology.

During the dark, cold winter months of 1092–3, prior to accepting the Archbishopric of Canterbury, Anselm began his treatise on the incarnation, *Cur Deus Homo*. Significantly, the idea arose and was encouraged through conversations with his friend Gilbert Crispin concerning the arrival in London of several learned Jews from Mainz. It is composed as a dialogue between Anselm and his pupil of seven years standing, Boso, who came over to England to help with the writing.[5] The theology, then, literally materializes and takes shape in and through a series of conversations.

The conversations are between fellow Benedictines; they materialize through friendship. By extension, the two figures exemplify the mutual edification that is continually occurring among members of the wider Church. For Anselm's theology of the incarnation and atonement rests upon an insight into the task of theology which he pithily announced in his earlier work *Proslogion* as 'faith seeking understanding'. Boso explains: 'As the right order requires us to believe the deep things of the Christian faith before we undertake to discuss them by reason; so to my mind it appears as a neglect if, after we are established in the faith, we do not understand what we believe.'[6]

We believe first and theology is the ongoing reflection upon that belief as we live and bring the experience of that living into a Christian understanding. It is the reflection upon a practising of what is, and what is continually being affirmed as, believed. Furthermore, Crispin and Anselm as Archbishop consider the Christian faith as they encounter the Jewish faith directly in London. Their reflections, which are the ruminations of the Church, seek to articulate (and therefore to represent) the logic and coherence of their Christian belief about salvation in the context of other belief systems. As such, theology brings together two horizons (to use an image made famous by the twentieth-century German philosopher of interpretation Hans Georg Gadamer). The first horizon is composed of those sources of our faith in which we have believed – the Scriptures, the Creeds and the teachings of the Church as they have been passed down and modified over the years. The second horizon is composed of all those things which constitute the context in which we practise our believing and which engage our theological thinking in the present. For Anselm that included the Jewish people arriving from Mainz, the socio-political structure of eleventh century Norman feudalism and a friendship with a pupil, Boso, who had been trained in Biblical exegesis and logic at Laon (a Cathedral school at the forefront of Mediaeval education). Theology, then, gives expression to an ongoing conversation between past texts and present contexts. It is a self-conscious form of what has come to be called 'intertextuality', in which one or more discourses are transposed by being re-articulated within another.[7] Because the conversation is ongoing, because contexts are always contingent, so theological expression will constantly change. In its examination of the doctrines of faith it will interpret and discuss these doctrines in terms available within, and comprehensible to, its contemporary context. Anselm's early medieval answer to the question '*Cur Deus homo?*' will not be ours. We will express the nature of the incarnation in a different way; a way which reflects the language and emphases of the present time.

Past texts and present contexts constitute the two voices being woven throughout Anselm's theological discourse. Augustine's theology, in *The Confessions*, can also be understood in a similar manner, albeit with the deeper dialogue between God and Augustine framing the whole work. We could schematize the differences in the relationship between theology and language as, the primary dialogue – between God and his human beings – and the second dialogue between present human beings and authoritative texts in which God has revealed himself to and through His Church. It is the nature and relationship of these interlaced dialogues which feeds that crowd of pressing questions concerning 'God-talk', 'God-reasoning' (*theo-logos*). Immediately, one of those pressing questions is identified: God does not exist in the world as natural science describes it. He is not an object visible among other objects. The statements 'oranges are fruit' and 'God is good' (or even Nietzsche's famous 'God is dead') are syntactically similar, but as kinds of statement, they are very different.

To what, therefore, do theological statements refer? What do they mean? In what relation do they stand to statements in other disciplines – aesthetic statements, ethical statements, philosophical and psychological statements, and so on?

Analogy

Traditionally, these questions have been answered with reference to the nature of analogy. Analogy describes a relationship between two objects; it is both a relationship of difference and also a relationship of similarity. In the case of theology the two 'objects' are God and aspects of his creation. If we said that nothing in our language could speak of God in a way that gives us any knowledge of God, then all theologians could only, at best, be agnostic (from *agnosko* – to be ignorant of). If we said that all our language referred to God with as equal a facility as it referred to things human, then God would become an extension of all things human. God would be anthropomorphized. Analogy offers a way between disparity or equivocity, on the one hand, and parity or univocity, on the other. It suggests a path between the twin dangers of agnosticism and anthropomorphism, a relationship of similarity-in-difference. Analogy offers some 'partial agreement and correspondence of our words with God's being'.[8] So Karl Barth wrote, in Chapter Five of his *Church Dogmatics*, which is concerned with discussing the relationship between language and our knowledge of God. We will return to Barth later. For the moment let us develop this notion of analogy through the famous exposition of the doctrine given by Thomas Aquinas.

With Suarez in the late sixteenth century a distinction was drawn between analogy of attribution (*analogia attributionis*) and analogy of proportionality (*analogia proportionalis*). In the former, a property *x* is held to belong properly to one object and improperly to a second. Aquinas discusses the example of the word 'healthy'. In the phrases 'I am healthy' and 'I have a healthy appetite' – 'healthiness' is understood to belong to the subject 'I' properly or directly, but it belongs to the appetite only by extension (because the appetite belongs to the 'I'). The appetite is a sign of the health of the 'I'. The 'I' here, or the object possessing the property directly, is then termed the 'prime analogate'. This is an example of *analogia attributionis*. In the analogy of proportionality both objects possess the same property properly and directly, though in different proportions. Here both share in common a third thing. In fact, this third thing becomes the basis of a certain univocity between them. In the late mediaeval world picture certain flowers were thought to contain properties relating them to the stars or the moon or the sun. Here both objects share in a third state in proportion to where they stand in the earthly and heavenly hierarchy. But Aquinas discusses the following example: 'the name of lion applied to God means only that God manifests strength in His works, as a lion in his' (1, Question 13, Article 6). The two objects share nothing in common; the name 'lion' is therefore used metaphorically in this case; for a word having provenance only within the creaturely realm is transferred to that which transcends the creaturely realm entirely. Aquinas concludes that only certain terms become analogues. Terms like 'wise', 'good' and 'love' can give us some partial knowledge of God for these are perfection terms belonging to God essentially and to his creatures by extension. But they are not just attributed, for we do really possess them in a creaturely form. When we employ them we suggest something is shared: for our love is not love, our goodness not goodness, nor our wisdom wisdom unless these qualities participate and share in the perfection of all things in God. Aquinas is developing here a notion which later became known, wrongly, as analogy of being, *analogia entis*. For we share these qualities because we, as creatures, exist only with respect to the perfection and source of being in God. But care must be taken here, for Aquinas will stress that our being and God's being are not the same. God's being is uncreated. So being itself is not a third thing that associates creatures and the divine such that creatures possess the same being only proportionally less because of their lower standing in a hierarchy linking all things to God as the most real thing. The later teaching on the *analogia entis*, which gave rise to natural theology and to the design and cosmological arguments for the existence of God is not Aquinas' teaching.[9] For the erasure of the difference between God's uncreated and perfect essence and our created existence would only compromise the transcendence of the divine. For Aquinas, then, most of our language about God is metaphorical and only those terms which can be infinitely extended can become a name for that which exists perfectly in God.

In this century, Karl Barth redefined the doctrine of analogy for Protestants. He did this by extending the analogy of attribution to cover all our language. He claimed that 'Our words are not our own property, but His ... We use our words improperly and pictorially ... when we apply them within the confines of what is appropriate to us as creatures. When we apply them to God they are not alienated from their original object and therefore from their truth, but, on the contrary, restored to it.'[10]

This he called the analogy of faith or the analogy of Christ. He describes this as an *analogia attributionis extrinseca* – in other words, creaturely reality does not intrinsically possess any property which belongs essentially and directly to God; it does not share or participate in anything divine. Creaturely reality can only be given such a property as a gift, by grace in revelation, from outside (*extrinseca*) itself.

Metaphor

Now there is no need at this point to detail the arguments which have raged over Aquinas' and Barth's doctrines of analogy.[11] We simply note here the continuing preoccupation of theologians with the nature of language and its representations of God. In fact, more recently, and continuing an ambivalent response to the sacramentalism of signs which emerged in the Protestant Reformation, there has been a move away from discussing analogy and the logic of theological discourse. Today, in the wake of an interest in symbolism throughout the early part of this century and the work done, both in the sciences and the humanities, on models and metaphor, the debates about the language of theology have taken a different direction. 'The Protestant tradition is, I would suggest, "metaphorical"; the Catholic, "symbolic" (or, "analogical" for contemporary Catholicism)', one leading American theologian writes.[12]

Investigations into the resources of metaphor have opened up new inquiries for Christian theology – from feminists, from ecologists, from those interested in Christianity's relation to other religions. In this move towards the evaluation of metaphor, theology cuts across one of the fundamental preoccupations of current critical theory. Discussions about metaphor (along with other forms of figural expression, such as metonymy and allegory) play a significant role in the diverse projects of Jacques Lacan, Paul Ricoeur, Jacques Derrida, Paul de Man and Jean-François Lyotard. The emphasis given to metaphor (and its opposite, metonymy) in structural linguistics has fostered the current interest in rhetoric and writing. Discussions about figurative language in post-structuralist and deconstructionist thought issues from the profound way in which language and linguistics have come to dominate discussions in philosophy, anthropology and ethnography in this century. What has attracted recent discussion in theology to metaphor can be summed up with reference to two important books on this topic, by Sallie McFague and Janet Martin Soskice.

McFague understands metaphor in terms of effective power. She asks 'What is it about a religious metaphorical statement which makes it more powerful than a symbolical statement?'[13] Metaphors have the ability to speak of that which is unknown or ineffable. Metaphorical thinking is the way we all think – by making comparisons between the known and the unknown. Effective comparisons in metaphorical statements shock or surprise – that is, they have an emotional effect upon readers. They are transformative. We will return to this in Chapter 4, when we examine reader–response theory. For the moment we are going to concentrate on metaphor as 'the way by which we understand as well as enlarge our world and change it'.[14] Metaphors transform our world by replacing the old and outworn with the new. In this way, metaphors comment critically on conceptual idols. For example, feminists will draw attention to the patriarchal idolization of God as a He. Metaphors do not fix meaning and so they cannot, therefore, become the object of idolatry. Their inherent instability of reference keeps meaning open, tentative and iconoclastic. They articulate and generate a surplus of meaning. By calling for interpretation, metaphors draw the reader into an engagement with the world they configure. They draw the reader into a relationship with the text, a world which is other than their world. Reading and interpreting metaphorical descriptions of other worlds (the world of the New Testament, for example) is an exercise in self-transcendence. The authority of the Scripture (always a key note in Protestant systematic theology) lies in its status as a 'classic' literary text – a text which forever opens itself to new understandings because of the fundamental openness of its metaphorical discourse.[15] Revelation (another key note in Protestant systematic theology) is now viewed as non-hegemonic, non-authoritarian. It is the constant unfolding of the transformative power of the Word in and through metaphorical discourse.

McFague's position owes much to critical theory, particularly the analysis of discourse in the interpretation theory of Paul Ricoeur. Ricoeur views metaphor as a revelatory event, 'an event in discourse'.[16] Metaphors have ontological value, a value which manifests itself when 'the literal sense is left behind so that the metaphorical sense can emerge ... The eclipse of the objective, manipulable world thus makes way for the revelation of a new dimension of reality and truth'.[17]

Where McFague emphasizes the existential function of metaphor (which heightens the role of the reader), Janet Martin Soskice concentrates upon the cognitive function of metaphor. Her book presents a much more analytical account of metaphor best suited to her concern to free religious language from a residual critique by positivists and empiricists who have denied the logical coherence of language employing transcendental terms. She analyses metaphor in order to define the conditions upon which we can speak of 'theological realism'. As with McFague, Soskice draws attention to how metaphor emphasizes 'the importance to Christian belief of experience, community, and an interpretative tradition'.[18] But she wants to make epistemological rather than ontological claims for metaphor. Rather than metaphors giving rise to a transcending experience of a new world (McFague), Soskice wishes to understand the reference of metaphor as the grounding experience from which the metaphorical articulation arose. Of the Scriptures, she writes: 'the touchstone of these chronicles of faith is experience, experiences pointed or diffuse, the experience of individuals and of communities which are believed to be experiences of the activity of the transcendent God'.[19]

Laying to one side the spectre of Gnosticism conjured, according to her critics, by McFague and the return of Soskice to an empirical correspondence theory of language, according to her critics,[20] theology's perennial concern with the nature of its discourse is evident. At the beginning of his monumental systematic theology, Karl Barth re-emphasizes that the task of Christian theology is 'the self-examination of the Christian Church in respect of the content of its distinctive talk about God'.[21] Traditionally, as we have seen, this has taken place through an examination of analogy and metaphor and, related to these, symbols, icons and models.

The study of theology

The question now is, given this dependence of theology upon examining its own language, what does critical theory's redescription of the nature and operation of language imply for the study of theology? We can only begin to ask this question having outlined critical theory's work on language. We will now do this by looking at the work of four figures: Jacques Derrida, Luce Irigaray, Gayatri Chakravorty Spivak and Judith Butler. We could have looked at this question through the work of Michael Foucault, Jean-François Lyotard, Jacques Lacan or Michel de Certeau – each of whom have written about the operation of language with respect to various fields: theories of power, jurisprudence, psychology and historiography. Derrida and Irigaray were chosen partly because the work of Foucault, Lyotard and Certeau will be discussed elsewhere and Irigaray is indebted to Lacan. Derrida and Irigaray were chosen partly also because the contributions these two thinkers have made to critical theory issue from the work they have both done on meaning and representation. Both Spivak and Butler extend and apply the work of Derrida and Irigaray; the former with respect to postcolonial and subaltern studies, and the latter with respect to the subversion or queering of gender. The work of all four thinkers has profound implications for theology as a discourse and how theology understands the practice of the faith it reflects upon.

Jacques Derrida

'I was born in El-Biar in the suburbs of Algiers in a petit-bourgeois Jewish family which was assimilated', Derrida informed one interviewer.[22] The year was 1930. Nineteen years later, he came to post-war France having gained a place at France's most elite academic establishment, the *Ecole Normale Supérieure* (ENS). Foucault had gone to the school three years earlier, but Georges Dumezil, Jean Hyppolite, Jean-Paul Sartre, Raymond Aron and Louis Althusser formed only part of the intellectual lineage into which Derrida was grafted. Philosophically, this was a time when Sartre was dominant, but in the ENS discussions of Hegel had the ascendency. There were other exciting subcurrents. Lévi-Strauss was publishing his articles on anthropology between 1945 and 1956, developing the structuralism that announced itself in *Structural Anthropology* (1958). Lacan, paying homage to Lévi-Strauss and reading for himself the work of Ferdinand de Saussure, was intensifying his attack on ego psychology that would find powerful expression in *Ecrits* (1966). Structuralism was emerging, and it is in the wake of structuralism that, in 1967, Derrida forcefully announced his presence to the academic world with the publication of *Speech and Phenomena and Other Essays on Husserl's Theory of Signs, Of Grammatology* and *Writing and Difference*.

Several commentaries upon and discussions of Derrida's work are now available,[23] but what we will examine here, bearing in mind what we have already noted concerning the language of theology, is the move Derrida makes beyond structural linguistics in his analysis of discourse. For this we need a brief account of the development of structural linguistics from Ferdinand de Saussure to Roman Jakobson and Louis Hjelmslev.

Structural linguistics

For Ferdinand de Saussure, the Swiss philologist lecturing in the early decades of this century in Geneva, the structure of language is constituted by two axes. There is the diachronic axis which reveals the morphology or changes which occur in any language. It is concerned with movement in time – 'Historical phonetics … is the first object of study in diachronic linguistics'.[24] History is mapped out along a chain of signifying elements, a chain of signs. Diachronic linguistics is concerned with *la parole* – the utterance or speech-act – its sound, the arbitrary signs it employs, and the way one of these signs (or signifiers) follows upon another in an endless sequence. As discussed in the Introduction to this book (p. xv), by 'arbitrary' Saussure means that the signifier 'has no natural connexion in reality',[25] the relationship between the signifier and what it signifies emerges from social convention. There is also the synchronic axis. This constitutes the timeless, abstract system of language (*la langue*) amenable to scientific study. It is an axis of simultaneity where certain general laws are evident. 'To synchrony belongs everything called "general grammar"'.[26] What is important in the operation of language along these two axes is that its mechanism (how it communicates) 'turns entirely upon identities and differences. The latter are merely counterparts of the former'.[27] What Saussure means by this is that signification takes place only through relations and differences between linguistic units. These relations and differences take two main forms. First, there are what Saussure terms 'syntagmatic relations'. For example, the meaning of any noun is related to its contextual difference from a verb, a definite article or a preposition. In the phrase 'to force someone's hand', the meaning of the phrase or syntagma depends upon the relation of, and the distinction between, the infinitive 'to force', the noun 'hand' and the indefinite pronoun 'someone'. The second of these relational differences is what Saussure terms 'associative relations'. For example, a 'boat' is not a 'ship', a 'yacht' or a 'dinghy', though its meaning arises from association with these other words. A 'boat' is also not a 'coat' or a 'moat' or a 'stoat'. The association may emerge through identical word-stems to which are added different prefixes or suffixes or the connotative freight any word carries. That the mechanism of meaning in any language depends upon this series of relations and differences will become very important for Derrida.

Saussure's work was taken up, criticized and developed by Roman Jakobson. Though Jakobson was not as convinced as Saussure that the nature of the sign was arbitrary (see his important essay 'Quest for the Essence of Language'[28]), he agreed that language functioned along two fundamental axes. He too characterizes these lines in terms of contiguity and simultaneity, but he calls the two axes metonymy (which operates diachronically) and metaphor (which operates synchronically).[29] He gives them the names of these tropes because these tropes are condensed forms presenting models of the two antithetical operations themselves. For Jakobson every symbolic process is located within the relations, and yet distinctions, between these two axes. However, certain symbolic forms give more emphasis to one of these axes than the other. Hence the metaphoric axis is more prevalent in lyric poetry and the metonymic in prose and realistic fiction.

It is by drawing upon these two writers (and the work of Jakobson's colleague in the Prague Circle, N.S. Trubetzkoy) that Lévi-Strauss announces his foundation for structural anthropology, and structuralism infiltrates the fields of cultural and literary criticism, and philosophy.[30] In several essays written in the mid-1960s, Derrida criticizes structuralism for its metaphysical presuppositions, and then in *Of Grammatology* he presents his own account of Saussure, Jakobson and Hjelmslev in order to develop his thesis that 'the idea of the sign ... must be deconstructed through a meditation upon writing' (*Of Grammatology*, p. 73). His central criticism concerns what he terms the 'phonocentrism' or the temporal and logical priority which structural linguistics gives to the spoken word over its written representation. Despite Saussure's observations that the sign is arbitrary and functions only through difference, his emphasis is not upon the inscribed nature of this sign but upon the communication which takes place through speech. Furthermore, he treats the idealization of this speech-act, *la parole*, by preferring to examine the synchronic rather than the diachronic operation of the sign.

Writing is an external event to language, for Saussure; not part of language itself. The spoken word is the direct and unsullied presentation of meaning now; phonetics is the science of the spoken word, the science relating speech to meaning. In this way all European linguistics from Saussure to Hjelmslev bind linguistics to semantics (*Of Grammatology*, p. 50). This privileging of the spoken (and the concurrent secondariness of the written) Derrida relates to 'logocentrism', a desire for, or a belief in, the possibility of the unmediated presence of the object signified. 'The system of language associated with phonetic–alphabetic writing is that within which logocentric metaphysics, determining the sense of being as presence, has been produced' (*Of Grammatology*, p. 43). The object of his own early work was 'to give to the theory of writing the scope needed to counter logocentric repression' (*Of Grammatology*, p. 51). That is, he wishes to show how the written works to undo the suggestions of meaning directly presenced through the sign and requires also an examination of the historical movement forward of language. Writing involves us in re-presentation, in mediated meaning and process. This desire for fully presenced meaning, for the sign as revealing the immediate truth, is ultimately, for Derrida, theological in nature. '[T]he humbling of writing beneath a speech dreaming of plenitude' such is the gesture 'required by an onto-theology determining the archeological and eschatological meaning of being as presence, as parousia' (*Of Grammatology*, p. 71). Full presence is summed up in the Hellenistic concept of the Logos and 'Infinitist theologies are always logocentrisms' (*ibid.*).

What is significant for theologians here is that Derrida is attacking a certain form of theology: the use of God within classical rationalism and Enlightenment Deism. The God Nietzsche declared dead. By 'infinitist' theology we take it that he is referring to a theology which does not recognize the limitations of its own language. He frequently mentions Leibniz or Hegel as examples of logocentric theologians. The discourse of such theologians is 'the discourse of someone who is satisfied with metaphors' (*Margins of Philosophy*, p. 267). Such 'theologians' do not question the nature of their own language and they fall victim to a conceptual idolatry.

The economy of *différance*

Derrida's critique of linguistics develops into his own analysis of the nature of language, and a host of terms emerge to aid such an analysis: deconstruction, *différance*, erasure, trace, iterability and supplementarity, are among the most well known. These terms are not used systematically or uniformly throughout Derrida's work. New terms are invented, picking up and expanding word plays within the various texts he is examining. However, these terms have more uniformity than most and describe processes at work in language-use (discourse) which have been Derrida's dominant concern. What remains uppermost in Derrida's employment of these terms is the heterogeneous nature of language. It is not simply that the written is now privileged over the spoken, absence of meaning over the presence of meaning. It is rather that language is understood to have a double origin or communicate through two voices. As Derrida describes it: 'Two texts, two hands, two ways of listening. Together simultaneously and separately' (*Margins of Philosophy*, p. 65). The doubleness, the radical difference between the spoken and written, the present and absent is seen to be older than Being itself. It is this difference which constitutes language and is itself constituted within language. 'Beyond Being and beings, this difference, ceaselessly differing from and deferring [itself]' (*ibid.*, p. 67). He terms this alterity a 'quasi-transcendental'. A transcendental is that which stands as the condition for the possibility of something, the unconditioned and foundation principle. Philosophy of religion since at least the Enlightenment has frequently viewed God as the foundational principle. By calling this alterity a quasi-transcendental, Derrida is drawing attention to an ability to substantiate difference. It is not a noun, the process of differing and deferring is continuous but allusive, always given in something else, always existing as a trace of what has passed. As such, this quasi-transcendental can never found or establish a philosophical system. In his more recent work – *Of Spirit* (English translation, 1989) and *Specters of Marx* (English translation, 1994) – the operation of this difference, this otherness or alterity is likened to a haunting. 'This logic of haunting would not be merely larger and more powerful than ontology ... It would harbour within itself ... eschatology and teleology themselves' (*Specters of Marx*, p. 10).

It is this doubleness, its production through the other, its economy as a gift which can never be grasped[31] and its consequences, which Derrida investigates in all his work. Derrida describes this doubleness most clearly in his early essay *'Différance'*, his reply to John Searle, *Limited Inc.*, and his reply to questions by Gerald Graff, 'Afterword: Towards An Ethic of Discussion' (see *Limited Inc.*). He begins by returning to Saussure's observations on the arbitrary nature of the sign and on its differential character. Signs represent a presence in its absence; the 'sign would be a deferred presence' (*Specters of Marx*, p. 138). *Différance* announces both the differential character of the sign and the deferral of the sign's meaning. *Différance* names the play between meaning and difference: 'we shall designate by the term *différance* the movement by which language, or any code, any system of reference in general, becomes "historically" constituted as a fabric of differences' (*Speech and Phenomena*, p. 141). Meaning is always already caught up in a system of signs which mediates it. Thus the ontological project of logocentrism is undermined, for 'Presence is a determination and effect within a system which is no longer that of presence but that of difference' (*ibid.*, p. 147). It is an economy because the desire for presence entails that language is always trying to overcome the deferral of meaning which it continually inscribes. Hence, there is the promise of a final eschaton in the economy of discourse itself.[32] In the communication of meaning, discourse needs and generates further discourse in an endless movement towards an ever-to-be postponed telos. Discourse is inseparable from a continual movement of displacement and dissemination (what Derrida will term 'supplementation'). However, each supplement, in trying to complete the meaning of that which went before it, also reproduces the inadequacy, with the result that communications, while generating further texts, require still further qualification.

In this way, Derrida suggests the openness of textuality to an indefinite future, a deferred eschaton – an openness which cannot be closed. We are always *in media res* – moving between an origin which can never be recovered or single and a conclusion which can never be determined. We occupy a place, as such, in the shifting sands of semiotic systems, haunted by the possibility of presence and stable identity, but forever unable to produce it. This state, for Derrida, is no apocalyptic crisis. For while the promise is deconstructable, it nevertheless remains as a witness to what is absolutely heterogeneous: the *nothing* which always remains outside and conditions the possibility for the text. What this absolute heterogeneity is, Derrida cannot say. In fact, it cannot be said, without falling into the clutches of deference. Throughout his work, Derrida reaffirms this promise or what he terms a quasi-transcendental. In his essay 'Ulysses Gramophone: Hear Say Yes in Joyce' (1987), he has spoken of an ineradicable 'yes' adhering to discourse. In 'Afterword' he writes: 'I have on several occasions spoke of "unconditional" affirmation or of "unconditional" appeal. This has also happened to me in other "contexts" and each time that I speak of the link between deconstruction and the "yes"' (*Limited Inc.*, p. 152). He continues, describing the double nature of *différance*:

> there are only contexts ... nothing exists outside context, as I have often said, but also that the limit of the frame or the border of the context always entails a clause of nonclosure. The outside penetrates and thus determines the inside. (*Ibid.*, pp. 152–3)

He has called this promise, this appeal, this unconditional affirmation which penetrates from outside, the trace (developing it from Heidegger's understanding of *die Spur* and Levinas' own use of the word 'trace').[33] The trace, for Derrida, is not the appearance of a transcendent present (as it is for Levinas), nor an immediate presentation of meaning within language, it is 'the simulacrum of a presence' (*Speech and Phenomena*, p. 156). The 'yes' is always a 'yes, yes'. The promise is always caught up in the doubling of being represented, mediated. The trace is always, in being discussed, effaced by the very language which makes it known. This is the central issue of what Derrida terms 'iterability' in language. That is, that signs must be repeatable if they are to mean anything, if they are to gain social currency. The very repeatability of signs destabilizes their meaning by setting up differences and deferrals of meaning or identity. Thus a logic of non-identical repetition is established in which the presence of the promise is always represented. The present, then – or, theologically, presence – is always twice removed from us. First, presence is always constituted through an act of remembering an event which already lies in the past. This implies there is a gap between event and consciousness. Secondly, presence has to be signified by signs which, by their very nature, announce the absence of that which is present; which substitute for that presence. The economy of the sign pushes the possibility for presence into the future. On the basis of this there arises Derrida's concern for time and our relationship to a future anterior (a verb tense in the French language).

Thus, while language raises the question of the transcendent and Derrida will continually ask concerning the economy of *différance* 'What differs? Who differs?' (*Speech and Phenomena*, p. 145) – it also radically qualifies any talk of revelation, epiphany, manifestation of truth. For no such immediacy is possible. The mediation of language and representation cannot be transcended. This does not, though, imply what is called a linguistic idealism. That is, that reality is always and only constructed through language. The point of Derrida's insistence on the quasi-transcendental, the promise and the trace, is that changes and developments in language are governed *both* by the immanent processes of socialization and by a beyond. The difficulty lies in the impossibility of stipulating the nature of that beyond. Arguing against his critics, Derrida writes: '*Différance* is not indeterminacy. It renders determinacy possible and necessary" (*Limited Inc.*, p. 149). Nevertheless, *différance* 'does mean that every referent, all reality, has the structure of a differential trace, and that we cannot refer to this "real' except in an interpretative experience' (*Limited Inc.*, p. 148). The question of what we might understand by 'interpretative experience' will be examined in Chapter 4.

Aporias and the theological question

In Derrida's model for the operation of discourse, then, it is not that rhetoric is all, but that the real is infected ineradicably by the metaphoric. Discussions of the real can only proceed therefore by becoming blind or deaf to the metaphoric. This, as we saw earlier, is how Derrida characterizes theological discourse. The signification of meaning always participates in an instability. Hence Derrida's fondness for titles and phrases which defy translation: *'Plus de metaphor'*, *'Des Tours de Babel'*. *'Plus de metaphor'*, for example, translates as 'more metaphor', 'more about metaphor', 'metaphor's excess' or 'no more metaphor', 'no more about metaphor' or 'no metaphor's excess'. The sheer untranslatability of the idiom instantiates a node of non-reducible meaning, a doubleness so antithetical ('more metaphor', 'no more metaphor') that, rather like Wittgenstein's portrayal of aspect-blindness,[34] we cannot accommodate two different possible meanings simultaneously. The sheer incomprehension, where one meaning counteracts the other, forces upon us the resistance of the text itself. The text itself becomes a sort of hole, or *aporia* through which we glimpse the indefinable. As Derrida has written very recently: 'this instability can even lead us elsewhere, and in truth can lead us to the limits from which the instability itself proceeds, at the very origin of the destabilizing movement' *(Aporias*, p. 65).

It is engaging in this kind of transcendental argument, where language folds in upon itself to offer a trace of the 'origin of the destabilizing' which has frequently led to Derrida discussing *différance* and deconstruction in terms of negative theology.[35] But Derrida is emphatic and, it seems, correct that the economy of *différance* is not a form of negative theology; for the unnamable space it opens up cannot be filled by 'some ineffable being ... like God, for example' *(Speech and Phenomena*, p. 159, also p. 134). In naming this site of absolute heterogeneity 'God' (as Levinas does), Derrida would move beyond the philosophical and embrace the theological; that is, he would make a move in faith, and construct an *a priori* argument. Nevertheless, Derrida has always recognized that descriptions of this economy 'will resemble ... those of negative theology' *(Speech and Phenomena*, p. 134). In his 1986 essay, 'How to Avoid Speaking: Denegations', he compares three modes of 'not-saying', explicitly drawing a comparison between the movement of discourse in negative theology (particularly the work of Pseudo-Dionysius and Eckhart) and *différance*. He concedes that a theological question concerning hyper-essentiality, remains lodged in the 'heart of any thought about difference' *(Psyché*, p. 542). The point for him is that '[I]t remains a question' that brings about a kenosis within signification, a continual pouring out of the meaningful. It cannot be named God and the question turned into a statement of identity. In remaining a question, it remains other, it remains different – outside the hegemony of reduction to the human subject. This is essential to Derrida's project – to locate and restore the place of the irreducible other as it is traced in discourse. It is not only traced, but it is the condition for discourse; a discourse constantly aware that it mourns the absence of this other:

> [as] an originary mourning, then the self-relation welcomes or supposes the other within its being-itself as different from itself. And reciprocally: the relation to the other (in itself outside myself, outside myself in myself) will never be distinguishable from a bereaved apprehension. (*Aporias*, p. 61)[36]

The condition of consciousness, of knowledge and language is '*un temps perdu*', an ancient memory and a futural promise of return upon which all else is founded and confounded, constructed and deconstructed.[37]

Luce Irigaray

When we turn to the work on representation by the French feminist, Luce Irigaray, some of the same themes we found in Derrida's work reappear. There is the concern with difference and alterity in an attempt to think the unthought; the concern to outline an economy in which difference creates a space (a space Irigaray will determine as the site of the sacred or divine); the concern with what is left out and external, and yet constitutive by being outside; a method of analysis which develops as an intertext – that is, a text which reads other texts, uncovering a hidden or forgotten voice within that other text. She too, in wanting to focus upon the semiotic – the realm of symbolic representation, its politics and its power – builds upon the work of Saussure and Jakobson. However, Irigaray's project differs from Derrida's in that her own emphasis is on sexual difference. The human thinking subject is always a sexed subject. With Irigaray representation and textuality, so important as we saw to theological study, encounters feminism. Her work on language and sexuality develops out of the impact structural linguistics had upon psychoanalysts working in the wake of Jacques Lacan.

Born in Belgium of a Catholic family in 1930, Irigaray's first articles, in the late 1960s, were concerned with psycho-linguistics. Some of these are now translated in her volume *Speaking is Never Neutral* [*neutre*].[38] In 1974, she published her Doctorate of Letters thesis for the University of Paris VIII, *Speculum of the Other Woman*, followed in 1977 by *This Sex Which is Not One.* These early books provide the theoretical background to what has become her central project: the recognition that culture is sexuate and that the female imaginary has had little or no representation in a culture that for centuries has been patriarchal.

Hence, the Western metaphysical concern with the one, the Logos, the logical, the coherent, the identified and the sexually neutral has suppressed the other scene, the feminine as other and not recognized how deeply hom(m)osexual it has been. The constitutive work of difference has gone unacknowledged.

We will explore the meaning of 'sexuate' and 'imaginary' later.[39] Before outlining Irigaray's project we need to understand its roots in the French concern this century with the metaphysics of desire and how they surfaced in schools of psychoanalysis.[40] Prominent among these schools was the *Ecole freudienne*, founded by Jacques Lacan in 1967, of which Irigaray was a member. She taught in its official department of psychoanalysis at Vincennes, until 1974 when she published *Speculum of the Other Woman.* She was then dismissed from her post.

Freud and Lacan

The impact of Freudian psychoanalysis in France in the early part of this century was felt considerably in literary circles developing a surrealist programme. Freud's own later concerns with language and artistic representation encouraged such a development. By the 1930s the stage was at least set for an evaluation of Freudianism and language through attempts by surrealists to tap into the unconscious by means of automatic writing.

Lacan, as he emerged in the post-Second World War period, deepened and challenged Freud's work on, and interest in, language at a time (the 1950s) when structuralism was emerging. Lacan was particularly influenced by the way Saussure had been taken up by Jakobson, Emile Beneveniste and Lévi-Strauss. As he wrote in his celebrated collection of essays, *Ecrits*: 'what the psychoanalytic experience discovers in the unconscious is the whole structure of language'.[41] For Freud the unconscious was silent; it experienced an aphasia that only interpreter, the analyst, gave expression to. Structuralist analysis ushered in a new model of self and its relationship to the world, in which the self no longer is the focus for attention. What is significant for any subject is the differential system, the structure, to which they belong and which gives them an identity. With Freud the centre of the psychoanalytic work is the subject, to whom the analyst gives a language, a voice. The language is an external symbolic representation invested with meaning by the subject. However, since the subject can never grasp the unconscious meaning this has to be given the subject by the analyst and, subsequently, the meaning is internalized by the one under analysis. Conscious explanation facilitates the healing of a lesion in the unconscious. With structuralism the language-system rather than the subject was foregrounded. The subject, like everything else, is constructed within the construal of language. Language speaks the subject; it was no longer the case of trying to get the subject to speak the language. It is not the subject who invests symbolic representation with meaning, rather meaning emerges from the relationship of the sign (and 'I' is a sign also) to the differential field of the language. Freud's analysis of sexuality and desire is now related to the structure of signification. As Lacan writes, in his essay 'The Signification of the Phallus,' 'The phallus is the privileged signifier of that mark in which the role of the logos is joined with the advent of desire.'[42]

Since so much of Irigaray's challenge to the nature of representation (particularly the maleness of representation) emerges from this connection explored by Lacan, we would do well to unfold the logic of Lacan's project a little further. Desire, for Freud as for Lacan, is a product of there being an other. Later we will be examining the morphology of sexual identity in relation to this desire. For the moment it is sufficient to understand, albeit briefly, that the boy's other is first his mother and then other women and the girl's other is her father and then other men. For Freud the emergence of this libidinal economy is associated with identifying whether we have or have not a penis. The desire is the product of believing the other is the key to satisfying our own needs. There is an element of demand then in the constitution of the other. The phallus is the symbol for the absent, distant yet constant promise of enjoying and sublating the other. For Lacan the acquisition of language is founded upon this rhythm of absence–presence – such language operates within an economy of desire. The desire can never be satisfied because it is the very demand for the other which constitutes and keeps the other as other. Desire longs to, reaches out to, but can never possess, the other (without bringing about the destruction of its own identity).

This economy of desire for the other is registered in the unconscious. As Lacan puts it, 'the unconscious of the subject is the discourse of the other'.[43] The entrance into sexuality, like the entrance into self-identity occurs at what Lacan termed the mirror stage of development. At this stage, the very 'junction of nature of grace',[44] the child identifies the configuration of itself as a whole (as an 'I') and yet also experiences an alienation. The 'I' is available only through the configuration, through the symbolic, through that which is other and external to itself; 'this maturation being henceforth dependent, in man, on a cultural mediation'.[45] Lacan regards the ability to configure and the ability to identify the image as oneself, as products of the imaginary – a faculty rather like the Kantian faculty of the imagination from which symbolic representation will emerge. The emergence of sexual desire and identity occurs with this entry into the realm of the symbolic as an expression of the male imaginary. The symbolic and the imaginary therefore organize the fragmentation of the sensory into an ego. It is because of this that the effects of the unconscious, that 'other scene', are

discovered at the level of the chain of materially unstable elements that constitutes language: effects determined by the double play of combination and substitution in the signifier, according to the two elements that generate the signified, metonymy and metaphor.[46]

What Lacan is doing here, and his essay 'Function and Field of Speech and Language' explicitly develops this, is mapping three structures, one upon the other, and creating a sort of palimpsest. The three structures are: first, Saussure's linguistic structure of language/speech-act (*langue/parole*); secondly, Jakobson's literary structure (metonymy/metaphor); and thirdly, Freud's structure for the nature of dreams (substitution or displacement/combination or condensation). For Lacanian psychoanalysis, the symptom is the speech-act, the particular cry and the metaphor, is the condensation in a dream around which the rest of dream-text focuses. Desire is the general economy, the language, the chain of signifiers substituting one for another in an endless differential movement towards an other, which can never be finally enjoyed. Lacan expresses this in an equation or algorithim S/s, where S is the signifier, s is the signified (the truth towards which the signifier refers, for which the signifer stands) and the / is the bar which can never be crossed. The bar is a break, a rupture within meaning itself. The significance of the signifier, its burden of truth, its reference, the Word of the word, is always absent, lacking or lost, like the phallus of Osiris. As Philippe Lacoue-Labarthe and Jean-Luc Nancy have written, in their much-acclaimed commentary on Lacan:

metaphor and metonymy borrowed from Jakobson, have lost their characteristics as complementary 'aspects' of language (whose respective preponderance may vary, according to literary genre, for example) and have become two autonomous entities whose association constitutes the law of language as the law of desire.[47]

The feminine other

The source of much argument, misunderstanding and contention is the realm of the symbolic and its relationship to the phallus. For if representation is governed by what Lacan called 'the law of the father' – if, in other words, desire is always phallic, always male, then the realm of the symbolic is being governed by the male imaginary and will therefore be patriarchal. This leads to a construal of culture itself as, according to Irigaray, 'hom(m)osexual' – that is, defined by men for men and monosexually orientated. In Freud's accounts of the morphology of sexual identity recognition of the possession or lack of the phallus determines your destiny as either a boy or a girl. The question arises as to whether there is a genuine female desire (other than a desire based upon the negative *lack* of a phallus) and therefore representations of the feminine. Can there be a female imaginary and symbolic representations giving expression to that imaginary? In Lacan, the phallus operates neither as a biological organ nor an emblem of masculinity. For Lacan it is the signifier itself, the law of the symbolic. Do women have access then to the symbolic without becoming men-*manqué*?

In an interview given in 1977, Irigaray rehearsed the analysis which formed the first part of her book *Speculum of the Other Woman*: 'the female sex is described as a lack, a "hole". Freud, and psychoanalysts following him maintain that the only desire on the part of a woman, when she discovers she has "no sex", is to have a penis.'[48] She then goes on to say:

> What we have to question is the system of representation ... Lacan, using a linguistic schema, concludes likewise, and repeats the same process, when he writes that woman is a lack in the discourse, that she cannot articulate herself, but [*sic*] does not 'exist' etc ... [F]emale sexuality cannot articulate itself, unless precisely as an 'undertone', a 'lack', in discourse. But why would this situation be unchanging? Why can one not transcend that logic? To speak outside it?[49]

This evaluation of Lacan is not quite fair, particularly in 1977. Even while Irigaray was preparing *Speculum* for press, in 1973–4, Lacan was beginning to discuss the whole question of feminine desire and female *jouissance*. In *Encore: Le séminaire XX* and his article 'Feminine Sexuality in Psychoanalytic Doctrine' (both published in 1975), Lacan is moving towards an examination of the Woman as Other. Even so, Lacan can only picture female desire as a determination of male desire. Irigaray wishes to go much further.[50]

In order to find a voice outside of this logic, Irigaray's early work deconstructs or submits the articulations of such a logic to a psychoanalysis. In *Speculum* she takes major texts in the canon of Western metaphysics, beginning with Freud's analysis of female sexuality and points to the feminine, the mirrored other, who is continually being repressed. With Freud, she asks whether a little girl really does have penis-envy and whether therefore this lack of the male sex organ is the origin and determining factor in the nature of her desire and sexuality (*Speculum of the Other Woman*, p. 50). It is not that she is offering an alternative account of the morphology of female sexuality, but rather that she wishes to ask 'Why does the term "envy" occur to Freud? Why does he choose it? ... Why not also analyse the "envy" for the vagina? Or the uterus? Or the vulva?' (*ibid.*, pp. 51–2). Secreted about these male texts (she also examines Plato's cave analogy in *The Republic*, and aspects of the work of Descartes, Kant, Hegel and Lacan) is the forgotten body of the woman, and it is this to which Irigaray draws attention. Deconstructing male reason and representation intertextually, she portrays the need for a feminine form of representation.

From portraying the repression of this feminine Other, Irigaray proceeded in her subsequent work to propose and announce a female thinking, a female 'syntax' which is irreducible 'by the standard of representation, or re-presentation' emerging from the male imaginary. This might be termed, *contre* Lacan, the word of the Mother. Here not the phallus but the two-lips, emblem of female sexuality, produces a different imaginary. 'Woman's desire would not be expected to speak the same language as man's', Irigaray writes, in her programmatic essay 'This Sex Which Is Not One' (*This Sex Which is Not One*, p. 25).

Towards a Sexuate Culture

Upon this basis, Irigaray's later project began to explore the notion of a sexuate culture.[51] The exploration took two directions. First, in her analysis and promotion of *'parler-femme'* ('speaking (as) woman') she wished to offer a critique of repressive elements in male symbolic representation: its obsession with the visual, the speculative (in terms of the conceptual), the defining power of language, its reduction of alterity to identity, difference to sameness. She speaks (and the difficulty of understanding Irigaray results from *the manner in which she speaks* or attempts to articulate what she believes has been represssed) of listening with 'another ear, as if hearing an "other meaning" always in the process of weaving itself, of embracing itself with words, but also getting rid of words in order not to become fixed, congealed in them. For if "she" says something, it is not, it is already no longer, identical with what she means' (*This Sex Which is Not One*, p. 29). The two-lips therefore express an irreducibility. 'She' can never be defined – can never be the subject in the male subject–object spatial structure. 'She' will always remain the unconscious of this symbolic representation.

The parallels with Derrida's understanding of the divided, irreducible nature of discourse are evident. Some of these concerns will be heard again in the work of Hélène Cixous (see Chapter 4). Like Derrida, Irigaray too wishes to provoke difference as it masks and saps the strength of identity in language. Like Cixous, she wishes to challenge products of the male imaginary by giving expression to the female imaginary. Margaret Whitford, in her excellent book on Irigaray, describes this heterogeneity well, returning us to the structural linguistics in the background of this project:

> What she [Irigaray] is trying to conceptualize is the double syntax, the possibility of a relationship between two economies, of which one would be metaphorical (the paternal one) and one would be metonymical (the maternal one).[52]

The first task, then, is to allow the female imaginary its own symbolic expression. To this end Irigaray writes mimetic texts, texts where meaning is elusive, subject–object syntax loose, main verbs absent, the authorial position or narrative voice pluralized or ambivalent. Texts emerge which hover between defining and demonstrating, like 'When Our Lips Speak Together' and *Marine Lover*. Here is a movement towards recovering the voice of the repressed.[53] The second task for Irigaray is relating this *parler-femme*, and the cultural products of the female imaginary, to the hom(m)osexual culture. Not, this time, defining the relationship as the female unconscious of a male symbolics; but rather attempting to envisage a bi-sexual culture: a culture aware and cultivating expression of its heterogeneous sexual origins.[54] It is in describing this sexuate culture that Irigaray develops her notion of fecundity and her writing is fired by a utopian vision.

Sexual difference would represent the advent of new fertile regions as yet unwitnessed ... it would involve the production of a new age of thought, art, poetry and language; the creations of a new *poetics*. (*Irigaray Reader*, p. 165)

It is clear that Irigaray envisages this new age as future, as a consequence of the first and more immediate task. It is only having come to speak as woman that women can then speak to men: 'Speaking (as) woman would, among other things, permit women to speak to men' (*This Sex Which is Not One*, p. 136).

Sexual Difference and Divinity

The development of an ethics, politics, epistemology and ontology of sexual difference has been the major preoccupation of Irigaray's most recent work. As Derrida has found himself constantly involved in discussing theological issues and theological texts, so with Irigaray's deconstruction there has emerged a concern with spirituality, angels, Jesus Christ, the Trinity and God. In her essay 'Belief Itself' she depicts sexual difference in terms of the two angels on either side of the ark of the covenant. The two are

facing, close, just far enough apart to prevent the uncountable touch of the flesh from blending into contact with the two ends. Between them the flesh holds back and flows forth before any mastery can be exercised over it ... a *fort-da* of the possibility of presence and of sharing in something divine that cannot be seen but can be felt, underlying all incarnation, which two angels, facing but not looking at each other, set up between them. (*Sexes and Genealogies*, p. 45)

A new age of spiritual incarnation is suggested, of a transcendent which is material (what Irigaray has termed a 'sensible transcendental'). It is an age brought about by a love mediated through sexual difference; a love that is integral to a libidinal economy. It is a love which, while being divine, is also human and corporeal. Irigaray's early work concerned itself with deconstructing the fixation upon the conceptual and visual which she associated with male discourses. The concern with the higher, spiritual ground of the concept and with visibility was understood as phallocentric. Speaking (as) woman, on the other hand, emphasizes the materiality of language, the relationship between textuality and bodies. Text is also tissue.

In giving expression to female desire and *jouissance*, Irigaray has been drawn to redeveloping the four-fold material structure of the cosmos according to pre-Socratics like Empedocles.[55] She wishes to reintroduce the material elements, the passions, the viscous and tactile into the philosophical (governed almost entirely by the conceptual, the logical). She does not do this, and neither does she speak of angels and Greek goddesses, to revitalize Romantic notions of the primitive (*à la Rousseau, à la Gauguin*), the pagan or the mythic. She does this as part of that deconstructive strategy, that articulation of the other in and through the same; to recover the different, the repressed of phallocentric discourse. As with Derrida at his most playful, the body of the text (the writing) is allowed to assume its consonant status in the generation and communication of what is meaningful. The angels we are told 'are of a different sex ... So it must be if the flesh of God is become flesh' (*Sexes and Genealogies*, p. 45). We are to become divine.[56]

With Irigaray's envisaging of a new culture, we are involved in a certain future eschatology. The 'chiasmus or a double loop in which each [sex] can go toward the other and come back to itself' (*An Ethics of Sexual Difference*, p. 9) having come about, Irigaray can entertain the hope for a new relation, a new covenant, which hangs loosely from a theological chain. In an interview given in Bologna in 1985, Irigaray commented: 'the question of our relation to the divine is not irrelevant and can help us in this task of seeking a personal and collective identity' (*Irigaray Reader*, p. 193).

In an essay devoted to analysing the New Testament exegesis of the American feminist, Elizabeth Schüssler Fiorenza, entitled 'Equal to Whom', [57] and in the final part of *Marine Lover*, entitled 'The crucified one: epistle to the last christians', Irigaray explores the incarnation of Jesus Christ. She creates a particular space for Jesus Christ as embracing both the male and the female.[58] In her call for a divinity which will function as a transcendental subject for women in the way the Judeo-Christian God-as-Father functions for men, she examines religion as a cultural expression, in the wake of Ludwig Feuerbach. We must be careful in extracting and building upon explicit theological themes in Irigaray's work,[59] while recognizing that difference and otherness remain, and the transcendent is not just a linguistic or cultural construct.

Gayatri Chakravorty Spivak

By including an account of the contribution to the question of representation by the Anglo–Indian critical theorist Spivak,[60] an explicitly political voice is heard. It is a voice informed by the work of Derrida and Irigaray. In their more recent writings Derrida and Irigaray have been developing the political implications of deconstruction, on the one hand, and sexual difference, on the other.[61] But Spivak, like Judith Butler whose work we will also examine, imports her critical theories for other uses: namely for developing a post colonial feminism. For Spivak, herself a diligent student of Marx, has consciously built upon the work of Derrida (whose book *Of Grammatology* she translated into English), particularly employing the tool of deconstructive criticism. Similarly, as a feminist she has appreciated the work of Irigaray, particularly the thesis that language is sexed ('every voice is inhabited by the sexual differential' – (*In Other Worlds*, p. 132). Her criticisms of both stem from her discipleship – her recognition that there is a deconstruction of Derrida (and Irigaray) yet to be performed. Central to her espousal of deconstruction and feminism is the desire to prevent deconstruction from becoming 'complicit with an essentialist bourgeois feminism' (*ibid.*, p. 91). This is part of a much larger project: the recognition that she, like any one else working within cultural studies, is involved in a politics of interpretation and readership. Thus Julia Kristeva, as 'an apologist for Christianity' (*ibid.*, p. 264) is harangued for privileging the roles of mother and psychoanalyst, and denigrating political interpretation (*ibid.*, pp. 126–9).[62]

Spivak's politics of interpretation are a development of her work as a translator. She is keenly aware of the difference between First and Third World discourses, and the degree of distortion that occurs in any interchange between these discourses. In her outspoken article 'French Feminism in an International Frame', she reminds First World feminists that, on the one hand, their information about the Third World issues from privileged informants, while, on the other, that 'the First World feminist must learn to stop feeling privileged *as a woman*' (*In Other Worlds*, p. 136). Pointedly, she demands we ask, 'not merely who who am I? but who is the other woman? How am I naming her? How does she name me?' (*ibid.*, p. 150).

With this explicit political agenda, and biography, the work of the Subaltern Studies Group,[63] examining the complex cultural currents in the history of South-Asian colonialism, would inevitably draw her interest. The focus for the Group's attention is those places where there are attempts to displace the dominant colonial discourse and therefore to affect a change in the chain of significations. The subaltern is an insurrectionist. The attempt to change the system always fails and the group analyses the nature of that failure of the subaltern or peasant consciousness within the dominant culture. For Spivak, this project is remarkably akin to deconstruction. In fact. she defines Subaltern Studies as deconstructing historiography. This is strategic, for she wishes to supplement (and therefore add to, modify and critique) attempts to discover and figure subaltern consciousness in colonial culture with 'First World post-humanism, post-Marxism' (*ibid.*, p. 210). She finds it necessary to do this because of the 'negative' readings of subaltern consciousness in the early work of the Group; a negativity which she relates to the way in which the members of the Group are themselves practitioners of the dominant educated discourse which the subaltern consciousness cannot disrupt. Recognizing that the subaltern voice cannot be recovered without betrayal, she suggests a strategy whereby the very elusiveness of the subaltern consciousness is, in fact, not only disruptive but also actually founds the possibility for the dominant cultural discourse. Subalternity is the difference which enables the elite to be elite. Hence, the economy of such a discourse, inscribes a lack, an *aporia*, an ineradicable difference – similar to the economy of *différance* – uncovered through deconstruction.

In her essay 'A Literary Representation of the Subaltern: A Woman's Text from the Third World', through a short story by the Indian writer Mahasweta Devi, Spivak examines the elusiveness of subaltern consciousness. She details the ways in which it refuses to be caught and defined by various Western, interpretive strategies (from Marxism to Lacanism). The subaltern in this story is, furthermore, a woman – the figure Spivak criticized earlier volumes of Subaltern Studies for not taking seriously enough. She develops, therefore, a more sophisicated means of evaluating subaltern material in a way which celebrates 'the text's apartness [*être-à-l'écart*]' (*ibid.*, p. 286).

Spivak's work is open to probing criticisms: where does she position her own discourse and her political agenda (in 'creating' the subaltern consciousness is she not further repressing it?)? She attacks First World globalizations, but is not her own employment of the 'Third World' a globalization also? For our purposes, what remains important is the kind of supplement she provides to Derrida's and Irigaray's work on representation. Judith Butler's work provides another. Spivak's thinking extends the question of representation politically (and ethically), to include ethnography, gendered ethnography.[64]

Judith Butler

Judith's Butler's work[65] issues from a total immersion into contemporary critical theory. Many of the continental thinkers whose work is sketched in this book have left their traces in Butler's writings: Derrida, Irigaray, Foucault, Lacan, Levinas, Kristeva. Her work debates with and synthesizes different analyses: a Foucauldian account of power, a psychoanalytic account of the subject continually negotiating its desires, a Derridean account of discourse as both conferring and simultaneously deferring identity, and a lesbian, feminist's account of gender. Her first book, *Subjects of Desire: Hegelian Reflections in Twentieth-Century France*, plots the development of a dynamic concept of subjectivity from its emergence in the Romantic idealism of Hegel, through the existentialism of Sartre and the darker readings of Hegel's project made fashionable by Kojève in the 1930s in France, and on into the preoccupation with desire by the French poststructuralists, particularly Lacan and Deleuze. She concludes that work with: 'From Hegel to Foucault, it appears that desire makes us into strangely fictive beings' (*Subjects of Desire*, p. 238). It is the constitution of those 'fictive beings' in and through desire that is the focus of her work. In her second book, *Gender Trouble: Feminism and the Subversion of Identity*, this focus is explicitly linked both to feminism and to performance and in her third, *Bodies that Matter: on the Discursive Limits of 'Sex'* to homosexuality. It is this later work that has put her at the forefront of a field of critical theory known as 'queer theory'.[66]

The subject

Butler's subject neither has the Cartesian mind which can affirm its own reality and assert that fact ('I think therefore I am'), nor a body with which it is in immediate contact and by means of which it has direct access to things as they are in the world around it. Following Foucault (whose work we will examine in Chapter 2), the subject is formed through social practices, through various strategies of power which constitute and discipline the self. Both the body and the psyche are composed. It is at this point that representation becomes paramount. As Butler has written recently on embodied subjectivity: 'Subjection consists precisely in this fundamental dependency on a discourse we never chose but that, paradoxically, initiates and sustains our agency' (*The Psychic Power of Life*, p. 2). As with Derrida's famous 'there is nothing outside the text', so here Butler is not advocating a linguistic idealism. Notions of our own identity are closely related to the discourses we are born into and learn to make our own. Language *forms* these notions of identity, it does not *cause* them to be. The *of* in 'subjects of desire' is both objective (we are subjected to desire) and subjective (we desire). What is inside and what is outside breaks down within this ambiguous grammar. The Cartesian construal of an inner 'I' who operates upon an outer world through a body which, at best, can cause misunderstandings, and, at worse, deceive us entirely, is rejected. And along with that rejection is a critique of the liberal humanist account of individuals whose moral aim is integrity and the personal freedom to be true to oneself. For the liberal humanist these aims are possible because of a personal autonomy which guarantees agency. What is required for the logic of this position is a volitional, pre-linguistic subject. For Butler, on the other hand, we are subjects because we are already under subjection. We will come upon a similar conception of the self in Levinas, whose work we will examine in Chapter 3.

Butler foregrounds four aspects of this process of selving that makes her work distinctive: the sexed body, gender, performance and representation. The languages we learn, the social relations we imitate, the institutional practices we participate in and perform all subject us to a ruling which forms our notions of who we are. Minds are not the controllers of bodies; thinking here is part of the ongoing reflexivity whereby persons learn to live within the various force-fields operating within a specific culture. Thinking is inseparable from embodied agency; and agency is inseparable from the cultural production of subjects as agents.

These ideas can appear deterministic, and Butler, along with other critical theorists who would support a non-foundational or non-substantial notion of the subject, has been criticized on two counts associated with determinism. First, for all her attention to gender troubling, and the disturbance of the dominant rules of social behaviour (particularly with respect to a queering of a heterosexual social order), her notion of the subject implies that even resistance is simply going to reinforce the *status quo*. There seems little scope therefore for change or transformation; the troubling is always operating already within the dominant cultural logic. Secondly, and related to this, if the subject's identity is always being produced and reproduced by the subject him or herself, then identity politics – which inaugurated recent changes in legislation and opinion with regard to the marginalized and persecuted (including homosexuals) – becomes impossible.

To counter these criticisms we need to appreciate that, for Butler, the psyche and the body are both excessive to cultural determinism. It is part of her critique of Foucault's work that his attention to the disciplining, punishment and production of subjects pays so little attention to the relationship there has to be between the psychological and the sociological. In particular, Foucault gives scant space to the psychology of desire or the psychic life of power. Butler rectifies this. This is one of the more important syntheses she produces in her work: Foucault (or Louis Althusser[67]) meets Freud (or Lacan). '[T]he psyche is precisely what exceeds the imprisoning effects of the discursive demand to inhabit a coherent identity, to become a coherent subject,' she writes (*The Psychic Life of Power*, p. 86), affirming the important contribution of psychoanalysis. At the same time the body is not an effect of the psyche. It has a materiality, but this materiality, as Foucault shows, is produced. As any account of how the body has been understood between Plato and Freud, or any overview of the way the body has been depicted in painting and medical manuals, demonstrates.[68] It is necessary

> to concede and affirm an array of 'materialities' that pertain to the body, that which is signified by the domains of biology, anatomy, physiology, hormonal and chemical composition, illness, age, weight, metabolism, life and death. None of this can be denied. But the undeniability of these 'materialities' in no way implies what it means to affirm them, indeed, what interpretive matrices condition, enable and limit that necessary affirmation ... [E]ach of those categories have a history and a historicity ... The linguistic categories that are understood to 'denote' the materiality of the body are themselves troubled by a referent that is never fully or permanently resolved or contained by any signifed. (*Bodies that Matter*, pp. 66–7).

The realm of ideas is never a separate realm, the realm of the material is never an empirical given subsequently engraved upon by various social practices. There is no interiority and no exteriority, only a continuous reflexivity, a performance of the subject of *desire* as the *subject* of desire. In the chiasmic performance of those two desires subjectivity is produced.

There is nothing arbitrary or wilful about this production. A subject cannot become anything he or she desires. For always the subject is historically located such that certain options are not available. There is a historicity of norms. But there is nothing deterministic about this production either. The indeterminacy of both psyche and body offer resistances to any cultural hegemony. They exceed their representations. Identity politics themselves are seen as the productions of 'a state which can only allocate recognition and rights to subjects totalized by the particularity that constitutes their plantiff status' (*The Psychic Life of Power*, p. 100). Such a politics do not disturb the *status quo* because what resistence and critique they offer is already circumscribed by what Butler calls 'the historical hegemony of the juridical subject' (*ibid.*, p. 101). What she, like Foucault, is demanding is a certain making of new forms of subjectivity, but understanding the way specific subjectivies are produced now is a necessary preliminary to offering an alternative account. In particular, the cultural production she analyses is that of the homosexual subject, and she does this while attempting to map out how subjects become gendered. She concludes (and we will unfold the logic of this statement in a moment) that

> The institution of a compulsory and naturalized heterosexuality requires and regulates gender as a binary relation in which the masculine term is differentiated from a feminine term, and this differentiation is accomplished through the practices of heterosexual desire. (*Gender Trouble*, pp. 22–3)

Performance

It is in this context that Butler develops her concept of gender as 'performance':

> *gender* is not a noun ... gender is performatively produced and compelled by the regulatory practices of gender coherence ... gender is always a doing ... There is no gender identity behind the expressions of gender; that identity is performatively constituted by the very 'expression' that are said to be its results. (*Ibid.*, pp. 24–5)

For Freud (and Butler's construals of a compulsory and naturalized heterosexuality and gender as performance modifies, critiques, but fundamentally accepts Freudian psychoanalysis), the sexual identity of a subject emerges from a domestic drama. A self-conscious theatricality is announced in the naming of the various stages in the development of the gendered subject after Sophocles' play, *Oedipus Rex*. Male and female subjects come through the process differently but involved for both is a series of denials, prohibitions, separations, displacements of desire and identifications. For the male, separated from the mother initially, he turns to the mother as an object of desire, for the mother first produces desire within him through her various ministrations upon his young body. The male desire is focused on the penis, and recognition that the woman does not have the penis, coupled with the prohibitions against incest installed by the father, brings him into the castration complex. Turning from the mother, the male child identifies with the father and in doing so establishes his gendered, masculine identity. The girl, on the other hand, also first separated from the mother, also turns to the mother as the object of her desire. This makes her, according to Freud, much more susceptible to homosexuality. Like the boy she recognizes the mother does not have the penis (as she likewise lacks the penis) and turns to the father (who possesses the penis), playing out her identification with the mother. As Butler notes: 'the assumption of femininity and the assumption of masculinity proceed through the accomplishment of an always tenuous heterosexuality' (*The Psychic Power of Life*, p. 135). It is tenuous because what she draws attention to is the way this drama pre-empts other forms of attachment than heterosexual ones. The assumption of a stabilized gender, masculine or feminine, is guaranteed only if there is a repudiation of homosexual attachments. In fact, the prohibition against homosexual attachments is there prior even to the law against incest. The girl must repudiate her love for her mother, and yet identify with her. The boy must identify with his father but not take him as the object of his desire. Butler wishes to demonstrate how the psychological processes regulate gendered identity – and, indeed, how they construct a culture in which heterosexuality is naturalized, but naturalized only by insisting upon the radical otherness of homosexuality. This naturalization and foreclosure of other possibilities has, as one of its repercussions, what Butler terms a 'heterosexual melancholy'. That is, the loss of possible homosexual attachments gives rise to hyper forms of being masculine and feminine. Gender production at the moment is governed then by a pathology that generates tacit cruelties.

Having argued for this, Butler can then call the heterosexual presupposition into question:

> I would argue that phenomenologically there are many ways of experiencing gender and sexuality that do not reduce to this equation, that do not presume that gender is stablized through the installation of a firm heterosexuality. (*Ibid.*, p. 136)

Uncoupled from the binary logistics of heterosexuality (stabilizing masculinity and femininity, prohibiting and yet preserving homosexuality) gender can be acted out in other ways. Uncoupled also from substantive notions of the subject and identity, gender can be seen as a process, an acting out which troubles or subverts 'those naturalized and reified notions of gender that support the masculine hegemony and heterosexist power' (*Gender Trouble*, p. 34). Such notions are not just related to heterosexuality, for the production of coherent gender identities would include 'coherent lesbian identity, coherent gay identity, and within those worlds, the coherent butch, the coherent femme' (*Bodies that Matter*, p. 114). In this queering of the heterosexist power new gender configurations can proliferate promoting alternative sexed bodies. With this we return to a cultural politics similiar to Irigaray's and Spivak's: new representations will install a new imaginary, will produce transformative power. 'If the power of discourse to produce that which it names is linked to the question of performativity, then the performative is one domain in which power acts *as* discourse' (*Bodies that Matter*, p. 225).

Theological implications

Irigaray voices the revolutionary nature of all four projects when, speaking of her own, she states:

> We need to reinterpret everything concerning the relations between the subject and discourse, the subject and the world, the subject and the cosmic, the microcosmic and the macrocosmic. Everything, beginning with the way in which the subject has been written. (*An Ethics of Sexual Difference*, p. 6)

What implications does Derrida's economy of *différance*, Irigaray's culture of sexual difference, Spivak's evaluation of subalternity and Butler's queering of current constructions of gender have for the theologian concerned with representation? To date, several books and articles have been published exploring or applying Derrida and Irigaray's work in a theological context.[69] If we turn back to theology's own concern with language, outlined in the Introduction to Chapter 1, we can perhaps begin to sketch a direction for theology's future consideration. Whatever Derrida's own relationship to negative theology or Jewish Messianism or Irigaray's notion of the divine, three aspects of their work seem to be relevant for theology's own concerns.

First, theology's concern with analogy – and, more recently, metaphor – has tended to emphasize the static and referential nature of certain nouns and adjectives. This is one of the effects of a nominalism that has been so dominant in our understandings of language since William of Ockham. There has been little sense that meaning, even for theological discourse, is part of an economy. To some extent, it is simply that we have forgotten the lessons Augustine taught – concerning the operation and participation of signs in the dialogue between divine (Trinitarian) and human desire. God is not an object like other objects in the world, and therefore attention to proper nouns and predicates falsifies our representations of God as it distorts our understanding of language. Language is a praxis, a use, a movement. Analogies and metaphors are part of a dynamic chain of signification, a narrative. If Derrida, Irigaray and others are correct in the new models for the operation of language they are describing, then names defer their meaning in a more general economy of desire. Theologians must ask, 'What model of language is being presupposed?' in doctrines of analogy or metaphor. If the model changes, then what happens to our understanding of discourse on, from or about God? Perhaps a theological examination of 'God-talk' should examine allegory rather than analogy, narrative rather than metaphor, as a means of establishing the nature of our knowledge of God.[70] In the wake of Derrida and Irigaray, theology must re-examine its own understanding of 'realism'.

Secondly, and to some extent subsequently, with Derrida, Irigaray, Spivak and Butler's emphasis upon the cultural construction and politics of stable identities, of meaning – the question of language's relationship to the immediate is raised. Philippe Lacoue-Labarthe succinctly emphasizes what is theologically at stake here: 'For it is not enough to affirm in the mode of belief that there is something "anterior" to representation if one is to "overcome" the logic of the said representation, which is, rigorously speaking, the interdiction of revelation.'[71] If language does not simply re-present, if immediacy and presence are questioned by double-nature of language, then some of our theological notions of 'revelation' or sacramental presence are problematized. Affected will be those proponents of metaphorical theology who wish to speak of an experience of the transcendent. We commented, when discussing Sallie McFague's work, on the incipient Docetism that wishes to see metaphor as a ladder to the divine, a ladder to be left behind. Derrida, Irigaray and Butler wish to emphasize the ineradicable materiality of the text. The body cannot simply be a vehicle for the spiritual and transcendent. The transcendent (for

Irigaray), the quasi-transcendent (for Derrida) is itself sensible. We cannot avoid mediation. But then we need to go back to our models of sacramental presence and revelation with a more balanced view of creation as God's graced medium.

Theologians of the ilk of Schleiermacher and Barth (and more recently Jean-Luc Marion[72]) constantly battle with the immediacy of revelation (as the feeling of absolute dependence or as the Word of God) and its material mediation – through human perceptions, conceptions and words. At the centre of their discussions is the incarnation of Christ himself, the human manifestation of the divine.

Negatively, then, in the light of Derrida, Irigaray, Spivak and Butler's work, theology must be constantly vigilant to the limitations of its discourse and the politics of meaning. Positively, theology must recognize those limitations as they relate to Christology: the language of theology understood theologically must relate to the doctrines of creation and incarnation. Perhaps a way forward is being sketched by several French Catholic theologians who are currently using phenomenology to attempt a description of the economy of the 'gift', the 'event' and grace. Since phenomenology is concerned with the structure of our relations to the world, it perhaps offers a means of exploring what Jean-Luc Marion has termed *'médiation immédiate'*.[73] Theological attention must also be paid to liturgy and prayer – the two forms of textual practice most often forgotten by systematic theologians.

It is with a closer attention to practices of the faith that Butler's work becomes helpful. Traditonally, when the church spoke about 'formation' it was with respect to becoming persons in Christ. Formation was a process of discipleship that required the subjection of the subject to the will of God, but not a subjection that demanded passivity. The subject was formed in the image of Christ by participating in a work that confounded activity and passivity, giving and reception. Butler's work gives an account of the performance and production of a gendered subject, but it might be a helpful account for the development of a doctrine of the gendered church. Too often in the past theological discussions of men and women in the church have suffered from what Irigaray would term its hom(m)osexual bias and Butler would view as its heterosexual world-view.[74] Discussions of sexual difference and the construction of gendered subjects has featured little. But Butler's work enables us to think through traditional doctrines of the church in terms of the performance and formation of one's gendered subjectivity in Christ. In the light of her work new kinds of gay theology are possible, for example. For the gay theologies of the liberal schools have been dominated by identity politics and the immediate experience of being gay.[75] Butler's work profoundly questions the presuppositions for such theologies, and, in doing so, opens up new paths for exploration.

Thirdly, and consequently, Irigaray's work on the female imaginary and the divine, and Spivak's work on the gendered subaltern must have an effect upon feminist theologies and projects for an inclusive language in Bible translations and liturgies.[76] Feminist Christian theology (as opposed to the post-Christian theologies of Mary Daly and Daphne Hampson) must answer the challenge Irigaray's work poses that it is simply reworking products of the male imaginary. What would constitute a feminine representation of the divine, how would this affect Christology and the doctrine of the Trinity? There has been much historical work done on women in Patristic and Mediaeval theology.[77] This work forms an important resource for future explorations, but to date, very little work has been done attempting to re-examine the traditional doctrines of systematic theology out of the female imaginary.[78] Can there be a feminine systematic theology, and if there can what would it look like? We are only beginning to ask these questions – but the consequences are enormous, both for men and for women. Such questions harbour the possibility for a new anthropology, a new understanding of sexual difference and relatedness within a theological purview. The notion of the *imago Dei* has never been so open and in need of re-examination.

With specific regard to Spivak's work, a host of questions concerning the relationship between Christianity, translation and cultural politics emerge. What happens to Judaism or Jewish Christianity when being surveyed and promoted through the educated language of Greek (even *Koine* Greek)? What happens when this Greek gives way to Latin and this Latin to the vernacular? Can the New Testament be read as subaltern material? Furthermore, Spivak's work has profound implications for multicultural dialogue and the representation of other faiths within a First World Christian discourse. Debate along these lines is occurring – but not within the study of Christian theology itself.[79]

Finally, the concrete attention all four of these thinkers pay to the politics of meaning and the attempted erasure of difference will necessitate that theological discourse too asks questions concerning its power and authority to speak: who does it address, on whose behalf, in whose voice?

2
Theology and History

Introduction

At the Spanish border town of Port Bou, late one night towards the end of September 1940, the German culture critic, Walter Benjamin, took his life in despair at being unable to leave Nazi-occupied France. Like the Master in Kafka's parable 'The Departure' who hears in the distance the sound of a trumpet, Benjamin, panic-stricken, simply wanted 'Out of here, nothing else, it's the only way I can reach my goal.'[1] His predicament, the very facts of what occurred in the dark on a frontier promising deliverance, might have come from Kafka's pen. Hannah Arendt underlines the tragic irony, the fatalism, of Benjamin's position: 'Only on that particular day was the catastrophe possible.'[2] History and story – how distinct are the categories?

Prior to his suicide, Benajmin had completed what has become one of the most talk-about documents in modern historiography, his 'Theses on the Philosophy of History'. In particular, attention has been constantly drawn to thesis IX, in which he describes a painting by Paul Klee named 'Angelus Novus':

> This is how one pictures the angel of history. His face is turned toward the past. Where we perceive a chain of events, he sees one single catastrophe which keeps piling wreckage upon wreckage and hurls it in front of his feet. The angel would like to stay, awaken the dead, and make whole what has been smashed. But a storm is blowing from Paradise; it has got caught in his wings with such violence that the angel can no longer close them. This storm irresistibly propels him into the future to which his back is turned, while the pile of debris before him grows skyward. This storm is what we call progress.[3]

It is a beautiful, if somewhat disturbing and apocalyptic passage. It serves to remind us, emblematically, of three interrelated points. First, we are the history makers: we 'perceive a chain of events' and we perceive in this chain a progress. Secondly, there is another view of time within which this human history takes place, a theological view: with Paradise and an angelic Messiah who would 'awaken the dead, and make whole what has been smashed'. How the first point relates to this second is part of the complex exploration of time and eternity in which all theology is involved. Thirdly, there is Benjamin's own narrative; Benjamin as storyteller and the mediator, who 'joins the ranks of the teachers and sages'.[4] Therefore there remain these three: history, theology and story – each interwoven and inextricably implying the others.

We need to bear this in mind as we begin to evaluate the importance of history for the study of theology and the extent to which recent critical theorists challenge our notions of 'history'.

Theology's concern with the question of history is profound. The Jewish and Christian (and Islamic) faiths are rooted in historical events. The Scriptures purport to be accounts of those events. However scholars might disagree about the accuracy of such accounts, when the writer of Isaiah frames his work with 'in the days of Uzziah, Jotham, Ahaz, and Hezekiah' and when the writer of Luke's gospel opens with 'in the days of Herod, the King of Judaea', then both writers are specifically rooting the significance of their stories in world history. Despite the variety of Christian Creeds, from the age of St Ignatius and Justin Martyr in the second century, the mapping of Jesus's life onto the history of the Roman Empire by the dating of the crucifixion 'under Pontius Pilate' was routine.[5]

Some theologians, like Karl Barth, wish to see the whole period of Christ's life as a special time in history. For them, the very authority of the New Testament lies in its status as a testimony to the singular historical event of Jesus Christ. 'The revelation attested to in Holy Scripture ... is a statement about the occurrence of an event.'[6] The importance of determining, in the most exact way possible, the nature of the event of Jesus Christ, led, in the early part of the nineteenth century, to the quest for the historical Christ. At a time in Germany when a new historical consciousness was giving rise to the academic discipline of historiography (shaped by historians like Leopold von Ranke, Johann Gustav Droysen and Wilhelm Dilthey[7]), theology's inextricable concern with history was raising serious questions.

David Friedrich Strauss was only 28 when he launched his *The Life of Jesus Critically Examined* into public debate. The year was 1836. The crucial question he nailed down in that work was the relationship between historical event and its representation. More pointedly, he explored the relationship between history and myth in the New Testament. Strauss distinguished between the time of Jesus, the formation of the first Christian community and the writing of the gospels. In the spaces between these three periods, Christians began to read the events of Jesus's life in the light of Jewish and Babylonian legends or myths. In the gospel accounts, therefore, we perceive 'the transference of messianic legends, almost all ready formed, to Jesus, with some alterations to adapt them to Christian opinions and to the individual character and circumstances of Jesus'.[8]

The important question raised and tackled by Strauss, and the demythologizers who followed in his wake, concerned historical reference and historical writing. Where did the facts end and their representation begin? What are the facts about the life of Jesus and how are they to be determined? It was a short step from Strauss to studies (in the New Testament) on the composition and transmission of the gospel narratives. Strauss introduced into the study of theology a philosophical question preoccupying German idealism – the relationship between reality and its representation.

The quest for (and the question about) the historical Jesus did not end with Albert Schweitzer's famous summary *The Quest for the Historical Jesus*. Schweitzer charted the project from Hermann Reimarius in the mid-eighteenth century to William Wrede at the end of the nineteenth. Though Schweitzer concluded that 'there is nothing more negative than the result of the critical study of the Life of Jesus',[9] the quest still continues today. Contemporary New Testament exegesis may no longer be concerned with discovering the real man behind the story, but historical–critical method nevertheless remains committed to accurately reconstructing the historical context within which the work of Jesus took place and, subsequently, was understood. This new quest is evident in the recent work of the New Testament scholar, James D.G. Dunn. Committed to a historical exegesis, he sees his task in charting the origins of the doctrine of the incarnation as

> trying to hear the words of the text as the writer of these words intended those for whom he wrote to hear them. Our only real hope of achieving that goal is by setting the text as fully as possible into the historical context within which it was written.[10]

It is within this new project of historical reconstruction that the work on the Jesus of history by the Dutch theologian Edward Schillebeeckx and the writings of E.P. Sanders, continue the quest of Reimarius and Strauss.[11]

Historie and *Geschichte*

Theology's concern with history does not stop at its meditation upon the founding events of the Christian religion and their representation. The changes and transformations of the Christian religion itself is a history – a history of dissemination and traditions. It is a history given particular theological validation in terms of relating how the salvation wrought then, with and through Jesus Christ, still remains relevant and effective now. The coming of the Christ then raises theological questions concerning not only the history between then and now, but the history between then and what came before it. The question here is between what Karl Barth terms 'God's Time and Our Time'.[12] Why does Christ come at that moment in Jewish history and not when the Maccabean brothers rose up against their Greek overlords? Why did the Messiah not come earlier, when the Temple was first razed and the people deported in Babylon? In other words, the question of the Christian tradition, the formation and development of the Christian Church (and its relation to the Kingdom of God), raises further questions about God's Providence and human destiny.

With Eusebius of Caesarea in the fourth century, we have the first conceptions of salvation history. In the twentieth century, Reinhold Niebuhr succinctly expressed the reason for theology's concern with salvation history:

> Historical religions are therefore by their very nature prophetic–messianic. They look forward at the first to a point in history and originally towards an eschaton (end) which is also the end of history, where the full meaning of life and history will be disclosed and fulfilled.[13]

H.R. Niebuhr wrote: 'To be a self is to have a god; to have a god is to have a history, that is, events connected by a meaningful pattern; to have one god is to have one history'.[14] The founding historical events for theology (Jewish, Christian or Islamic) require that there be a theology of history as such.

The nineteenth-century concern with history as progress was reinforced by scientific paradigms of evolution – in geology and biology.

History, as a cultural science, began to be conceived as a body of knowledge with its own methods of enquiry and proof. The rise of History as an academic discipline in the nineteenth century led, in the early twentieth, to a philosophical interest in the problem of time. In the first half of this century, it was common for theologians to distinguish between two forms of historical temporality emerging from two distinct German words. There was *Historie*, by which was understood the sheer historicity of existence in all its contingency; and there was *Geschichte*, by which was understood the historic, the epoch-shifting events, which were determinative for all that followed them. The first was material, the second was causal and participated in a certain logic. The two words, and the theological distinction made between them, do have some New Testament basis in the difference between *chronos* (the time of clocks and calendars) and *kairos* (specific and decisive moments). Rudolf Bultmann, in conversation with Martin Heidegger, used the difference between *Historie* and *Geschichte* to examine 'the temporality of eschatological existence'.[15] There is 'the historical process' understood as 'phenomena and incidents determinable by time – "what happened"' and there is *Geschichte* as 'event in time'.[16] This event is a present encounter with the Word of God. It is not, Bultmann always insisted, a difference between the historical and a super-historical, but an encounter with the very meaning of the historical, the kerygma, which demands decision. The resurrection, for Bultmann is not an occurrence in the everyday historical process; but an event of faith whereby the early church receives and comprehends the meaning of the crucifixion. The resurrection is a narrative account of the experience of God's presence breaking in and turning temporality into eschatological existence. The question of time and history turns into a question about revelation and into a dialectical tension between the temporal and the eternal.

For Oscar Cullmann, the distinction between *Historie* and *Geschichte,* leads to an understanding of *Geschichte* as salvation history or *Heilsgeschichte*. He develops his arguments for this in his influential book, *Christ and Time*.[17] Salvation history views Christ as the midpoint in time to which all that came before him and all that comes after him must be measured. It is an argument that would find significant parallels both in Friedrich Schleiermacher's notion of the development of God-consciousness in history and Karl Barth's doctrine of Christ as the Lord of time. A 'golden thread', or what Cullmann calls 'The Continuous Line of Salvation', runs through time and reveals the acts of God in human history. What came before

Christ prepared the way for him; what came after is the working out and establishment of the final Kingdom. History thus becomes the theatre for redemption and a medium for revelation. Theology, as Rudolf Bultmann saw,[18] is close to dissolving here into philosophy of history.

Nevertheless, following in the wake of Hegel's conflation of theodicy and history and Marx's secularization of this in the nineteenth century, the work of the contemporary German theologians, Jürgen Moltmann and Wolfhart Pannenberg, insists that any revelation of God has no other content than the world, human beings and their history. For both of them, the involvement of the Trinitarian God in creation cannot simply be limited to the birth, death and resurrection of Jesus Christ. In fact, this Christ-event is, for both, meaningful only in terms of God's whole plan for history.

Pannenberg writes: 'the event of revelation [i]s an anticipatory fulfilment of the realisation of God's historical plan and the manifestation of God's glory at the end of history'.[19] The Christ-event has eschatological significance, proleptically looking forward to the consummation of history in the Kingdom and affecting the course of history itself. Thus, until that time at history's end the divine plan remains a mystery – for the truth (which always assumes 'the coherence of all that is true')[20] is, as yet, incomplete. Only the doctrine of the Trinity makes sense of time as God's grace for our redemption.

Both Moltmann and Pannenberg are frank about their dependence upon Hegel's philosophical system, and the work of both theologians raises the question about whether any final separation can be drawn between the philosophy of history and a theology of history. Both continue in the tradition of German Romantic historicism. As Leopold von Ranke, the father of the German science of history said: 'Every event is truly part of world history, that never solely consists of sheer destruction, but rather is able to engender in the fleeting present moment something for the future.'[21] The historical event is part of the teleological development of History itself. Ranke pictured the historian as a priest serving an omniscient Deity, learning to think like God thinks. The science of history, as Ranke considers it, necessarily implicates theology in the philosophy of history. This philosophy of history then informs the various historiographic tools employed in its enquiry. The subject matter of history is chosen. Its boundaries are drawn and, given the gamut of possible subject matters, is necessarily drawn artificially. The subject matter is investigated, connections are made and findings are given meaning by considerations which are themselves non-historical and abstract. Even if, in fact, most particularly if, the subject matter is God. As one recent philosopher of religion has put it (commenting upon the work of the British theologian, Maurice Wiles, who was also deeply concerned with the God who acts in history): 'reflection upon the relationship between events, records and faith indicates that Christian theological understanding ultimately depends upon metaphysical convictions.'[22]

Theology, history and critical theory

Let us draw out three significant aspects of the relationship between theology and history, aspects with which contemporary critical theory is concerned. The first is the investigation into the nature of time and time's relationship to the eternal. How is time being understood in the various philosophies of history and therefore in various theologies? The classical perspective (evident in Aristotle and, more recently, Hegel) pictured time as circular, but time need not be circular. It could be linear. It could be multilevelled or like a palimpsest, a parchment which has been written on and then the writing rubbed out so that the parchment can be written on a second time. Time could be something we bring to our comprehension of the world, not a property the world has in and for itself. Is time indeed a property? When theology concerns itself about time then it is involved with existential questions (as Augustine and Barth both saw). In Chapter 14 of *Church Dogmatics*, Barth states that 'The Church of the New Testament lives in ... time-consciousness; that is, it is the Church of those who "wait" and "hasten."'[23] For Barth, with the entrance of God's time into our befuddled temporality, the present is caught between a time of expectation (the future) and a time of recollection (the past). This is the Christian experience of temporality.

The second aspect of this reflection is an investigation into what can be defined as an event. Theology here is involved with phenomenological questions. That is, how an object, in this case an occurrence, becomes meaningful to the observer. Can the event ever be evaluated as a pure event or is it only an event to the extent that it is made meaningful by being witnessed and reported as an event? At what point can the pure, pre-interpreted givenness of an event be assessed? Answering these questions is dependent upon a philosophy of action and agency, as well as a notion of time. Concepts of action, agency and time are bound to affect how one isolates, determines the nature and interprets the significance of any act.

The third aspect of this reflection returns us to those questions we considered in examining theology's relationship to questions of representation. How does the record of the event connect with the event itself? How does the reading of the report connect with its writing and the event written about? Here theology is involved with hermeneutical questions. Here also it must be recognized that the way in which an event is reported will depend to some extent (and just to what extent is an enormously complicated question to answer) upon the conventions and genres of such historical reportage. Such conventions and genres will, in turn, depend upon how and why one event among a myriad is seen as significant. They will depend also upon one's world-picture and conception of time. Hence in the work of Bultmann, Cullmann and Pannenberg, one has to begin interpreting Biblical accounts of history by trying to assess Jewish and Hellenic concepts of time and event. We begin then with the exegesis of the Scriptural text; with a configuration of time and event. But any reflections upon time and event are inseparable from the examination of texts of some kind, from language, from representation, from narrative.[24]

In our analysis of the relationship between theology and representation, the incarnation, or Christ as the Word of God, is the key doctrine in systematic theology which concerns itself with representation. Here, discussing theology's relationship with history it is the work of both the Son and the Spirit in Creation. As Pannenberg has put it: 'by the creation of the world and the sending of his Son and Spirit to work in it, [God] has made himself dependent upon the course of history.'[25] The key doctrines of systematic theology – revelation, the event of incarnation, the work of salvation, the work of the Spirit, the edification of the Church and the Kingdom (with its implied eschatology), the relationship between the immanent and the economic Trinity – are implicated in and influenced by our construals of history and the methodological tools used to evaluate and justify such construals. Theology, reflecting upon its own historical roots and concerns, leans heavily upon secular historical methods. If we call this theology's concern with the techniques of historiography, there are other more philosophical and doctrinal questions which stand, often presupposed, in the wings of such techniques. We need now to bring out these other questions. For any attempt, by critical theorists, to reconceive historical methodology will affect that reflection which Christian theology must undertake. It will affect not only the employment of historical techniques, but also the philosophical and doctrinal issues presupposed by those techniques.

Paul Ricoeur

It was as a prisoner of war that Ricoeur gained access to the thought of the great German phenomenologists and existential thinkers Edmund Husserl, Martin Heidegger and Karl Jaspers. Their writings fed a mind already educated in the existentialism of Gabriel Marcel and Jean-Paul Sartre. At the centre of existentialism and phenomenology is the human condition – its relation to, its knowledge and construction of, the world. Ricoeur's early books explore the work of these seminal philosophical figures. From his book, *Freedom and Nature* (1950) to his most recent *Oneself as Another* (1992), Ricoeur's fundamental concern has been in developing a philosophy of the will.[26] That is, his work has consistently explored notions of intention ('I decide'), action ('I move') and personal identity ('I consent'). His exploration has taken him into the realms of representation (particularly symbolism, metaphor and narrative), as we noted in Chapter 1, and ethics, as we will note in Chapter 3. Central to his work on the will has been an analysis of time, event, history, hermeneutics and the interdependence of such analyses. For the purposes of this chapter we will be examining two monumental works, *History and Truth* (a collection of essays published in 1955) and *Time and Narrative* (three volumes published between 1983 and 1985). We will trace the differences and development in thinking between these two works and examine what happened in the philosophy of history during the thirty-year period which separates them.

History and Truth

It was Reinhold Niebuhr who remarked that 'the problem of the meaning of history is always the problem of the meaning of life itself'.[27] It is a remark that might well have been made by the young Ricoeur building his philosophy of history on the basis of Marcel's existentialism and Husserl's phenomenology. History cannot be divorced from anthropology, that is, for Ricoeur, from human finitude ('their right to error', *History and Truth*, p. 10). Therefore questions of objectivity and scientific method in historiography are made complex by the fact that we are, ourselves, experiencing and making history. Epigrammatically, Ricoeur writes: 'the object of history is the human subject itself' (*ibid.*, p. 40). This definition and this emphasis lies at the heart of the historical problematic as Ricoeur conceives and works with it.

The objectivity of history is three-fold. First, it is an objectivity in terms of 'traces' (the word employed by François Simiand and Marc Bloch). The objects of history (events, situations, institutions and the people who generate them) leave traces in documents. The historian's task is to reconstruct the event from these traces and 'in this way establishes historical facts' (*History and Truth*, p. 23). The historian, in reconstructing these events, is not simply returning the past to us, but is involved in the activity of trying to explain the past to us and therefore bringing us to a certain historical understanding. Secondly, then, the historian's 'supreme effort to put history in order' (*ibid.*, p. 24) is another form of manifesting the objectivity of history. On this two-fold basis Ricoeur concludes that 'history is thoroughly faithful to its etymology: it is "research", *istoria*' (*ibid.*, p. 25). Thirdly, in putting history in order, the objectivity of history assumes a totality within which each moment or part relates to a whole. While Ricoeur, wrestling with Hegel, wishes to see history as open-ended – as an ongoing dialogue between the universal and the particular that cannot, from the point of view of fallible human nature,[28] attain a synthesis – nevertheless there remains an eschatological horizon, an end of history, within which historical objectivity becomes possible. If history is to be made meaningful, if the historian's task lies in rendering an account of this meaningfulness, then there can only be one history assumed, one unity of truth within the boundaries of which we hope we remain and work (*ibid.*, p. 54–5).

We need to be alert to two associated features of this historical objectivity as Ricoeur outlines it – because these features determine his approach to historiography from his early work to his late. First, since traces are located in documents history is concerned, primarily, with texts. At a more primordial level history is acts and events. These acts and events always exceed our ability to grasp their full import. An 'ultimate meaning remains hidden' for 'we do not know when we influence persons' (*History and Truth*, p. 109). However, these acts and events whose meaning is irreducible, nevertheless only become known, only constitute a body of knowledge, through representation, through the traces they leave behind in texts testifying to their occurrence. Secondly, by analysing the historian's task in terms of explanation/understanding, Ricoeur is viewing the historical investigation as a hermeneutical enterprise. Historiography involves a politics of interpretation. Though unlike the historiography of Michel de Certeau (see Chapter 4), Ricoeur rarely handles the political as such.

The distinction between explanation (which is what the physical sciences attempt to attain) and understanding (which is what the human sciences are attempting to attain), goes back to the late work of Wilhelm Dilthey in the first years of the twentieth century. Dilthey's concern is explication of the relationship between scientific knowledge and the knowledge available in the cultural sciences (*Geistwissenschaften*). He presents a critique of a positivism which gave supremacy to scientific over social knowledge, by pointing out that explaining is a lower, though necessary, level of knowledge, than understanding. Understanding has to grapple with issues concerning the interpretation of representations and expressions of life. The objectivity of history for Ricoeur, then, is not based on positivism (the actuality of events and the concrete nature of historical data). It is based upon texts and their interpretation within the horizon of 'ultimate meaning'. We have no access to this ultimate meaning except through faith. It remains as a determining hope, a determining Utopia. It suggests the possibility of a Lord of history whose intention towards Creation is one of love. This position has two implications. First, 'a theology of love ... would at the same time be a theology of history' (*History and Truth*, p. 112). Secondly (as Ricoeur begins to see more and more), questions of history (and theology) turn upon the nature and interpretation of language or, more precisely, discourse.

It is because historiography is inseparable from interpretation that Ricoeur then details the nature of subjectivity as it operates dialectically within the objectivity of history. He draws attention to four aspects of this subjectivism. First, 'the notion of historical choice' (*History and Truth*, p. 26). Here the historian, selecting a field within which to research and the details in that field deemed worthy of attention, works always with an implicit theory of what counts as history. Secondly, historical explanation is founded upon seeing and clarifying certain causal connections and 'this ordering will always remain precarious' (*ibid.*, p. 26). Thirdly, because a certain historical distance comes into play between the historian and the past being investigated, then there is necessarily a 'withdrawing from his customary environment' and a projection of the historian 'hypothetically into another present' (*ibid.*, p. 28). Such projection is a form of imagination. Finally, fourthly, the historical investigation is always an intersubjectivity. For it is governed by 'a will for encounter as much as by a will for explanation' (*ibid.*, p. 29). Historians are therefore part of the past they are making explicable, since 'the men of the past are part of the same humanity' (*ibid.*, p. 29).

History, for early Ricoeur, is caught between a 'surrational meaning' (*History and Truth*, p. 94) which is theological, a concrete objectivity traced only in forms of representation and a subjective interrogation and appropriation of the meaning of such representations. What is constituted by these three relations is an 'existential scheme of historical ambiguity' (*ibid.*, p. 97). The truth of history is endlessly deferred. There are only histories – fragmentary, pragmatic and ephemeral. Again, a comparison with Michel de Certeau on this point is illuminating (see Chapter 4).

The Annales School

Ricoeur's early views on history and historiography (like Certeau's) were deeply influenced by the approach to the subject of Lucien Fèbvre and Marc Bloch. The School they founded, just before the opening of the Second World War, *Annales d'histoire économique et sociale*, brought about what Ricoeur later called 'the eclipse of the event in French historiography' (*Time and Narrative*, 1, p. 96). Where history no longer revolved around events engineered by great and influential people, then history was divorced from narrative. Here was a rejection of the Hegelian view of history with its great men like Napoleon bringing about events made meaningful within the whole pattern of history as it was emerging. Here was a rejection of Leopold von Ranke's insistence that history was comprised of 'scenes of freedom': 'A long series of events – succeeding, simultaneous to, one another – linked together in this way constitute a century, an epoch.'[29] The Annales School, though reacting against the excessive positivism of earlier French historiography, emphasized the complex factuality of history, rather than any concept of History founded upon metaphysical *a priori*. They subscribed to and built upon Raymond's Aron's view that no 'such thing as a *historical reality* exists ready made, so that science merely has to reproduce it faithfully'.[30] In his influential book *The Historian's Craft*, Marc Bloch advocates careful research of documents, but research conducted with an acute awareness of what it is to be human. In a famous chapter which undermines the possibility for historical objectivity by drawing attention to the frauds and human errors in any documentation, he writes:

> The truth is that the majority of minds are mediocre recording cameras of the surrounding world.... There is no reliable witness in the absolute sense. There is only more or less reliable testimony.[31]

Historians select and interpret, but the selection and interpretation always reduces and therefore betrays the shifting sands and kaleidoscopic complexity of time and place, cause and effect.

Reality offers us a nearly infinite number of lines of force which all converge upon the same phenomenon. The choice we make among them may well be founded upon characteristics which, in practice, fully merit our attention; but it is always a choice.[32]

History is always a construct, therefore, not a record or a reconstruction. Furthermore, as a construct it is always written, always a discourse.

Bloch will emphasize the need for historians to be interdisciplinary. The historians must consider the linguistic context, the geographical context, the religious and cultural context of any document or artefact bearing a 'trace' of the past. The historical 'fact' exists within a vast and expansive social reality. This social reality extends towards and embraces our own – for texts and archaeological documents will address us only in the light of the questions we have put to them. History must be, then, this total human phenomenon. It must deal with careful and scrupulous analysis, not philosophical synthesis and historical dogmatism. For Fernand Braudel, the short time span of event-dominated history must be replaced by history concerned with the *longue durée* which opens up a space within which changes can be understood and mapped. His own work *The Mediterranean and the Mediterranean World in the Age of Philip II*, is a leading example of history no longer taking as its object principal human actors in the political sphere.

Bloch and Fèbvre, like Aron, were students of the *Ecole Normale Supérieure*. Bloch was shot as a member of the French Resistance by the Nazis in 1944. Two years later Michel Foucault entered the same school. Foucault too was considerably challenged by the development of the Annales School in French historiography, which Jacques Le Goff christened *'L'Histoire nouvelle'* (quoted in *Time and Narrative*, 1, p. 246). Ricoeur, while excited and challenged by the work of Bloch and Braudel, became increasingly critical of their anti-narrative and anti-event stance. It is in this (and the metaphysical presuppositions narrative coherence infers) that he differs from Michel de Certeau (see Chapter 4). In *History and Truth* certain tensions are evident though not analysed. Ricoeur sees the work of the Annales School as a resource for countering the Hegelian move towards synthesis and the absolute. He utilizes their reflections upon historical 'traces' in documents and the human elements in both the making and the interpretating of such documents. Nevertheless, the German philosophical tradition – epistemological, ontological and, therefore, hermeneutical –

profoundly affects Ricoeur's thinking. For all his emphasis upon the positive nature of ambivalence – parallel to Bloch's insistence upon the 'nearly infinite number of lines of force' which constitutes reality – Ricoeur wishes to appeal to an overarching meaning, an eschatology or end of history which makes each event meaningful. Standing fully in the hermeneutical tradition, he wishes to move from 'explanation' to 'understanding'. In other words, Ricoeur demands that history, historical knowledge and historiography be grounded in the more primordial category of narrative understanding. This appeal to an ultimate emplotment of time, Jean-François Lyotard will term a 'grand narrative' or a 'metanarrative'. This is a universal narrative, such as Hegel or Marx's views of history, which claims to organize and explain the real meaning of other small narrative practices.[33] This dialectic between existential ambivalence and the horizon of what is ultimately meaningful, will constitute the determining problematic in Ricoeur's *Time and Narrative*, as we shall see.

Hayden White

Later, Ricoeur will observe that the relation of history to narrative was not 'directly at issue in the first phase of the debate during the forties and fifties' (*Time and Narrative*, 1, p. 111). It became an issue partly because of an accelerated interest in narrative which became pronounced in France in the wake of structuralism. Prior to this, a landmark in the development of narratology was established in 1928 by the Russian formalist Vladimir Propp. He took a hundred Russian folk tales and attempted to determine the fundamental elements in their structure. *The Morphology of the Folktale* became a classic only much later when Russian formalism and the linguistic investigations of Ferdinand de Saussure came together in the first wave of French structuralism. Claude Lévi-Strauss, A.J. Greimas, Gerard Genette, Roland Barthes, Jacques Lacan, René Girard, Michel Foucault and Jean-François Lyotard all began to pay great attention to the nature of narrative. On the basis of their work (and the work done in the 1960s by Arthur C. Danto and William H. Dray on the philosophy of history) the American historian, Hayden White, began to examine the relation between narrative and historiography. His work represents an important attempt to grasp 'the deep structure of the historical imagination' as it creates and configures the 'historical field' (the raw data of history prior to analysis or representation). White insisted on treating 'the historical work as what it most manifestly is: a verbal structure in the form of a narrative prose discourse'.[34] With White the 'writtenness' of history is foregrounded; the work of new historicism only takes this one step further, as we will see towards the end of this chapter.

Briefly, White begins by creating a four-fold classificatory system, each section of which subdivides also into four. First, every historian configures history according to a certain type of narrative plot. There are, following Northrop Frye's typology,[35] four major forms of emplotment: the romantic, the tragic, the comic and the satiric. Secondly, historians not only emplot history, they also seek to explicate what it all adds up to. They argue for what happens in their stories in such a way that they invoke 'putative laws of historical explanation'.[36] There are four forms such arguments can take: formist (emphasizing 'the uniqueness of different agents, agencies and acts'[37]); organicist (in which every event is a part of the whole); mechanicist (where history is governed by divine laws and their operations); and contextualist (where events take on their meaning only in relation to their contexts). Thirdly, every 'idea of history [is] attended by specifically determinable ideological implications'.[38] Following Karl Mannheim's typology, there are four forms such ideology can take: anarchist, radical, conservative and liberal. Finally, historians emplot, argue and ideologically structure their own work in a particular historiographical style. Following French structuralism, White employs 'four basic tropes for the analysis of poetic, or figurative, language':[39] metaphor, metonymy, synecdoche and irony. In good structuralist company, White asserts that the linguistic 'prefiguration' of the historical field is primordial. The synchronic and diachronic axes of discourse is maintained throughout and the forms of emplotment, argument and ideology are determined by that primary 'linguistic act which is tropological in nature'.[40]

The four-by-four grid represents what White calls 'the ideal-type structure of the "historical work"'.[41] Having thus outlined the ideal, he can then plot specific works of the historical imagination on this map. In his most influential work, *Metahistory* (1973), he plots the work of famous nineteenth-century historians (Michelet, Ranke, Tocqueville and Burckhardt) and philosophers of history (Hegel, Marx, Nietzsche and Croce). White wishes also to make a further claim that historical analysis in the nineteenth century shifted from metaphoric to ironic as, increasingly, reflection upon the nature of historiography brought about a crisis of historicism. By the end of the nineteenth century, in the world of history there was an 'irreducible relativism of all knowledge'.[42]

Arguably, the importance of White's work lies not in his evaluations of particular historians (for example, Michelet thought himself a Liberal was, in fact, an Anarchist, 'came to rest in the mode of Metaphor, and emplotted history as Romance'[43]) – although those evaluations are much more subtle than he is often given credit for. The value of White's work lies in his method of examining history as a form of discourse. As such, historiography opens itself to an investigation which employs tools devised by textual criticism, critical theory and narratology. Questions of history cannot be separated from questions concerning representation. History is written (although White, in true neo-Kantian fashion, will still maintain it is 'out there' as the primary historical field). No objectivity in historical science is possible. History is not even determined by authorial intention. It is determined by the structure of language itself. Historical 'explanation' and historical 'realism' are simply effects of writing. Nor is any evaluative judgement possible between these modes of representing the historical. White concludes that 'the only grounds for preferring one over another are moral or aesthetic ones'.[44] However, surely, a moral judgement relates to an ideological perspective and is also, therefore, determined by tropology. So, the only ground for evaluation is then aesthetic. New historicism will concur with White.

We move closer here to the postmodern question of the 'end of history',[45] the view that history itself is a product of modernity. White, of course, would want to claim that the metahistorical 'grid' upon which all acts of history writing can be mapped, transcends all historiography. What is the status of this grid, this ideal? In what relation does it stand to the pre-critical data which constitute the historical field? Is the grid simply a regulative ideal, in a Kantian understanding of that word? Is it the structure of human consciousness itself, and so an epistemological structure? Or is it the structure of reality itself? White does not say, and that is fundamental. For without detailing the status of his grid then he leaves unanswered the question of the relationship of truth and history. In fact, he opens the way for the eradication of the distinction between history and fiction which new historicism exploits when it overthrows White's metaphysical assumptions about structuralism.[46]

Ricoeur and narrative

Ricoeur, indebted to White, nevertheless perceives the unanswered questions: 'White's recourse to tropology runs the risk of wiping the boundary between fiction and history' (*Time and Narrative*, 3, p. 154). It is exactly the epistemological and ontological status of the historical (in terms of both the temporal condition of being human and as a form of discourse) which concerns Ricoeur's return to the problematic of history and truth in the three volumes of *Time and Narrative* (see n. 26 above). '[W]e shall give this debate between the ontology of historicality and the epistemology of historiography the attention it fully deserves' (*ibid.*, p. 73). In volume 1 of that work he acknowledges his debt to both *l'histoire nouvelle* and Hayden White. He differs from White in his commitment to a diachronic analysis of the relationship between time, history and narrative. White continually draws us back from the emplotment and its argument to the synchronic structure of discourse itself. In brief, White lacks Ricoeur's commitment to, and examination of, the problem of time; more particularly, the relationship between cosmological time, the human experience of time and narrative time.

Along with this concern to investigate the problematic of time (examined through Aristotle, Augustine, Kant, Husserl and Heidegger) is an equal concern to investigate the nature of mimesis or representation. In fact, these two foundational themes of Western metaphysics are related through narrative which configures the two antithetical forms of time (world time and human time), and in doing so refigures the nature of temporality for the reading subject. As Ricoeur puts it: 'the hypothesis that governs our inquiry, [is] namely, that the effort of thinking which is at work in every narrative configuration is completed in a refiguration of temporal experience' (*Time and Narrative*, 3, p. 3). This second concern, with mimesis, has preoccupied Ricoeur from his *Fallible Man* (1960) which developed his ideas on the correlation of the human will and understanding through attention to language, particularly the verb (*Fallible Man*, p. 36). In the second part of *Fallible Man*, *The Symbolism of Evil* (1960), Ricoeur delves deeper into the nature of representation in terms of myth, symbol and metaphor. In *The Rule of Metaphor* (1975), Ricoeur then analyses how the function metaphor in the sentence is to open up an irreducible surplus of meaning. As he writes at the beginning of *Time and Narrative* (a book Ricoeur conceived as complementing *The Rule of Metaphor*), he now extends his analysis to the new horizons of meaning opened up by larger units of discourse, namely narrative emplotment. The point is that history (both in the sense of an historical science and the actions of human beings in the world) cannot be divorced from philosophical reflections upon time and its configuration. The historian does not handle events, but the traces of those events in documents which emplot those events. This is because narrative is both the condition of our temporal existence (*Time and Narrative*, 1, p. 52) and the expression of all historical consciousness.

Hence, central to Ricoeur's investigation is examining 'the dissymmetry that occurs between historical narrative and fictional narrative when we consider their referential implications, along with the truthclaim made by each of these two great narrative modes' (*Time and Narrative*, 3, p. 5). This examination was absent from his earlier analysis of history and truth (though there are references in those essays to the importance of narrative). His examination proceeds by outlining the difference between historical intentions and the intentions of fiction and, on the basis of this, raising two ontological questions. First, what we mean by 'the word "reality" when applied to the past' (*ibid.*, p. 100). Secondly, what the ontological status of reading literature is which 'returns to life, that is, to the practical and affective field of experience' (*ibid.* p. 101).

The intentions of historiography are determined by three features which Ricoeur lists: the calendar, which presupposes a founding event from which it is possible to 'traverse time in two directions' (*Time and Narrative*, 3, p. 106), a past and future, and which determines set units of measurement; the succession of generations (whereby a community of time is constituted with reference to a 'remembered past, a lived present, and the anticipated future' (*ibid.*, pp. 112–13)); and archival documents in which the past has left a trace in so far as this material bears witness to that past. The important characteristic of these three features, for Ricoeur, is that each mediates the fundamental *aporia* in time between human time and cosmic time. Each refigures time, creating what Ricoeur names 'historical time'. The calendar time evidently relates to cosmic time, but '[i]f we did not have the phenomenological notion of the present, as the "today" in terms of which there is a "tomorrow" and a "yesterday", we would not be able to make any sense of the idea of a new event that breaks with the previous era' (*ibid.*, p. 107). Similarly, each generation 'is a mediating structure between the private time of the individual fate and the public time of history' (*ibid.*, p. 113). Finally, each document in every archive is the result of an institutional activity which has chosen 'what should be conserved, what thrown away' (*ibid.*, p. 116). Such documentation constitutes historical proof. Such documentation nourishes the claim that history is based upon facts, but the authority of such a document lies in the significance of its trace of the past. Also it is a trace of an event which is absent and constructed by human testimony to its passing. The trace of the past in archival material then also interweaves 'the phenomenological perspective and the cosmological perspective on time' (*ibid.*, p. 123). In the trace the existential and the empirical overlap. Each of these features is mediated through an inscription which requires interpreting. The past as such does not appear. It is absent. Only traces of its passing remain. Historical positivism is based upon these mediations. Historiography as such, therefore, is the narrative refiguration of the interweaving of human and cosmic temporality.

In this way, Ricoeur (unlike White) can distinguish the task of historiographer from that of the writer of fiction. For the writer of fiction is removed from the constraints of cosmological time documented in archives to which the historian is obliged to pay respect. The writer of fiction can then explore 'the resources of phenomenological time that are left unexploited or are inhibited by historical narrative' (*Time and Narrative*, 3, p. 128).

In what relation does this historical narrative stand to the reality of past events? This becomes the second part of Ricoeur's analysis. It also opens up a second major difference between the historian and the novelist. For Ricoeur, drawing upon the rich resources of the German language for talking about mimesis, distinguishes between representation as *vertreten* ('to stand for' or 'to take the place of') and representation as *vorstellen* (to create a mental picture of). The narrated event 'stands in for' and, therefore, bears a certain correspondence to, the real event.[47] Ricoeur introduces here his work on metaphor and analogy (and White's work on tropology). For this 'standing in for' is the basis of analogy and metaphor. Ricoeur concludes that 'between a narrative and a course of events, there is not a relation of reproduction, reduplication, or equivalence but a metaphorical relation' (*Time and Narrative*, 3, pp. 153–4). The analogical character of historical narrative means that there is some relation of identity between the present narration and the past event and yet there is also a recognition of difference, a recognition that the 'past is a foreign country, they do things differently there'.[48] This is an important move for Ricoeur because he has consistently argued throughout his work on metaphor for the epistemological and ontological import of this trope: '"seeing-as", which sums up the power of metaphor' is 'the revealer of a "being-as" on the deepest ontological level' (*Time and Narrative*, 1, p. xi). It is this epistemological and ontological import which Ricoeur now attempts to locate in narrative discourse. It is in this way that

Ricoeur can affirm that although 'we have to combat the prejudice that the historian's language can be made entirely transparent' (*Time and Narrative*, 3, p. 154), nevertheless the analogical correspondence between a course of events and a historian's configuration of those events ensures that 'the being-as of the past event is brought to language' (*ibid.*, p. 154). The trace of the past is retraced and so 'historians can, absolutely speaking, be said to refer to something "real"' (*ibid.*, p. 157). The reality to which historians refer is not the naive empiricism of positivists, but it bears nevertheless the trace of having actually occurred. We cannot discover the past without also inventing it to some extent. His realism is therefore a qualified one. Hence, after Volume 1 of *Time and Narrative*, Ricoeur drops the use of the word 'reference' with its positivistic freight.

If historiography is indebted to the literary imagination and 'history is quasi-fictive' (*Time and Narrative*, 3, p. 190), the crux of Ricoeur's argument for the truth in history pivots upon the ontological import of metaphor: that the past event and the present configuration share the same ontological horizon. If they do not, then the distinction between historical narrative and fiction cannot be founded upon a distinction between *vertreten* and *vorstellen* and 'historians do not know the past at all but only their own thought about the past' (*ibid.*, p. 146). The first distinction, about the constraints of cosmological time on the historian remains. However, on its own, this distinction can never argue for the truth of the historian's work. If the writing of history is governed by the illusion of truth rather than truth itself then *la recherche du temps perdu* is open to ideological manipulations, the deliberate manufacture of illusions to truth. It is at this juncture that we meet the work on history by Michel Foucault.

Michel Foucault

Born in Poitiers in 1926 and, significantly, educated in Catholic schools before proceeding to the *Ecole Normale Supérieure*, Foucault's early interests were primarily in philosophy and psychology. However, although he was always concerned with historical methodology, he was, unlike Ricoeur, also a writer of 'histories'. For the last fourteen years of his academic career (1970–84), he held a chair in the History of Systems of Thought at France's most prestigious institution the *College de France*. It was an institution that had honoured several of the leading members of the Annales School – Lucien Fèbvre, Fernand Braudel, Georges Duby and later (proposed and supported by Foucault)

Philippe Ariès. From his early publication, *Madness and Civilization: a History of Insanity in the Age of Reason* (1961), which catapulted him to intellectual fame, to the four volumes of *The History of Sexuality* (the final one still in draft when Foucault died of an AIDS-related illness in 1984), Foucault's work is both philosophical and historical in nature.[49] Like the Annales School, his historical work refused to concentrate upon the explanation of major events and the significance of major figures. Rather, it too examined long periods of time beneath political events. *The Birth of the Clinic: An Archaeology of Medical Perception* (1963), *The Archaeology of Knowledge* (1969), *Discipline and Punish: The Birth of the Prison* (1975), all work with what the Annales School termed the *longue durée*.

Foucault's historiography was also shaped by the work of his own teachers: Garston Bachelard's concern with the philosophy of science and epistemological ruptures; Georges Canguilhem's concern in the history of science with the displacement and transformation of concepts.[50] From another teacher, Louis Althusser, Foucault learned the intractability of ideology. The way, then, he approached the writing of history and the kinds of histories he produced, articulated a distinctive philosophy which stood firmly against the metaphysics of essences, subjects, objects, reality and truth. In a debate staged in 1978 between French historians and philosophers, Foucault explained: 'My books are neither philosophical treatises not historical studies; at most, philosophical fragments on historical building sites.'[51] Ricoeur's problematic of history and truth was never Foucault's because for Foucault historiography is not concerned with any ultimate truth, any eschatological horizon of meaning. The truth of History, the ontology of historiography, was of no interest to him at all. Foucault will rather speak of 'the games of truth' (*jeux de vérités*) (*The History of Sexuality*, 2, p. 6) and histories (plural and in a lower case). For truth as knowledge (*savoir*) is wedded to discourse and social disciplines. Discourse then is wedded to power relations as they emerge and operate within society. The objects of Foucault's histories are specific practices and the power-knowledge discourses which maintained, justified and policed them. This understanding of truth has its roots in Kierkegaard and Nietzsche. It was Nietzsche, in *Daybreak* who first announced that 'All historians speak of things which have never existed except in imagination.'[52] Nietzsche stands in a tradition therefore opposed to the explanation/understanding of a general hermeneutics which informs Ricoeur's approach to history and truth. With Foucault, following Nietzsche, we face the 'epistemological mutation of history' (*The Archaeology of Knowledge*, p. 11).

We can see from this why Foucault is more interested in specific practices rather than causation, tradition, influence, development and evolution. He is more interested in drawing maps of the various principles involved in 'games of truth' rather than attempting to reconstruct as accurately as possible the event, the situation, as it had once been and its connections and continuity with other events. So, for example, in Volume 2 of *The History of Sexuality: The Use of Pleasure*, Foucault is concerned not with the evolution of pagan ethics of sexual behaviour into Christian, but with mapping the 'restructuration of the forms of self-relationship and a transformation of the practices and techniques on which this relationship was based' (*ibid.*, p. 63). Three specific terms enable us to grasp the nature of Foucault's historical project, its philosophical presuppositions and implications: archaeology, genealogy and eventalization (*événementialiser*). It is these presuppositions and their implications that we are interested in, along with how Foucault's approach to historiography may challenge and change the methods for constructing histories of Israel and the Church.

Archaeologies

In the Introduction to *The Archaeology of Knowledge* – a book which reflects upon changes in the field of historical knowledge and their implications – Foucault acknowledges his debt to the Annales School in the development of his concept of an 'archaeology'. For the Annales School, in their emphasis upon long periods, unearthed the 'unmoving histories' beneath 'the rapidly changing history of governments, wars and famines'. Beneath the surface of events they distinguished 'various sedimentary strata' and so histories as 'linear successions ... have given way to discoveries in depth' (*ibid.*, p. 3). However, Foucault's debt to the Annales School is not without criticism. For the Annales School in its search for stable structures in the sediments of change suffered, like the structuralists, from a certain tendency towards idealism. Bachelard and Canguilhem were discovering and teasing out the discontinuities, a 'substructure ... implied by the interplay of transmissions, resumptions, disappearances, and repetitions' (*ibid.*, p. 5). It is the notion of discontinuity which Foucault's 'archaeology' explores and affirms. Such a notion was the enemy of philosophies of universal history (still influencing Ricoeur), which sought to establish patterns of homogeneous relations and dissolve radical differences along the line of a single ontological horizon.

What both the work of the Annales School and the work of

Bachelard and Canguilhem agreed upon was the centrality of the document as a monument to the past. 'History is that which transformed documents into monuments' (*The Archaeology of Knowledge*, p. 7). Archaeology is concerned with the relationships between such documents as monuments, how they constitute distinctive series 'which are juxtaposed to one another, follow one another, overlap and intersect, without one being able to reduce them to a linear scheme' (*ibid.*, p. 8). Foucault takes up a series as it has already been defined – psychopathology, for example, in *Madness and Civilization* or codes of correction and punishment in *Discipline and Punish*. He then assesses the politics and the power relations that enabled such a series to be constituted, and charts the differences and correlations between one series and another. The basis for this work was hours spent digging into archival materials, spending a large proportion of each day in the *Bibliothèque Nationale* and, later, the *Bibliothèque du Saulchoir*.

In allowing the discontinuities to emerge in any series and between any series, Foucault problematizes the object (whether it be madness, the clinic or the penitentiary) which seems to unify all the discourses that make up this series. Madness in the seventeenth century is not the same object as the illness which preoccupies early psychopathology or the object being policed through the development of legal procedures for judging the insane. Sexuality for the ancient Greeks was not the same object as that which emerged as a consequence of the Christian redescription of the flesh and the regulative practices (like confession) engineering new models of selfhood and desire. What an archaeology attempts to do is to present the interplay of rules governing the social and intellectual space in which the object can emerge, locate itself in relation to other objects in the field, be transformed, even forgotten or replaced. The object, then, only exists 'under the positive conditions of a complex group of relations' (*The Archaeology of Knowledge*, p. 45). The object does not exist constantly and essentially in its own right. It is dispersed and an archaeology maps out that dispersal; it traces the rules for its formation, its constitution. As Foucault writes concerning his analysis of psychiatry in *Madness and Civilization*:

> on examining this new discipline, we discovered two things: what made it possible at the time it appeared, what brought about this great change in the economy of concepts, analyses, and demonstrations, was a whole set of relations between hospitalization, internment, the conditions and procedures of social exclusion, the rules of jurisprudence, the norms of industrial labour and bourgeois

morality, in short a whole group of relations that characterized for this discursive practice the formation of its statements. (*The Archaeology of Knowledge*, p. 179)

This mode of analysing objects can also be employed in analyzing the formation of concepts, and with the same result. Concepts arise only in and through a group of rules and a series of practices which govern them. They do not arise because they exist independently, essentially, as transcendental forms or ideas. What applies to the formation and transformation of concepts, applies also to the human subject. It too is constituted. It too is given an identity. We saw the influence of this approach to subjectivity in Chapter 1 with the work of Judith Butler. The de-centring of the primacy of the subject or consciousness (fundamental to philosophy from Descartes to Kant, from Hegel to Sartre) is axiomatic to Foucault's project (as it was also for structuralists like Lévi-Strauss and Lacan). The collapse of the subject required the end of humanism.[53] For Foucault, the self issues from and with reference to a certain infrastructure of discourses; it is therefore both created and able to create itself. Later, Foucault develops his thinking here beyond the archaeology of discourses into non-discursive 'games of truth' which provide the modern soul and its body with certain technologies for its creation and recreation. Foucault the homosexual, who looked forward to 'a culture which invents ways of relatings, types of existence, types of exchanges between individuals which are really new',[54] will develop a concept of freedom on the basis of the construction of selfhood. 'We have to promote new forms of subjectivity', he wrote, towards the end of his life.[55] We will return to this again when outlining the new models of selfhood and ethics which have emerged in critical theory in Chapter 3. For the moment we can allow Foucault to sum up the function of archaeology:

To define [these] objects [concepts, subjects] without reference to the ground, the foundation of things, but by relating them to the body of rules that enable them to form as objects of a discourse and thus constitute the conditions of their historical appearance. (*The Archaeology of Knowledge*, pp. 47–8)

Genealogies

Although, in his archaeological work, Foucault's concern seems to have been with the formation of institutions (the asylum, the hospital) and an analysis of power as it is manifested in specific discourses and knowledges, towards the end of his life Foucault described his true goal as ethical. 'To create a history of the different modes by which, in our culture, human beings are made subjects.'[56] In this he was consciously building upon Nietzsche's examination of the development of moral consciousness through the repression and socialization of the animal instinct in *Genealogy of Morals*. Foucault's archaeology is now complemented by 'genealogy'. In fact, some would say that genealogy becomes Foucault's main method of analysis in his later work.[57] It emerges as a term at a time when Foucault begins to give a new emphasis to the subject of the body, its pain and confinement, its pleasures and ascesis.[58] Archaeology is concerned with diagnostic rules (for formation and transformation of discourses and knowledges). The theory of archaeology, propounded systematically in *The Archaeology of Knowledge*, owes much to the structuralist climate in France in the 1960s. In his Conclusion to that book Foucault starts to ask himself questions which, though refuted, begin to question his methodology. What his new emphasis upon genealogy fostered was a much clearer rejection of the reality of rules or orders for historical appearance. He termed these rules and orders in that book historical *a priori* (*ibid.*, pp. 126–31). Although he insisted on archaeology's anti-transcendental position – it was not concerned with identities, universal reason, the correlation of part to whole – nevertheless, his whole theoretical examination of archaeology was an attempt to identify objective, universal rules for the formation and transformation of various discourses. Like structuralism, its aim was both ahistorical and highly theoretical.

The task of 'genealogy' was to reveal that things 'have no essence or that their essence was fabricated in a piecemeal fashion from alien forms' (*Language, Counter-Memory, Practice*, p. 142), but without formulating rules. The emphasis is not upon structures and discourses but fluid and multivarious non-discursive power relations which play in certain 'games of truth'. What Foucault is attempting to do through the method of genealogy is analyze, with more sophistication and subtlety, a concern that has remained fundamental to all his work: the relation of power to knowledge. The model of the subject or the object as it emerges in genealogy is the site for 'a perpetual battle rather than a contract regulating a transaction or the conquest of a territory' (*Discipline and Punish*, p. 26). Foucault goes on to add that these power relations 'are not univocal; they define innumerable points of confrontation, focuses of instability, each of which has its own risks of conflict, of struggles' (*ibid.*, p. 27). In *Discipline and Punish*, Foucault wished to analyse these relations as part of tracing the historical transition away from the body to the genealogy of the modern 'soul'. This was a soul which he affirmed existed though it was no longer defined by a Christian ideology. We would come to see this soul 'as the present correlative of a certain technology of power of the body' (*ibid.*, p. 29). The importance of this notion lay in the fact that it was upon this soul that certain modern concepts and discourses were constructed: the psyche, subjectivity, personality, consciousness and the ethics of humanism. It is in this sense that Foucault can reverse the Platonic heritage and state 'the man described for us, whom we are invited to free, is already in himself the effect of a subjection [*assujettissement*] much more profound than himself ... the soul is the prison of the body' (*ibid.*, p. 30).

In *The History of Sexuality*, we turn from the genealogy of the modern soul and its power to discipline the body to the construction of knowledges about the body's pleasures and desires. Foucault develops his notion of bio-power which he viewed emerging in the seventeenth century as a political technology concerned with population and labour force. His concern is the relations between history and life. Throughout both of these books the aim is to locate areas of dense power relations; sexuality seeming to Foucault to be the densest of all (*The History of Sexuality*, 1, p. 103) and that which has brought about a radical intensification of the body.

What is significant in this work is the questioning of certain common, transcendental assumptions about knowledge. We are called upon to abandon a whole tradition that has conceived knowledge, truth and the appeal to reason as objective and outside historical, geographical, personal, social and economic interests. History for Foucault, then, unlike Ricoeur, can appeal to no suprahistorical or apocalyptic objectivity (*Language, Counter-Memory, Practice*, p. 152):

> We should admit rather that power produces knowledge (and not simply by encouraging it because it serves power or by applying it because it is useful); that power and knowledge directly imply one another; that there is no power relation without the correlative constitution of a field of knowledge, nor any knowledge that does not presuppose and constitute at the same time power relations. (*Discipline and Punish*, p. 27)

Power is not simply institutional and repressive here. Power is universal and immanent. It is part of the very nature of society as the actions of any group of people modify and affect each other. Power is also constitutive – it determines focuses for attention and therefore creates the objects of knowledge that emerge in discourses; it creates forms of rationalization and invests them with a credibility. It is for this reason that in *The History of Sexuality* Foucault stands against the repressive hypothesis – that the truth of sexuality is becoming more evident as sexual repression is overthrown. For Foucault, both the discourses which appear to offer the new truth about our contemporary understanding of sexuality, and the discourses which seemingly repressed this truth in the past, are constructs masking the power relations which have brought them to birth. In particular, both discourses maintain a negative view of power – power as constraint and coercion. In rejecting this view of power, Foucault is not wishing to construct an alternative theory of power; rather he wishes to develop an analytics of power using archaeology and genealogy as his tools. It is in mapping out the various discourses on and of the desiring human being that archaeology and genealogy come together and the constitution of our contemporary sexuality can be mapped. We can see now why he became such a resource for Judith Bulter's work. In Volume 2 *The History of Sexuality: The Use of Pleasure*, it is from the archaeology of discourses on diets, marriage and management of the household, and the courting of boy-lovers that the genealogy of the aesthetics and ethics of the subject in classical antiquity emerges. This is offered as a comparative model to a sexual conduct governed by 'desire and its purifying hermeneutics' (*The History of Sexuality*, 2, p. 254) – a Christian understanding of the flesh which has governed modern notions of sexuality.

Eventalization

We can see from this brief survey that Foucault's work is concerned with the present – where we have come from (as subjects, with souls and bodies); where institutions have come from; where certain discursive practices that form our social sciences (like psychiatry and psychoanalysis) have come from. It is not a history of the past in terms of the present (where the genesis of certain modem phenomena is retraced or the past is viewed through contemporary contact lenses) so much as an excavation revealing various levels or transformations within which these phenomena were made significant, changed their significance or disappeared altogether. The force-fields within which these phenomena form and transform are termed *dispositifs*, which

Hubert L. Dreyfus and Paul Rabinow translate (not accurately but intelligently) as 'grids of intelligibility'. It is Foucault's purpose to isolate these grids and the social practices of which they consist. Foucault is not searching for origins or causes; he is not trying to give us a more accurate picture of the past, a truer history. No accurate picture of the past can be given; no reconstruction of all the possible relations constituting an object of knowledge is possible. There is no true history.

It is in these 'grids of intelligibility' that specific practices are found inscribed by specific rationales and constituted by specific sets of power relations. Foucault's focus upon these he terms 'eventalization' (*événementialiser*). Eventalization is a product of genealogy – for it too redirects us towards non-discursive practices rather than simply the archaeology of discourses. Such eventalization might take the form of Damiens' horrific punishment for regicide (the account of which opens *Discipline and Punish* and operates as a cultural metaphor for the problematic Foucault wishes to analyze) or Charcot's methods for investigating women's sexuality in Salpetrière in the 1880s. However, each practice eventalizes a form of knowledge, its legitimation and verification. Each practice evidences its own logic, its own rationality. Therefore no one practice can be more true or more rational than any other. There can be no hierarchy of logics. Truth is a product of the practice itself. 'Each historical event has its own formal level and localisation' (*The Archaeology of Knowledge*, p. 189).

This return to the 'event' flies in the face of Annales School theory, but it is an event within which the subject is sidelined or decentred – neither Damiens nor Charcot interest Foucault. It is an event which is not examined as a catalyst for other events. While being singular and individual the event has no one meaning. Foucault's analysis of it diffuses its meaning; deconstructs it in terms of the force-field from which it emerges. In this way he can foreground his analytics of power and its symbiotic relation to knowledge. Michel de Certeau will engage in a similar activity with respect to the demonic possessions which took place in a seventeenth century convent in Loudon, as we will see in Chapter 4. Eventalization anchors analysis in the concrete and historically particular. This fact goes some way to counter the criticisms levelled at him by Jürgen Habermas and Charles Taylor among others,[59] that Foucault is attempting to do what he says cannot be done: deduce universal, ahistorical principles for the operation of power. Foucault is aware that his own work is part of another 'game of truth':

I am fully aware that I have never written anything other than fictions. For all that, I would not want to say that they were outside truth ... One 'fictions' history starting from a political reality that renders it true, one 'fictions' a politics that does not yet exist starting from a historical truth.[60]

Being aware that he too is involved in a power/ knowledge symbiosis does not mean that his work is self-refuting, that it collapses beneath the weight of pronounced relativism. Eventalization returns us always to what is specific and the plotting of technologies of subjection within precise locations. Foucault offers us a mode of historical critique which enables us to assess the political dynamics of our present condition and to affirm or resist those dynamics in the search for 'new forms of subjectivity'.

New historicism

On 4 September 1986, Professor Stephen J. Greenblatt (Professor of English literature at the University of California, Berkeley) gave a lecture at the University of Western Australia which he began by stating:

A few years ago I was asked by *Genre* to edit a selection of Renaissance essays, and I said, OK. I collected a bunch of essays and then, out of a kind of desperation to get the introduction done, I wrote that the essays represented something I called a 'new historicism'. (*Learning to Curse*, p. 146)[61]

So the labelling of a literary and historiographical practice, which Greenblatt had already developed and demonstrated in his 1980 book, *Renaissance Self-Fashioning*, began in 1982, and Berkeley became its centre. As a practice of analysis, it exalts in Foucault's 'game of truth'. It is playful (evident in the ironic tone of Greenblatt's confession, its rhetorical debunking of academic discourse, and its pleasure in pronouncing an intellectual act as arbitrary) and undertheorised. But its values, methods of inquiry, its focus on power, production and the market, and its views on what constitutes a culture, are indebted to a marriage between Foucault and the American anthropologist Clifford Geertz.

Influences

In developing what was termed variously as a 'cultural semiotics' and an 'interpretive anthropology,'[62] Geertz developed the term (coined by the Oxford philosopher Gilbert Ryle) 'thick description'. This covered a form of analysis in which a particular event, ritual, custom, object or idea was interpreted through determining its particular social grounding. The task of the ethnographer, as he put it, was to relate any form of symbolic action to its 'multiplicity of complex conceptual structures, many of them superimposed upon or knotted into one another ... which he must contrive somehow first to grasp and then to render'.[63] Influenced by Wittgenstein's work on 'language games' and 'life forms', and his attack on private theories of meaning, influenced also by the structural anthropology of Lévi-Strauss, Geertz established a theory of culture as a collection of socially established systems of meaning in terms of which people act and communicate. These socially established systems constitute the context for any strange object, practice or experience encountered by the anthropologist. As such the anthropologist can describe these forms of human behaviour either thinly (that is, reductively – merely as observable 'facts') or thickly (that is, disclosing their meaning by examining the manifold layers of the social semiotics in which they are located and produced). Such a description offered an interpretation of what, to the outsider, was alien and other. In this way, events of anthropological and ethnographical interest can be treated as 'texts'. So, in Geertz's famous essay 'Deep Play: Notes on the Balinese Cockfight',[64] he reads the Balinese interest in cockfighting as indicative of the 'styles of feeling' of the people themselves: how they stage a repressed violence through these fights.

Significantly, both for the method of 'thick description' and, later, the practices of new historicism, Geertz is explicit that interpretive anthropology produces only 'fictions', in the sense that they 'are made' and that, as such, this raises problems of verification for those who wished to construct anthropology as a strict science. Furthermore, even though practicing 'thick description' fosters a concern for the local and microscopic, nevertheless interpretive anthropology wishes to draw more general conclusions. Geertz tackled the various objections by emphasizing that, given the complex overlay of symbolic systems, 'Cultural analysis is intrinsically incomplete'[65] and necessarily contestable. That, therefore, one analysis builds on, develops and extends the thickness of another. And that, given the symbolic nature of social actions, analysis of micro-practices will inevitably speak to larger issues, possessing, intrinsically, wider implications for social discourse and the politics of meaning. It was important, given that Geertz was attacking other reductive ethnographical methods that were theory-driven, that the process of analysis in interpretive anthropology was seen to be inductive rather than deductive. It may make some generalizable claims, it may employ various theoretical frameworks in approaching its material, but (unlike Lévi-Strauss' structural anthropology) it is not based in a theoretical position. Likewise, returning to new historicism, Stephen Greenblatt can say that it is 'a practice rather than a doctrine, since as far as I can tell (and I should be the one to know) it's no doctrine at all'. But it is evident that a certain circularity appertains to Geertz's method which will be significant for the methodologies of new historicism: for Geertz reveals the manifold and complicit layers of social semiotics that he assumes to be there to start with. His model of culture is both the lens through which he views the particular situation and the object he finds presented for his view. In other words, Geertz's 'thick descriptions' elide a difference between what is out there and his description of what is out there; the object under study and his interpretation of the object.[66] We will return to this.

The other major influence, as I said above, is the work of Foucault. Foucault in fact spent the last five or six years of his life teaching at Berkeley. His impact upon Greenblatt's work is evident in the concern about power and the formation of the self, central themes of new historicism's *locus classicus*, *Renaissance Self-Fashioning*. Here Greenblatt studies the ways in which selfhood was created through power embodied in various institutions such as the court, the church, colonial administration and the patriarchal family. As with Foucault the analysis of power is always an analysis of specific practices and disciplines and therefore, also like Foucault, power lacks a focused agency. In Marxism the dominant agency is captialism, for example, working through various organs like labour and by a number of economic means. What Greenblatt adopts is Foucault's revisionist Marxism, where power is not simply a matter of economics and state governments, but adheres to the practices (and resistances) of everyday life. Here, although there are named individuals who act – like Thomas More who passes judgement upon the exorcisms performed by the Protestant heretic James Bainham – these individuals act on behalf of institutions larger than themselves against other institutional forms of power, some of which they are hardly conscious, of nevermind attempting to control. Power is anonymous and diffuse. It is every-where and yet ungraspable.

The sociological and anthropological descriptions of Geertz's 'cultural semiotics' new historicism supplements with Foucault's cultural politics. This combination is further supplemented by close textual reading developed with respect to literary texts by I.A. Richards and New Criticism. Greenberg was trained by exponents of New Criticism at Yale. What coheres in these three critical methods is an attention to representation itself; the way we represent the world and our experience within it to ourselves, and the way in which those representations substantiate and form those selves. It is not simply that new historicism views the sharp distinction between literature and social life as wrong. Nor is it simply trying to avoid the reductions and pitfalls of an ideological critique of literature (such as that offered by Marxism), on the one hand, or the organic unity and therefore autonomy of the literary text, on the other. New historicism is making greater claims than that. These are cosmological claims, in fact, for they announce the profound participation of the social in the literary to the extent that each is interpretable only with reference to the other.

What is foundational here is a universal intratextuality or an appre-ciation of 'the larger networks of meaning in which both the author and his works participate'. As such, every action is social and 'embed-ded in systems of public signification'; systems empowered and legitimated by institutions that form and fashion bodies, souls and how they are to be understood.

'Invisible bullets'

What this gives rise to is a new investment in the literary form of the essay and the anecdote; the anecdotal often provides the critical lever in an essay that then takes on a distinctive shape and function. If we take Stephen Greenblatt's essay 'Invisible Bullets', for example, the following characteristic form is evident. It opens with a quotation from a police report on Christopher Marlowe in which Marlowe is claimed to have said Thomas Harriot (an Elizabethan mathematician, navigator and cartographer) could work more and better miracles than Moses. We then examine the charge of atheism levelled at Harriot, looking closely at his book *A Brief and True Report of the New Found Land of Virginia*. This examination, which brings to light a 'relation between orthodoxy and subversion' is then used 'to understand the far more complex problem posed by Shakespeare's history plays' (*Learning to Curse*, p. 23). The problem is that of how the plays can be read as pronouncing both the political conservativism of the status quo and the radicalism of political critique, political alternatives. Though, before embarking on a close reading of three particular plays *(Henry IV, Parts 1 and 2* and *Henry V)* we delve into Machiavelli and the function of religion as a civic discipline, the atheism of Ralegh, and Harriot's encounter with the Algonquin Indians (an encounter which confirms Machievelli's thesis). Then comes an analysis of Prince Hal in *Henry IV, Part 1*, which points up the self-conscious theatricality of Hal over against Falstaff. Hal is forced to play his part in the scheme of state power, whereas Falstaff's performance is the manifestation of a natural disposition. The essay then moves to Hal's role in *Henry IV, Part 2*, but only by first looking into Thomas Harman's pamphlet *A Caveat for Common Cursitors*. The common point between the texts is

> that the founding of the modern state, like the self-fashioning of the modern prince, is shown to be based upon acts of calculation, intimidation, and deceit. And these acts are performed in an enter-tainment for which audiences, the subjects of this very state, pay money and applaud. *(Ibid.,* p. 53)

Henry IV, Part 2 ends, of course, with Hal's acceptance of the estab-lished order. Nevertheless, the subversion and criticism of that order is staged and the audience is implicated in legitimizing (by applauding) that staging. And so we proceed to *Henry V*, returning to the theatrical display of the charismatic authority of the king. Greenblatt now draws a comparison between Hal and Elizabeth I before returning to Harriot (where he began) and concluding:

> Like Harriot in the New World, the Henry plays confirm the Machiavellian hypothesis that princely power originates in force and fraud even as they drew their audience towards an acceptance of that power. *(Ibid.,* p. 65)

The intratextuality does not end there. We contemporary readers, with our own historical particularity, are brought into (and made complicit with) the text of Greenblatt's essay. For what we define as principles of subversion and order or authority in the Renaissance reflects some-thing about ourselves and what we define or avoid defining subversive in our own situations. New historicism, as such, is a symptom of our present cultural and political ethos; and we are challenged by it to ask why we do or do not legitimate its practices; why we find its window on the past interesting.

As for the title of the essay, 'Invisible Bullets', this becomes a metaphor on several levels: first it refers to a conception of disease, coined by Thomas Harriot, that killed off hundreds of the Algonquin Indians. Secondly, it refers to the ideologies of subversion (like atheism) produced by the establishment whereby we build up an immunity so as 'to contain alien forces effortlessly' (*ibid.*, p. 39). Thirdly, the 'bullets' are the various ploys and rhetorics of the essay itself with which the reader is infected – either to the point of being cured (understanding some unrecognized truth about Shakespeare's history plays) or to the point of being poisoned (that is, taken in by the clever historical dexterity of the writer, Greenblatt himself). But then who can say, who can legislate here? Has something been learned, have some new connections been made, or have we simply been chasing a wild goose up a garden path or reading a shaggy-dog story?

Social energy

It is evident from this synopsis that the literary text – in this case, Shakespeare's Prince Hal trilogy – remains central. Greenblatt was trained by the leaders of New Criticism – Cleanth Brooks and Maynard Mack. Indeed part of the exercise is to provide what literary criticism has been doing since at least Johnson's time: interpretations of specific texts. Some critics have suggested that, like the cultural liberalism it eschews, new historicism, privileges classical literary masterpieces. But this centralization of the text is, simultaneously, being decentralized as the investigation proceeds through the interpretation of other texts (and an interpretation of the relationship of each of these texts to that particular literary *corpus*): Harriot's, Machiavelli's and Harman's most particularly. This way of proceeding maps a perceived problematic in Shakespeare's history plays on colonialism, American history and ethnography (through Harriot), modern political theory (through Machiavelli) and sociology (though Harman). It is important to realize that Greenblatt is not saying that these discourses produced Shakespeare's trilogy or even directly influenced it. Such inferences belong to old historicism which thought in terms of cause and effect, held to a sharp distinction between the literary products of the imagination and the hard, stable facts of the social and historical background, and embraced a correspondence notion of language such that words passively reflect a world which is 'out there' and prior to its representation. The positivism of old historicism, founded upon a scientism rooted in the origins of the modern university with its call for educational disciplines to constitute their autonomous fields and methods, is rejected. Shakespeare's theatre as much produces the Renaissance emphasis upon spectacle and monarchial power as reflects it. Both are caught up with what Greenblatt terms 'social energy'. 'We identify *energia* only indirectly, by its effects: it is manifested in the capacity of certain verbal, aural, and visual traces to produce, shape, and organize collective physical and mental experiences' (*Shakespearean Negotiations*, p. 6), he writes. And further:

> What then is the social energy that is being circulated? Power, charisma, sexual excitement, collective dreams, wonder, desire, anxiety, religious awe, free-floating intensities of experience: in a sense the question is absurd, for everything produced by the society can circulate unless it is deliberately excluded from circulation. Under such circumstances, there can be no single method, no overall picture, no exhaustive and definitive cultural poetics. (*Ibid.*, p. 19)

Where what is paramount is representation, the endless promulgation and exchange of signs, then any particular text can be described 'thickly' by locating it with a field of cultural forces, and in this way the cultural critic can move from observations of a literary and concrete nature to more general observations concerning not only Elizabethan culture but also our own. Concentric circles of significance emerge from a literary textual epicentre, circles which modify the nature of the literary artefact. The literary texts – whether with Greenblatt on Shakespeare or Marlowe, or with Catherine Gallagher on George Eliot[67] or with Jane Tompkins on Harriet Beecher Stowe[68] – become allegories of cultural and political tensions. In this respect, new historicism is still continuing the cultural materialist investigations of literary critics like Raymond Williams. The fundamental difference is the degree of reflexivity in the writing.

The unavoidable concern with our present cultural habitus is part of the self-reflexive nature of new historicism. The historian or literary historian is himself or herself embedded in history and all of these histories are made, written. We will see some close correspondences here with the work of Michel de Certeau on the literary nature of historiography, in Chapter 4. The correspondences are not accidental. As with Foucault, Certeau also spent time teaching in the 1980s at Berkeley. Greenblatt stages the reflection upon the present by bringing in references to contemporary history, reading Lacan's construction of the self in psychoanalysis into *Othello*, introducing memories and experiences (his own and his father's), and employing a self-consciously modern idiom (like 'zany' and 'a bunch of'). Nevertheless, it remains true that although there are new historical examinations of Mediaeval, Romantic and modern literature and even studies of the *Rambo* movie series and the Reagan era, there is a particular investment of new historicist interest in Renaissance literature. This is not by chance. The concerns of Foucault with cultural practices and the fashioning of the self come together in the literature of early modernity. The disassociation between the political and the imaginative, the social and the literary, promoting in literary studies a division between text and context, is frequently understood to have taken place in the Romantic period. In the Renaissance period, what another new practitioner of new historicism, Jon Klancher, terms the 'delicate semiosis of history, culture and power' is more in evidence because 'politics and literature were still undifferentiated realms'.[69] There is also another reason why the Renaissance is a suitable period in literary studies for new historicism – and this will lead us into the metaphysical undertow of this intellectual project: the Renaissance was an age concerned with homology. In Greenblatt's Renaissance world, where the fluid relationship between the church and the theatre has its economic manifestations in the sale of liturgical clothing to the players' wardrobe, and where the exorcisms performed in the theatres and in the church have structural similarities, similitude is fundamental. As Frank Lentricchia incisively comments about new historicism: 'similitude is the invisible expressive centre, a "world-view" which functions as the principle of making sense of all things, causing ... all things to be visible and coherent in a relation of similarity.'[70] Greenblatt himself has declared that 'We are dealing ... with a shared code, a set of interlocking tropes and similitudes that function not only as the objects but as the conditions of representation' (*Shakespearean Negotiations*, p. 86). This cosmos of cultural symbols participating in flows of anonymous power is an analogical universe and as such bears fitting proximity to the Renaissance world view propounded by the likes of older literary historians such as E.M.W. Tillyard in *The Elizabethan World Picture*[71] and Arthur Lovejoy in *The Great Chain of Being*.[72]

The invisible power of similitude prevents new historicism from simply exulting in the arbitrary, although critics of Greenblatt's work have not always seen this. The persuasive power of new historicism lies in the way in which what may seem like 'an assemblage of disparate and fragmentary things, arbitrarily juxtaposed, their asserted cultural interconnections all too often depending on Greenblatt's skill at arrangement' (as one of his severer critics has commented),[73] does both enlighten aspects of the literary texts and argue for important, complex and elusive exchanges between institutions. Observations are made on the relationship between Church and society in Elizabethan England which will be of interest to ecclesiastical historians. For example, in his notorious essay 'Resonance and Wonder', which begins with an anecdote about Cardinal Wolsey's hat in a case at Christ Church, Oxford, Greenblatt argues for a shift in dramaturgy from Catholic concerns with ritual to post-Reformation theatre: a conscious secularization of the aesthetic. Another aspect of this shift is given attention in his essay 'The Improvisation of Power', where he states:

> The Anglican Church and the monarch who was its Supreme Head did not, as radical Protestants demanded, eradicate Catholic ritual but rather improvised within it in an attempt to assume its power.

More importantly, new historicist methodology espouses the metaphysics of monism; that is, that all the various forms of materiality in the world constitute reality as one substance. For Greenblatt, as for Aristotle, Hobbes and Spinoza (and more contemporary monists like Gilles Deleuze and Jean-François Lyotard), all is in flux or motion. In fact, Greenblatt's employment of *energia* when speaking about social energies is directly taken from Aristotle. Like more recent monists, the world-view of new historicism is deterministic (everything is bound up with everything else), and yet it is a determinism without a *telos* or development towards a higher or more perfect condition (unlike the monisms of Hegel and Marx).

The politics of history

This idealist metaphysics is in tension with the desire of the new historicist to touch the authentic and historically real in the past. This desire is testified to both by the appeal to the anecdotal ('rooted in the real' Joel Fineman comments[74]) and Greenblatt's own confession in a recent interview: 'I long for the touch of the real in the way that earlier generations longed for the touch of the transcendent.'[75] But the real is always mediated and so even the anecdote can only 'produce the effect of the real, the occurrence of contingency'.[76] This is close to a linguistic idealism; that is, there is nothing but the flux of matter which our representations shape and make meaningful. The consequent determinism of this metaphysics is also a source of tension. For new historicism's critical engagement with and exposure of the mechanisms of ideology and the economies of power commits it to a political vision. It is concerned with the marginal, for example, and the politics of the academic institution (which canonizes certain writers and abandons others to obscurity). In the same interview, Greenblatt states that 'One of the impulses for me deeply over the last 20 years is some idea of a democratic literary space'.[77] But how does this political impulse for change operate within a deterministic worldview? Does not new historicism's form of analysis simply suggest this is the way things are and always will be? Does not new historicism find itself inevitably affirming the status quo and challenging the liberal dreams that great art educates and provokes? Greenblatt's examination of Shakespeare's Prince Hal trilogy demonstrates how the ambiguity of plays that can be read as either politically conservative or radically subversive is part of a wider economy of power which produces and stages its own subversion *that it maybe more powerful*. The plays do not voice a criticism of the social and political; they are caught up with, reflect and promote the same power-relations evident culturally. Several critics of new historicism have raised this question of whether 'Ironically, with new historicism, critique may be diminishing its own socio–political efficacy'.[78]

To some extent, the tensions are a consequence of the method and return us to the apolitical 'descriptions' of Clifford Geertz. How can there be a movement from 'description' to 'perscription'; from the activity of interpretation to the activities of critique and transformation? From what 'higher ground' can new historicism's analyses advocate something better, when they recognize only too well that these analyses too are implicated in specific cultural force-fields? It is no accident that new historicism emerges when it does and is, by and large, an American (even Californian) affair. New historicism enables us to grasp the cultural transactions which empower or disempower certain literary forms, but since all literature is understood to be inseparable from such cultural transactions how can new historicism's analyses effect change? Marxist criticism escapes this tension between determinism and the impulse for change through its teleology, that is, it accepts an historical movement towards the liberation of the labourer and the transfiguration of capitalism. But new historicism does not work with such a teleological view of history. All is in flux and history is the ongoing representation of this flux, the textuality of time. There is no Darwinian sense of progress or development through time; there are simply new figurations of power-relations. Furthermore, because of the flattening out of time and space – the levelling out of the democratic literary playingfield – it is difficult to see how one can evaluate a better or worse ideological figuration of power-relations or a valuable or less valuable interpretation of a literary work. For the ideologies, literary works and the subsequent interpretations of literary works are all 'heterogeneous and unstable, permeable and processual',[79] to quote another leading new historicist, Louis A. Montrose. And we are all implicated in them. At the end of his article, 'The Poetics and Politics of Culture', Montrose argues that:

> If ... we bring to our students and to ourselves a sense of our own historicity, an apprehension of our own positionings within ideology, then we are at the same time demonstrating the limited but nevertheless tangible possibility of contesting the regime of power and knowledge that at once sustains and constrains us.[80]

This is a fine rhetorical flourish, and new historicism is about performing a certain persuasiveness, but one notes that it is framed by the subjunctive ('If') and while positing a 'limited ... possibility of contesting' seems to have to create a certain cultural hegemony (*the* regime of power and knowledge) in order to destabilize it. But is there one regime of power/knowledge and how would we know and how would we know that we position ourselves correctly with respect to it and therefore how would we know when we were contesting it? Ultimately, this flourish produces the effect of authority, but an authority without substance.

Montrose's rhetorical act repeats Greenblatt's observation: power (this time academic power) produces and stages its own subversions in order to become more powerful. But there are two problems arising from this conclusion which have bearing upon the political engagement of new historicism. First, there is no room here for genuine subversion; for all subversion is staged and already complicit. Secondly, and we found this too with Geerzt, the interpretation is yet another manifestation of the object it sought to interpret: the analytical process engages in a self-confirming circularity.

It is possible to see, then, how new historicism avoids radical indeterminacy, even the charge of being arbitrary; but it is less possible to see how it avoids the charges of nihilism, circularity and political quietism. Quietism because new historicism operates at the level of textuality, representation and description even though it appears to be diagnostic in its technique. As H. Aram Veeser points out: new historicism 'accepts the inevitability of emptiness'.[81] And Jonathan Goldberg, another practitioner of new historicism, only confirms this when he points to what historical truth new historicism unveils: 'restless energies, disorderly desires, aspiration.'[82] We return to the play of agonistic forces, the violence which generates representations to constain it, found in Geerzt's analysis of the Balinese cockfight; found also in the work of another critical theorist, René Girard.[83] As such, new historicism's methodology is keyed into a profoundly non-theological world-view. Nevertheless the question remains as to whether as a method which refuses the autonomy of any academic discipline and alerts us to the politics of meaning, it might prove useful to the study of theology.

Theological implications

This chapter has presented a series of different historiographical projects, focusing on three of the most important – Ricoeur's, Foucault's and the practices of new historicism. For each 'event' is crucial to the analysis, though for Foucault and new historicism, the emplotment and consequent configuration of that event (that is, relating that event to other events in a history such as Ricoeur pictures it) cannot give us access to any deeper truth about history than is already there on its very surface. Both Foucault and the new historicism are suspicious of narrative as a explanation; in fact, suspicious of the ideology of narrative itself. While not denying that there is temporal succession, Foucault and new historicism view narrative as reducing complexity to continuity, to a logic of cause and effect. Narrative neutralizes the event by dissolving its singularity and hence its power to resist both a cultural hegemony or a later historical interpretation of that hegemony. The micro-politics of the event, the local and situated knowledges it bears the traces of, these are fundamental to the historical projects of Foucault and new historicism. In the name of its own dynamic, narratives fail to be reflexive enough about the power relations constituting, and the logic located in, the event itself. Narrative is not, therefore, a privileged tool for truth about the event. It is for this reason that the field of events Foucault chooses to concentrate on resists continuity: the insane, the silence of the imprisoned, the polymorphous pleasures of the impassioned. As one feminist reader of Foucault has recently pointed out, 'genealogy as resistance involves using history to give voice to the marginal and submerged voices which lie "a little beneath history"'.[84] The purpose of historiography is cultural critique. When the past has powerfully affected the practices of our living today (and the way we theorize and think about those practices), then the historical task is to offer 'thick descriptions' of that past which point up the suppressed alternatives. Narrative, for Foucault and new historicism, remains too Hegelian, too imperialistic. But the appraisal of Nietzsche, for Foucault, turns even his own works into 'fictions'. And while new historicism still wishes to claim it is being true to the historical contexts within which literary production is embedded, nevertheless, as we saw, its commitment to cultural semiotics means that it cannot privilege its own accounts of the historical configurations whereby literary texts are interpreted. Thick description can always get thicker and these accounts say as much about our current cultural agendas as about the past's – and who can say whether they do not say much more?

In terms of theology's own concerns with history, Ricoeur's work offers the possibility of a hermeneutics of revelation and testimony. In fact, Ricoeur has quite explicitly provided these in his essays 'Preface to Bultmann', 'Towards a Hermeneutics of the Idea of Revelation', 'Towards a Hermeneutics of Testimony', and more recently, '*Experience et langage dans le discours religieux*'.[85] Ricoeur reveals that he sees his work developing in a line extending from Bultmann to the new hermeneutics of Ernst Fuchs and Gerhard Ebeling. His interpretation theory, in which language operates at the boundary of a transcendental horizon, offers a more detailed analysis of the relationship between the Word of God and the words of human beings. For interpreting the Bible as a text, Ricoeur's work has proved fruitful and its results are interesting.[86] It emphasizes a reader–response to the text (see Chapter 4) and therefore develops a phenomenology of religious experience. However, Ricoeur's more general understanding of the relationship between narrative and revelation (history, story and event), the co-implication of revelation and narrative, still awaits an extended theological (rather than interpretive) application. It could be developed into a narrative theology by being given a wider theological structure in terms of the economy of the Trinity, for example. Rowan Williams, in an article written in 1986, makes this suggestion.[87] Since the possibility for knowledge of God rests, theologically, upon the operation of the Trinity in salvation, then a more extended analysis, on the basis of Ricoeur's work, of the relation between the Word and the Spirit lies waiting to be undertaken.

Like Ricoeur (and White), Foucault and new historicism's work draws attention to the fact that history is written, it is composed by means of specific rhetorical strategies. Like Ricoeur (and White), their work acts as a check against historical positivism, and the analyses of Biblical and ecclesial history built upon such positivism. Unlike Ricoeur, the work of Foucault and new historicism also acts as a check against notions of eschatological development, or Christian expansionism. It would invite us to examine the politics of such notions. Far more than Ricoeur (or White), Foucault and new historicism points to the politics of discourses of truth or knowledge. Foucault's historical tools – archaeology and genealogy – have as yet (as far as I know) not been applied rigorously to Biblical narratives and their accounts of events or aspects of the Christian tradition (other than his own brief allusions to Christian notions of the 'flesh'). To some extent, feminist evaluations of the Gospel materials have emphasized the way each text is located in a cultural field that has produced it.[88] There has been some work done on the relationship between rhetoric and praxis in the medieval and contemporary church.[89] George Lindbeck's post-liberal development of a cultural–linguistic model for religion, although based on the anthropological investigations of Clifford Geertz, seems also in the spirit of Foucault.[90]

Of course questions of pluralism and relativism bubble quickly to the surface, in Lindbeck's work, in Foucault's and in new historicism's. For Foucault and new historicism it is not a problem; for any universal notion of Christian 'truth' it is. Christian theology, unless it is going to remain wilfully naive concerning the relationship between power/knowledge and the discourse/practices involved in the dissemination of such power/knowledge, must face those questions. Christian theology is a cultural product – it must examine itself as such and examine, as a consequence, its own force-field of legitimation.

To some extent, Greenblatt's work is rewriting church history. He is clearly fascinated by the rise of Protestantism and the displacement of Catholic liturgical consciousness into Renaissance theatre. His work offers new ways of rethinking and practising ecclesial historigraphy. Besides his own comments upon religion,[91] Foucault's genealogical method has perhaps most to offer the theologian by way of enabling new sociological analyses of the Church and its practices past and present. This work has already begun. Talal Asad has extended Foucault's analyses of monastic disciplines and the fashioning of selfhood and employed such analysis with reference to practices of the Islamic faith.[92] Furthermore, some of the most interesting work in feminism and queer theory has been done by historians concerned to trace the cracks in the monolithic patriarchy, androcentrism or hetero-sexualism of the past. The work of Kate Cooper and Caroline Walker Bynum on gender and representation in the Patristic and Mediaeval periods;[93] the work of Alan Bray, Bruce Smith and Michael Roche on homosexual desire and friendships in the Renaissance;[94] the work of Daniel Boyarin on the resistence to androcentrism in the Talmudic culture[95] – all are examples of Foucault-indebted scholarship which is changing our understandings of the theological past.

3
Theology and Ethics

Introduction

The world of Jean-Paul Sartre's existentialism is a world without God and a world in which human dignity is suspect. In *Huis Clos* (translated as *No Exit* or *In Camera*) three people, two women and one man, are locked in an elegantly apportioned room following their deaths. We discover they are also locked in a circle of never-to-be-gratified sexual desire. One of the women, Inez, is attracted to the other, Estelle, while Estelle is attracted to the man Garcin. Garcin only wants Estelle if she can support his failing self-esteem, but he needs the presence of Inez because as a suicide she has known cowardice and it is cowardice as an aspect of narcissism which has been his own abiding vice. Inez offers the possibility to Garcin, then, of understanding or sympathy. The three characters are in Hell and as Garcin knows 'Hell is ... other people!' Each tortures and toys with the others, making and breaking promises, one constantly begging another for trust, love, 'just a spark of human feeling'. No such spark is evident or offered. At their most naked, their stories having been confessed so that each sees the others clearly and without illusions, they all recognize that 'Human feeling. That's beyond my range. I'm rotten to the core ... I'm all dried up can't give and I can't receive. How could *I* help you?' Each then is alone while realizing 'Alone, none of us can save himself or herself.' They cannot constitute a community, though they are inextricably linked to each other for eternity. Calculating, isolated, the three characters occupy a space empty of meaning and ethical concern. Their world is an amoral one. The logic of what is right for one ('right' understood as 'self-satisfying' or an appeal to their own intuitive sense of what would be good for them) is incommensurate with what is 'right' for another.

Such a logic perpetuates subjective relativism and social atomism. The Augustinian ethical distinction between things in the world to enjoy (*frui*) and things in the world to use (*uti*),[1] the Kantian ethical distinction between treating humanity as an end rather than a means,[2] and the virtue ethics of Aquinas that spring from love (*caritas*) and move towards union with the Good,[3] have no significance here. No overarching ethical rationality will resolve the game that Estelle, Inez and Garcin will play out interminably.[4]

Where hell is conceived as living with other people, society is deemed agonistic or conflictual. This is Hobbes' world of conflicting, independent egos who prey upon each other. An ethics in such a world is founded upon self-preservation. It can be established only on the basis of some form of social contract – which preserves the well-being of the majority – policed and ratified by some coercive power. For social stability, those who agree to such a contract must constitute a majority or they will not be able to enforce and promulgate that contract. In Sartre's play the social contract has dissolved – what remains is simply the greedy, self-deluding desires of Inez, Estelle and Garcin and a state of perpetual civil war. It is that naked revelation of tortuous moral relativism, with its Nietzschean echoes of the will-to-power, which invokes a sense of judgement in the audience. The action takes place in camera, constituting the audience as a jury. The fact that the drama takes place within a religiously conceived space – hell as the place of judgement, a judgement being lived out by the three characters in which each is the torturer of the others – reinforces the theological, even explicitly Christian, framework within which the action takes place: divine arbitration, human sin, the good and the evil. No heaven is posited; the group form an antitype of the Church. Nevertheless, within this Hell, there is the memory of, and the nostalgia for, certain virtues – love, faithfulness, honesty, compassion, truth, heroism – which enables their mutual torturing to continue. The audience-as-jury embodies the nostalgias of liberal humanism. In the play there is no concept of a pre-ethical situation in which human beings before a Fall into sin lived in alignment with a natural law and a divine goodness. However, the idea that human beings are the cause and agents of an immorality whose consequences return upon their own heads is emphatic. For Sartre even an account of amorality requires theological staging and a theological cast standing in the wings (or, in *Huis Clos*, beyond the door which shuts the three characters within the room).

The question of the ethics of human existence is inextricably bound up with theological and philosophical categories: the nature of love, desire, the good, the just, and personal integrity. Despite the endless circles of their violence towards each other, the three characters in Sartre's play meditate upon the nature of the human condition. And despite the bleakness and despair, Sartre continues to write – write well, write dramatically, write profitably. Moral, metaphysical and aesthetic intentions govern Sartre's vision; an entrenched nostalgia for a dead God yet remains. It is not, then, just that religious teachings frequently delineate ethical codes, but more that any analysis of the human condition and the way we behave towards each other demands the use of transcendental categories if only to frame an articulation which is critical of such categories. As Julia Kristeva has put it, concerning the ethical position of Hegel, it was 'founded, as it must be in the West, on the remains of transcendental idealism' (*The Powers of Horror*, p. 30).

Biblical ethics

Within Western forms of monotheism (Judaism, Christianity, Islam) God has been pictured as embodying, maintaining and promoting the ethical standard against which all human behaviour is measured, justified or condemned. The denunciations of the eighth-century BCE prophets – Amos, Hosea, Isaiah and Micah – against the social injustices perpetrated by wealthy landowners and the sexual immorality of those seduced by Canaanite fertility cults, were all made in the name of a righteous God before whom all the nations of the world would be judged. Humility, mercy, justice and obedience were enjoined upon the people as ethical marks of faithfulness to Yahweh. Codes of good social practice – sexual, commercial, medical, dietary and liturgical – emerged at an early date and within the theological framework of a 'covenant' were given legitimation under the name of Moses. Biblical law bears traces of earlier Mesopotamian roots where the king administered a justice that had been divinely revealed. It eventually constituted the Torah which, from the fifth century BC and increasingly under the influence of Hellenism (after 333 BC), came to represent a universal law – the true way to live righteously. Only by following this way would the people be blessed and made fruitful by Yahweh, while evildoers would be punished. Later, in the second century BC and with the development of the Pharisees and the oral commentary upon the Torah, *halakhah* emerged – prescriptions, some of which were moral. These, when written down and collated, came to constitute the *Mishnah* towards the end of the second century AD.

At the centre of Christian ethics is a new relation to the Jewish law and its oral traditions. Whatever the complexities of interpretating the Bible, of deciding which, if any, of the words Jesus spoke can in fact be identified as His, of deciding whether these alleged words are consonant with or distinct from Pauline ethics, nevertheless, the New Testament remains normative for Christian ethics. As Karl Barth has put it, 'If He were not the Judge, He would not be the Saviour.'[5] At the heart of this normativity lies the ethic of love, the summation of the law, as given by Christ: 'You shall love the Lord your God with all your heart, and with all your soul, and with all your mind.' This is the great and first commandment and the second is like it: 'You shall love your neighbour as yourself' (Matthew 22.37–9, Mark 12.30–1, Luke 10.27). The extent to which this injuction can be elaborated upon is a matter of intense dispute. Some have seen a move from the general to a special ethics in the Sermon on the Mount. Others have viewed the Sermon on the Mount as expressing only a Matthean ethics for a Matthean community, therefore not the basis for a Christian ethics as such.[6] Such attempts to elucidate the Biblical foundations for a Christian ethics stumble into some of the problems we have already looked at in Chapter 1: the problems of representation which continually demands the supplement of interpretation. Jack T. Sanders wishes to distinguish between the ethics of Jesus (which is inextricable from 'his awareness of the immanence of the righteous God'[7]), and the ethics of Mark, Matthew, Luke, Paul, John, James and 'the later Epistles and the Apocalypse'. They are each ethical codes issuing from their own time and within their own contexts. Moral injuctions are inseparable from the sociological conditions from which they emerge and to which they give expression. Nevertheless, attempts have been made to extract the core areas of ethical concern, notably the New Testament teaching on divorce, sexuality, political obedience, money and toleration of others.[8] Certainly, what can be deduced from the New Testament's presentation of Jesus' law of love is a concern with what may be broadly termed 'social responsibility'. The welfare of our neighbours is to be a reflection of our care for ourselves and part of the circulation and sacrifices of love (the Greek *agape*). The welfare of both neighbour and self is the concern of a God who relates to and communicates with persons. The Christian God is a personal God – theological ethics, as such, is therefore interested in personhood (its development, its destruction, its redemption). A distinct personality, in imitation of Christ, expresses this personhood. Paul outlines the characteristic conduct of such a person in his Epistle to the Galatians:

'the fruit of the Spirit is love, joy, peace, patience, kindness, goodness, faithfulness, gentleness, self-control' (Galatians 5.22–3). To these Christian virtues others might be added – humility, generosity, courage, perseverance, faith and hope. The realm for the establishment and manifestation of these virtues is the Church, the new community, the kingdom of God. Christian ethics cannot therefore be disassociated from ecclesiology and practices endorsed by the *ecclesia* for the cultivation of Christian virtues. Nor can ethics be divorced from pneumatology, as Galatians reminds us. For it is the Spirit of Christ which moves, as love, to nourish, vitalize and develop the community.

Agape and eros

Yet, if love is axiomatic for Christian ethics, it is not unambivalent. The most common Greek word in the New Testament for love may be *agape,* but there is also *phileo* and a consistent avoidance of the more common classical Greek term *eros.* What is distinctive about love as *agape?* How does it relate to and differ from love as *eros* – which to the Hellenistic mind (as later to the Christian Platonist mind) was capable of divine dimensions? Within Platonic thought *eros* was the dynamic for transformation in the personal pilgrimage towards the Good. Ethics was inseparable from *eros:* that which one desired to be conformed to. The impact on Christian theology of Anders Nygren's study, *Agape and Eros,* cannot be underestimated here. Based upon the fact that the only words for love found in the New Testament are *agape* and *phileo,* Nygren's thesis schooled a whole generation of theologians and Christian ethicists who wished to see *agape* as contrary to erotic desire with its demand for self-satisfaction.[9] Distinctively, *agape* is selfless, unmotivated, beneficient giving; whereas *eros,* at base, is indulgent and narcissistic. The first is divine grace which cannot be deserved; the second is, at best, human aspiration. While raising the question of where the two meet, Nygren wishes to insist that 'Eros and Agape are not only two entirely opposite motifs, but have also developed their own characteristic groups of representations'.[10] He concludes his theoretical section: 'The measure in which such a synthesis appears to have been successful is from the point of view of the Agape motif the measure of its failure, for it has meant the betrayal of Agape.'[11]

The total denial of self-love which Nygren views as fundamental to *agape* emphasizes sacrificial obedience. It is exactly the role of self-love which Kristeva's work wishes to reassess. In her book *Tales of Love,* Kristeva draws attention to the way in which this aspect of *eros* was transformed by the advent of Christianity. She introduces a parallelism between the development of the Narcissus myth by Ovid in Rome and the nascent Christian concept of *amor sui*. The difference between the two is that 'in Narcissus' universe there is no other' *(Tales of Love,* p. 113). Kristeva likens this to the world of Plotinus' *monos pros monon*. The Christian 'adoption-love' of the Father God, distinctively 'sets up the believer as subject of the Other' *(ibid.,* p. 145). Agape-love internalizes sacrificial giving in terms of obedience *(ibid.,* p. 146), but the whence of that love is always elsewhere – as gift or grace. The Christian *amor sui* – issuing from Christ's injunction to love the neighbour as you love yourself – is predicated on a love which descends and which is prior to the subject. *Amor sui* is one element in the establishment of a communal 'we'. Kristeva observes that 'The essential moment of this theocentrism is the inversion of Eros' dynamics, which rose towards the desired object or supreme Wisdom. *Agape*, on the contrary, inasmuch as it is identified with God, comes down; it is gift, welcome, and favour' *(ibid.,* p. 141). What is significant about this observation is that *agape* is the possession of God alone. In so far as it can inform and permeate human desire then human beings can participate in *agape*, but human desire in and of itself remains erotic.

There has been a long tradition in Christian thought which has wanted to read human participation in God's divine activity in the world (the creation of God's own *ethos)* as founded upon a divine *eros*/human *eros* co-respondence. As such, Christian ethics is the expression of a profound incarnational theology. We would find this in Cappodocian and Byzantine mystics like Gregory of Nyssa and Maximus the Confessor. We would find it in medieval theologians like Bonaventure and Bernard of Clairvaux. It is Bernard, in his sermons on the Song of Songs who writes:

> I think this is the principal reason why the invisible God willed to be seen in flesh and to converse with men as man. He wanted to recapture the affections of carnal men who were unable to love in any other way, by first drawing them into the salutary love of his own humanity.[12]

Nygren exhaustively investigates this tradition, understands it as a failure in Christian theology and views Luther as returning us to orthodoxy in this matter. But the idea of divine *eros* has been kept alive by the Orthodox Church and it receives expression once again in the work of the twentieth-century Swiss theologian Hans Urs von Balthasar and the Russian Orthodox theologian Paul Evdokimov.

Of course, the ambivalence and subjective involvement of such a love at the root of ethics raises more than potential dangers. First, it raises the spectre of antinomianism: love and do what you will, even if that means infringing the laws of the land (laws concerning incest and paedophilia, for example). Secondly, it can give precedence to the emotional colouring of a particular situation, hindering objective or a more long-term judgement. There is potential for tragedy here as Donald MacKinnon observed concerning the Samaritan's action in the Lukan parable.[13] A high degree of self-knowledge is required to 'help' another, ignorance even in assistance can list death among its consequences. The Samaritan bound the wounds of the injured man, 'pouring in oil and wine'. His action is the deployment of specific medical skills. If he had not had those skills and done something else the death of the man might have resulted which would only have exacerbated Jewish–Samaritan hostilities. The degree of self-knowledge (or relevant knowledge) in any situation is a vexed question; we cannot see all the consequences of what we might term an action in 'love'.[14] It is because of the twin dangers of antinomianism and situational relativism that ethics cannot be deemed a theological appendix. It has to be seen at the centre of a theological anthropology describing the work of redemption in terms of the actual praxis of the Christian faith; the manifestation and development of the incarnation itself. Aquinas recognized that.

At the head of the 170 questions that constitute Aquinas' teaching on Christian ethics in the second part of the second part of the *Summa,* stands the Pauline triad of faith, hope and charity. These he defines as theological virtues as distinct from moral virtues which are in accord with right reason, for these virtues have as their object God Himself. Of these three, charity is more excellent than faith or hope (and therefore all other virtues) because charity 'attains God Himself that it may rest in Him, but not that something may accrue to us from Him' (*Summa*, II–II, Question 23, Article 6). Charity stands, then, at the apex of all other virtues. It responds to God as the Supreme Good. For as Supreme Good 'all desired perfections flow from Him as from the First Cause' (*ibid.*, I, Question 6, Article 3). Goodness is intrinsically desirable. As Schleiermacher concluded his monumental *The Christian Faith*, 'the unfolding of the divine love conducts us here to the realm of Christian Ethics'.[15]

Theology's concern with a God who loves is necessarily caught up with its concern with the establishment of what is good. The object of love and the object of what is good must correlate. Love must find issue in forms of behaviour which express and perpetuate that love. As such, love involves a movement, an exchange and a participation. It is this correlative concern with the economy of love and the practice of what is good which so interests both Emmanuel Levinas and Julia Kristeva. It is the relationship between love and the way its circulation constitutes community which is of interest to Jean-Luc Nancy.

Julia Kristeva[16]

Born and educated in Bulgaria in a devout Catholic family, Julia Kristeva arrived in Paris at the age of 25 in 1966. Her father, Stoian Kristev was 'an intellectual, an eminent scholar who never integrated into the party cadres' (*Nations without Nationalism*, p. x, Leon Roudiez's translation). Nevertheless, in Paris, Kristeva mixed with the political left-wing. Introduced to *avant-garde* thinkers by her compatriot, the linguist Tzvetan Todorov, she began making her impact on the Parisan intelligentsia with articles in journals such as *Critique* and *Tel Quel*.[17] She had come to France on a research fellowship and two books soon emerged from that work: in 1969 *Semeiotike: Recherches pour une semanalyse* and in 1970 *Le Texte du Roman*. The development of her notion of semanalysis is the basis for all her thinking, and at the centre of semanalysis is the speaking subject governed by *'primary* processes (displacement, condensation – or metonymy, metaphor)' *(The Kristeva Reader*, p. 29). This is a subject of desire; the same subject whose emergence we saw Judith Butler predicate her work upon. Kristeva recognised, from the beginning, that semanalysis was 'a moral gesture', because it 'rocked the foundations of sociality' by restoring to the subject 'that negativity – drive-governed, but also social, political and historical – which rends and renews the social code' (*ibid.*, p. 33).

The Hegelian background

Before rehearsing the characteristics of semanalysis, this subject of desire needs to be put into its intellectual context. We have noted something of this context in Chapter 1 when outlining the projects of Irigaray and Butler in terms of the projects of Freud and Lacan. Kristeva, as is evident from the way she links the Freudian terms 'displacement' and 'condensation' with the Lacanian (and Jakobsonian) terms 'metonymy' and 'metaphor' is profoundly indebted to Lacan's school of revised Freudianism. Her work, like Lacan's, Irigaray's and Butler's examines the inner logic governing the binding of psychoanalysis to language and representation. However, coming out of a Marxist background Kristeva, more than Irigaray, has been aware that her work involves her in a re-reading of Hegel. She has observed that '*semanalysis* can be thought of as the direct successor of the dialectical method' (*The Kristeva Reader*, p. 31). It is with the introduction into French academic circles of Hegel in the 1930s and 1940s by Alexandre Kojève and Jean Hyppolite, and Freud in the 1920s by André Gide and Gaston Gallimard,[18] that the ego as the subject of desire took centre stage, philosophically.

The influential text by Hegel was his *Phenomenology of Spirit* (translated by Jean Hyppolite between 1939 and 1942). Hegel (developing the work of Kant, Fichte and Schelling) proposes in that early book a philosophy of subjective consciousness. It is an active consciousness, emerging from and transforming the natural world. The subject is then in process (an important aspect of Kristeva's work); it is caught up in time and history. As Hegel noted 'in a necessary manner [Mind] immanently differentiates itself and returns out of its differences into unity with itself'.[19] This movement towards difference and the sublation of difference in unity is the work of negation performed by the consciousness on that which is external to and other than itself. Negation mediates as the subjective consciousness moves forever towards absolute unity. This is the dialectical immanent process; the movement of this affirmative and constructive work of the negative is called force. In Sections 136–65 Hegel elaborates his notion of force as both the medium for the sublation of difference and that which is independent of the being-for-itself. Force is also that which is solicited by difference. The negative arises because of the recognition of difference. Force manifests itself because 'difference is nothing else than being-for-another'.[20] Otherness therefore solicits force while, from another point of view, it might be seen as force soliciting otherness. As Hegel puts it: 'Force has its determinateness only through the other, and solicits only in so far as the other solicits it to be a soliciting Force.'[21] This movement towards and from otherness constitutes sell-consciousness: 'self-consciousness exhibits itself as the movement in which the antithesis is removed, and the identity of itself with itself becomes explicit for it'.[22] For Hegel 'self-consciousness is *Desire* in general'.[23] From Section 167, Hegel initiates his inquiry into Desire *(Begierde* – animal hunger) which led to his famous analogy of Lordship and Bondage. If force, or rather the play of the two moments of force, is the universal law and medium of understanding, desire is its dynamic. Desire *is* the living self-consciousness which has before it its object to possess and be gratified by.

Alexandre Kojève and Jean Hyppolite had both given rather different readings of this Hegelian desire.[24] It was these readings which were being reacted against by their pupils. Foucault's essay 'Nietzsche, Genealogy and History', which we looked at in Chapter 2 and Derrida's essay 'The Pit and the Pyramid: An Introduction to Hegel's Semiology' – both of which offered radical critiques of the Hegelian subject – were essays offered as part of an anthology in honour of Jean Hyppolite (who had taught them at the *Ecole Normale Supérieure).* Kristeva's reassessment of the role of desire and negation in the speaking subject – roles which semanalysis is to clarify – is part of this continuing critique of Hegel's identity-through-difference.

Semanalysis

In *Revolution in Poetic Language* (1974), Kristeva maps out the textual topos which semanalysis examines. The speaking subject announces itself within a signifying practice. It is a practice characterized by two axes: the semiotic and the symbolic. Furthermore, it is a practice propelled by the 'unceasing operation of the drives towards, in and through language' *(Revolution in Poetic Language,* p. 17). Her analysis of the symbolic owes much to Lacan, but where she differs from Lacan is in wishing to investigate the nature of these drives prior to the mirror stage and their subsequent effects. These drives constitute primary processes which displace and condense energies that find expression in the metaphors and metonymies of discourse itself. They form what Kristeva, after Plato in his *Timaeus* terms a *chora*[25]: 'an essentially mobile and extremely provisional articulation ... analogous only to vocal or kinetic rhythm ... nourishing and maternal' *(ibid.,* pp. 25–6). All discourse takes place within and against this *chora* which leaves its traces upon the symbolic in terms of ruptures. If it can be seen as a place then it is that from which both generation and negation within discourse issues. Within this 'receptical', the semiotic is the 'psychosomatic modality of the signifying process' *(ibid.,* p. 28) and the symbolic (which includes the syntactical as well as the representational) is the sign system employed by the speaking subject in its interactions with other speaking subjects. The *chora* is frequently called the 'semiotic *chora';* it is what enables Kristeva to associate the dialectical movement of language and identity (of the subject) with material, even biochemical processes. Semanalysis is the examination of the traces of the semiotic *chora* in various forms of representation – the poetry of Lautréamont, the painting of Jackson

Pollock, the social structure of ancient Israel, the biographies of her own clients for analysis, among others. In a way which, once more, distinguishes her work from Lacan's, she develops a phase prior to the mirror stage. The mirror stage for Lacan, we recall, was the scene for the emergence of subjectivity as the comcomitant entry of that subject into the order of the symbolic. For Kristeva, the semiotic processes 'constitute a *pre-subject*' (*In the Beginning was Love*, p. 8), but the 'break in the signifying process, establishing the *identification* of the subject and the object as preconditions for propositionality' (*Revolution in Poetic Language*, p. 43), she terms the 'thetic'. The thetic is the rupture or boundary which establishes signification (thesis) and the subject – both of which will always remain in process for they will always be disrupted and displaced by the semiotic drives of the motile *chora*. Mimetic representation and poetic language (both rich in rhythm, connotative and therefore semiotic traces) become important reminders of what the thetic break and the symbolic conceal. Mimesis and poetic language

> prevent the imposition of the thetic from becoming theological; in other words, they prevent the imposition of the thetic from hiding the semiotic process that produces it, and they bar it from inducing the subject, reified as a transcendental ego, to function solely within the systems of science and monotheistic religion. (*Ibid.*, pp. 58–9)

At this point, her references to theology and monotheism owe much to Feuerbach's thesis that God is the projection of the human ego[26] given psychological depth by Freud in first *Future of an Illusion* and, subsequently, *Moses and Monotheism*. Her attitude to theology, and Christian monotheism in particular will change, as she widens her understanding of 'symbolic representation' and comes to see the Christian religion itself as a 'psychic modality':

> Christ's Passion brings into play even more primitive layers of the psyche; it thus reveals a fundamental depression (a narcissistic wound or reversed hatred) that conditions access to human language ... The child must abandon its mother and be abandoned by her in order to be accepted by the father and begin talking ..., language begins in mourning ... The 'scandal of the cross', the *logos tou stavron* or language of the cross ..., is embodied, I think, not only in the psychic and physical suffering which irrigates our lives

[*qui irrigue notre existence*] but even more profoundly in the essential alienation which conditions our access to language, in the mourning that accompanies the dawn of psychic life ... Christ abandoned, Christ in Hell, is of course the sign that God shares the condition of the sinner. But He also tells the story of that necessary melancholy beyond which we humans may just possibly discover the other ... In this respect too, Christianity wins adhesion of the masses; it supplies images for even the fissures in our secret and fundamental logic. How can we not believe? (*In the Beginning Was Love*, pp. 40–2)

As this quotation reveals, Kristeva, in her semanalytic exploration of the imaginary, rediscovered the deep associations between Christianity and psychoanalysis. These associations are twofold. First, Christianity expresses the role of the negative, the rupturing of the symbolic order (what Derrida would term the logocentric order). Christianity historically stages what Kristeva later, in her book *The Powers of Horror* came to term 'abjection'. Abjection manifests itself psychologically as melancholy. Here it is the melancholy of a child entering the order of the symbolic, but it is a melancholy which infects all artistic endeavour to the extent that such

creation is that adventure of the body and signs which bears witness to the affect – to sadness as imprint of separation and beginning of the symbol's sway; to joy as the imprint of the triumph that settles me in the universe of artifice and symbol. (*Black Sun: Depression and Melancholia*, p. 22)

The entry into the symbolic can be the catharsis of the melancholic and the abject, the creation of boundaries and order which keeps the chaotic, the *chora*, at bay. In *Black Sun: Depression and Melancholia* (1987) she performs a semanalysis of Hans Holbein the Younger's portrayal of 'The Body of Christ in the Tomb'. Here is a depiction of forsakenness 'without the promise of Resurrection' (*ibid.*, p. 110); the presentation of a 'dark, insolent, and senseless eternal power' (*ibid.*, p. 109). It is that melancholy moment which 'summoned up his aesthetic activity, which overcame the melancholy latency while keeping its trace' (*ibid.*, p. 128). Where theologians like Calvin, Barth and Balthasar develop from this a *theologia crucis*, Kristeva develops a *psychologia crucis*. Kristeva recognizes that with the Crucifixion, Christianity set 'rupture at the very heart of the absolute subject – Christ' (*ibid.*, p. 132). Because Christianity then endorses an identification with the sufferings of this Christ (its ethics of obedience, humility and agapaic self-giving issue from such an identification), Kristeva recognises that the 'Christian faith appears then as an antidote to hiatus and depression' (*ibid.*, p. 134). Christ represents abjection for us – the descent towards the threshold of nonmeaning, what Balthasar called the silence which is 'his final revelation, his utmost word'.[27] What theologically is termed *kenosis* is the melancholy moment of self-giving or abandonment without which for Kristeva 'there is no psyche' (*ibid.*, p. 4).

The second of the deep affinities between Christianity and psychoanalysis expresses the role of the positive, the transferential element of all discourse which is closely related to the symbolic. This is referred to above as the 'joy', the 'imprint of the triumph which settles' (*ibid.*, p. 22). The transference opens up an economy of giving and loving (of both ourselves and the stranger). However, before we examine this positive, even healing, transferential act, we need to clarify the picture of subjectivity or personhood which is emerging from Kristeva's work.

Personhood and the stranger

As with Judith Butler, the self in Kristeva's work is not the transcendental ego of either Kant, Fichte or Husserl; the ego that is projected into the monotheistic Father-God. It is a fissured ego, like Freud's and Lacan's, and because it is fissured it is an ego that is part of an economy. It is a subject in process (and therefore a subject with a narrative) because through the fissuring arises the perennial desire to regain the unity and statis of the *monos*, while recognizing the impossibility of such a state. The self-in-process is an ecstatic self – that is, while remaining profoundly narcissistic, it lives beyond itself in an attempt to reappropriate the unity of itself. The stranger is therefore within the self as well as beyond it, substantiating it. In her *Tales Of Love*, Kristeva examines this fissured subjectivity in terms of primary narcissism (which is revisited in various forms in the philosophical tradition, culminating in Descartes' concern with the *cogito*) and the not-I, the idealized other which affects us, invoking our desire (what Bernard of Clairvaux describes as the *Ego affectus est*). Love is birthed in this fissuring. As Kristeva puts it: 'Love is a death sentence which causes me to be' (*Tales of Love*, p. 104). What is important about this fissuring is the psychic space it opens up; a space between the ego and the mirror it faces which Lacan paid little attention to and which Kristeva explores. At the end of *Tales of Love*, Kristeva calls human beings 'extraterritorials'. As subjects which become narcissistic from the earliest moments of our separation from the Mother, in that psychic space opened by separation lies all our potential for loving, integration and transformation. We are, as Levinas graphically described it, 'hostages of the Other'. Subjects-in-process are subjects-in-community. Our subjectivity is profoundly ethical. Kristeva concludes, in a way which leads us back to the Catholic Christianity she frequently draws upon:

> As long as the Western Self could think of itself as an *Ego affectus est*, with Bernard of Clairvaux for instance, its psychic space … remained safe and was constantly able to integrate crises … The discontent always arises out of a repudiation of love – of the *Ego affectus est*. (*Tales of Love*, p. 378)

These two profound associations of Christianity and psychology are reflected upon in several short lectures she gave in a convent school, collected as *In the Beginning was Love: Psychoanalysis and Faith*. 'In both religion and psychoanalysis a destabilized subject constantly searches for stabilization' (*In the Beginning Was Love*, p. 19), she writes. In the Christian religion that stabilization or healing of identity (in which welcoming the other has an intrinsic and necessary role) is expressed in the celebration of a divine love which affects personal transformation. 'This fusion with God, which … is more semiotic than symbolic, repairs the wounds of Narcissus' (*ibid.*, p. 25). It does this through a process of faith, where one identifies with and imitates the other. Kristeva asks: 'Is it not true that analysis begins with something comparable to faith, namely, transferential love?' (*ibid.*, p. 52). In this love between analyst and analysand a trust in the other and an exchange with the other is established. Transference becomes a secular synonym for love and faith – it recognizes separation, loss, alienation while desiring always to overcome them. In this sense it offers a 'way of life in fragile equilibrium between hedonism and concern for transcendent meaning' (*ibid.*, p. 62). There remains, certainly, a sense for Kristeva that psychoanalysis is a kind of lay religion which is better than Christianity because it is not tied to what she terms 'its fundamental fantasies' (*ibid.*, p. 52). Psychoanalysis, on such a reading, is demythologized Christianity. On the other hand, others might point out that Kristeva provides no grounds or argument for why Chistianity could not be read as demythologized psychology. As Kelly Oliver, has written concerning Kristeva's continual appeal to religious metaphors:

this is perhaps a symptom of Kristeva's nostalgic relationship to Christianity. Certainly, using religious metaphors in order to describe the psyche and analytic processes privileges and recreates the Christian imaginary.[28]

Leslie Hill speaks likewise: 'Kristeva takes us back here to a ground some no doubt thought they had left: the idea of the Christian substratum of all modern art.'[29] Like Irigaray (and Cixous), Kristeva is asking 'who is God for contemporary feminism?'[30] However, what interests us here are the ethical implications of Kristeva's 'religious' thinking. This she sums up as: psychoanalysis's 'vital efficacy is inseparable from its ethical dimension, which is commensurate with love: the speaking being opens up to and reposes in the other' (*ibid.*, p. 61).

It is an ethics of alterity, governed by a law of love as desire – traditionally a Christian ethic (as in the theologies of Augustine, Pseudo-Dionysius, Aquinas, Schleiermacher and Balthasar) – that Kristeva's work proposes. The more recent book, *Strangers to Ourselves* (1988) and the essays collected in *Nations Without Nationalism* (1994) have concerned themselves directly with the politics of such an ethical position than any of her previous work. The question of the other as separate yet integral to the subject-in-process becomes a political question concerning the identity of the nation (France). With the rights of the foreigner (particularly suing for the rights of the French foreigner to vote) political reason confronts moral reason; the rights of the citizen confront the rights of man (*Strangers to Ourselves*, p. 98). This is inseparable from the practicalities of jurisprudence and State legislation. Kristeva attempts to move beyond personal to a social ethics of alterity with relation to France's contemporary dilemma – national fundamentalism, on the one hand, and the increasing demands of and for immigration, on the other. The cry for integration is concomitant with the contemporary movement of labour across Europe and, more generally, the globe. The sense of identity in crisis and the loss of national particularities she holds responsible for adding 'to the membership and votes of the National Front' and 'a resurgence of French national spirit' (*Nations Without Nationalism*, p. 39). She wishes us to extend the notion of the foreigner by applying it to ourselves, exploring it within ourselves and, in doing that, respecting the privacy that ensures the freedom of democracies (*Strangers to Ourselves*, p. 195). Then, in a utopic strain which has always been part of the ego ideal Kristeva's psychoanalysis inherited from Freud, a new community will emerge. This will be a paradoxical community … made up of foreigners who are reconciled with themselves to the extent that they recognize themselves as foreigners. The multinational society would thus be the consequence of an extreme individualism, but conscious of its discontents and limits, knowing only indomitable people ready-to-help-themselves in their weakness, a weakness whose other name is our radical strangeness. (*Ibid.*, p. 195)

In a letter written in February 1990 to Harlem Desir, founder of SOS Racisme, she endorses the politics of an *ésprit général,* which she takes, and adapts from the French Enlightenment thinker Montesquieu. In doing so, Kristeva turns from psychoanalytic and literary discourses (where we began) to politics, sociology and ethics (the practical implications of her work). As a paradoxical community we are a pilgrimage people – the subject-in-process is the foreigner with a promise (like Abraham), the one who has nowhere to lay his head (like Christ) or a Pauline missionary. We will meet this conception again with Jean-Luc Nancy's 'inoperable community' and the nomadic existence which characterizes Michel de Certeau's project. Personhood is constituted in the *aporia* between atopia (foreigness) and utopia (blessedness).

The ethical, religious and political implications of Kristeva's work have been heavily criticized. We have already mentioned those who find Kristeva's nostalgia for Catholic Christianity unpalatable. There are others who see in her work a dominant heterosexual position which overlooks or denies homosexual relations. Her attitude to certain forms of 'tribal' feminism is critical (see 'Women's Time', *The Kristeva Reader*, pp. 188–213).[31] However, it is not the purpose of this study to explore the rights and wrongs of such criticisms. Here we simply wish to see what the implications of Kristeva's notions of subjectivity, desire and difference could mean for theology's necessary engagement with ethics.

Emmanuel Levinas

Kristeva's concern with the ethics and politics of difference parallels a similar concern in the 1980s by 1970s *avant-garde* thinkers. Michel Foucault, Jacques Derrida, Philippe Lacoue-Labarthe, Jean-Luc Nancy, Paul Ricoeur and Luce Irigaray have all concerned themselves with the social and political implications of their critical theories.[32] There was a concern to understand poststructural critiques 'as an ethical demand which provides a compelling account of responsibility as an affirmation of alterity, of the otherness of the Other: "Yes, to the stranger".[33] Hence, as celebrity intellectuals they felt that it was important to be active in civil rights and social justice movements. The father of such a postmodern ethics was certainly Emmanuel Levinas, who has been exploring the very issues of alterity and the ethics instituted by the presence of the wholly other, since his early phenomenological interest in Husserl in the late 1920s.

Levinas, like Kristeva, is himself an outsider. Born in 1906 into an orthodox Jewish family in Lithuania, at the age of 17 he came to Strasbourg, while Lenin was establishing himself in control of Russia. It was 1923. At Strasbourg he met his lifelong and influential friend Maurice Blanchot. At Strasbourg he also came under the influence of phenomenology as it was being preached by Husserl and Heidegger at the nearby University of Freiburg. By 1928 Levinas was studying Husserl, whose ideas were already being disseminated through a French Catholic, Jean Hering.[34] In 1930 Levinas, to critical acclaim, published his dissertation on Husserl's theory of intuition. In 1929 Husserl himself came to Paris to give a series of lectures that became known as his *Cartesian Meditations*.[35] With Gabrielle Peiffer, Levinas translated these lectures into French and published them (before, in fact, they were published in Germany). The question at the centre of these lectures, a question which was to dominate Levinas' own thinking for decades, was: the 'Uncovering of the sphere of transcendental being as monological intersubjectivity' or 'experiencing someone else' (*Cartesian Meditations*, p. 89). Though Levinas was to criticize Husserl, at first through the work of Heidegger (with which eventually he also became very critical), he consistently examined (with the help of the Jewish thinkers Martin Buber and Franz Rosenzweig) the question of the relationship between self and other. This question, along with its philosophical, theological and ethical implications, is most fully explored in his foremost works: *Totality and Infinity* (1961) and *Otherwise than Being or Beyond Essence* (1974).

Working on the basis of the divided subject, as it had emerged in German idealism and developed through the existential investigation into the authentic and inauthentic possibilities of *Dasein* with Martin Heidegger, Levinas came to picture the ego as always 'being hostage, hostage for all the others who, precisely *qua* others, do not belong to the same genus as I, since I am responsible even for their responsibility (*Collected Philosophical Papers*, p. 150). Buber and Rosenzweig (in Germany), Gabriel Marcel (in France) and Ferdinand Ebner (in Austria) were all, following the horrors of the First World War, independently developing a theological ethics based upon dialogue. Their work constituted a social ontology – that is, it examined the nature of inter-subjectivity as the basis for identity. The fundamental axiom for their investigations was the relationship between the I and the Thou.

Martin Buber

Buber's book, *I and Thou*, is to some extent representative.[36] Buber proposes that our relatedness to the world is one of two paradigms: an I–It relationship or an I–Thou. The I–It perspective is where the subject utilizes the object for its own purposes; it subordinates its meaning to the intentions of the I. The I totalizes any significance the object (or person as an object) might have in and for itself. In a different way, this is the relationship of the world exemplified and analyzed in their different ways, by Kant's transcendental ego, scientific positivism and market consumerism. The I–Thou perspective is a surprising encounter that takes place when the other comes to the I. Buber will talk of the other addressing the I. The encounter is oppositional, but in the event of the encounter a 'between' is opened up in which the I transcends itself and its I–It relations with the world. Both the I and the Thou participate in a common ground, a mutuality. This primary relatedness or interdependence affects three spheres: first, our relations with nature; secondly, our relations with each other; thirdly, our spiritual life. Buber concludes:

> In every sphere in its own way, through each process of becoming that is present to us we look out towards the fringe of the eternal *Thou*; in each we are aware of a breath from the eternal *Thou*; in each *Thou* we address the eternal *Thou*.[37]

Each of us is twofold because this primary Thou is innate and it is because of this that we can recognize the Thou as such. Only God is absolute Person. Authentic meaning, identity, personal salvation all take place in this encounter which reveals to us the presence and mystery of the divine Thou, God. The relationship between ourselves and our neighbours is therefore not only paradigmatic of, but a par-ticipation in, a relationship with God. Buber emphasizes that 'we earthly beings never look at God without the world'.[38] Furthermore, in that looking at the world there is always going to be a dialectic between the two fundamental perspectives, the I–It and the I–Thou, because although the I–Thou is an immediate encounter, all represen-tation and consciousness of such an encounter must rely upon I–It, subject–object distinctions. The movement and directness of speech, for Buber, seems at times to transcend this mediation – hence the ecounter is dialogical. However, 'in accordance with our nature we are continually making the eternal *Thou* into It, into something'.[39]

I discussed Buber's philosophical position and its difficulties in the book *Barth, Derrida and the Language of Theology*.[40] Here, what is important is the way certain emphases of dialogicalism (and therefore the ethics of relationalism) are taken up and transformed by Levinas. Three of these are central – the notion of the twofold I, the notion of relational and transcendental encounter and the recognition that language is the scene within which this alterity is traced. Levinas was quick to discern a philosophical problem in Buber's thinking (to which Rosenzweig had alerted Buber much earlier). Levinas complains that Buber can see only the I–Thou relations as a spiritual friendship and 'the pure spiritualism of friendship does not correspond to the facts' (*The Levinas Reader*, pp. 72–3). Levinas, speaking after the devastation of the Jewish Holocaust, wishes to emphasize the misery of the other and how it totally questions the I. It

> may be conjectured that clothing those who are naked and nourishing those who go hungry is a more authentic way of finding access to the other than the rarefied ether of a spiritual friendship. (*Ibid.*, p. 73)

At stake is taking seriously the difference, the separation, between the I and the Thou. Levinas speaks not of dialogue but 'dia-logue', which 'contrary to certain descriptions by philosophers of dialogue' is a thought 'beyond what is given' (*Le Dieu qui vient a l'idée*, p. 230). Unlike dialogue, 'dia-logue' emphasizes not correlation but rupture, not humanism but 'an-arche.'

The self, the other and language

The self for Levinas, in its twofoldness, is a 'me' prior to being an I. It is placed in the accusative (the object of the wholly other who is, alone, subject). As Levinas can express it in French, *me voici* – 'here I am'. As accusative it is always accused and held responsible for the other. The term Levinas coins to describe this anterior passivity in the self is *ipseity*, because this is 'the signification of the pronoun *self* for which Latin grammars … know no nominative form' (*Otherwise than Being or Beyond Essence*, p. 112). The self is subject to the other who always has priority. Like Kristeva, Levinas is offering an alternative model for the Cartesian (and Husserlian) ego, the autonomous one, the monad for whom relations with the world can only be I–It. His ethics issue directly from this self who realizes its prior responsibility to live for the other – to live out a servitude, a kenosis, or what Levinas will describe as an endless act of substitution for the other:

> Subjectivity *signifies* by a passivity more passive than all passivity, more passive than matter, by its vulnerability, its sensibility, by its nudity more nude than nudity, the sincere denuding of this very nudity that becomes a saying, a saying of responsibility, by the substitution in which responsibility is said to the very end, by the accusative of the oneself without nominative form, by exposedness to the traumatism of gratuitous accusation, by expiation for the other. (*Collected Philosophical Papers*, p. 147)

If there are echoes here of Isaiah's suffering servant (Isaiah 53), of Jewish Messianism, of Christianity's Christ, the echoes are intentional. Only in accepting that this is our condition as human beings can the Good be traced. Outside this recognition of our condition only violence can ensue: 'Violence is to be found in any action in which one acts as if one were alone in the act: as if the rest of the world were only there to *receive* the action' (*Difficult Freedom*, p. 6).

In Husserl's analysis, the transcendental ego is governed by the structures and strictures of its intentionality, so that the other, the neighbour, can only be apperceived. That is, perceived as existing analogous to ourselves, as an analogy of ourselves. The sense of there being a body over there can only be derived 'by an apperceptive transfer from my animate organism' (*Cartesian Meditations*, p. 110). Levinas (like Buber) wants to speak of a more immediate encounter with the neighbour and it is frequently on this point that he has been criticized (most particularly by Jacques Derrida).[41] It is with the face of the Other (*autrui* – other person) that the immediacy and negativity of their presence issues:

> The face is not the mere assemblage of a nose, a forehead, eyes, etc; it is all that, of course, but takes on the meaning of a face through the new dimension it opens up in the perception of a being. Through the face, the being is not only enclosed in its form and offered to the hand, it is also open, establishing itself in depth and, in this opening, presenting itself somehow in a personal way. (*Difficult Freedom*, p. 8)

With the face of the other we are drawn out of ourselves, realizing the primacy of our *ipseity*, recognizing a responsibility for this other which is prior to the appearance of this other. It is this situation which constitutes us as a society and constitutes society as just. The 'temptation to murder and this impossibility of murder constitute the very vision of the face. To see a face is already to hear "You shall not kill", and to hear "You shall not kill" is to hear "Social justice"' (*ibid.*, pp. 8–9). Levinas employs the term 'proximity' to suggest the immediacy of this event. This proximity occurs prior to consciousness or knowledge. The moment we become conscious of it, the moment we begin to conceptualize its nature, then we have stepped back from the immediacy of the encounter into representations (the intentional constructs of our Kantian Ego). Transcendence, therefore, lies in the event itself. However, it is not an empty transcendence, but a transcendence in which we are wrenched from ourselves, the autonomy of our consciousness and intentions, by the demand of the other and the responsibility this lays (and has always laid) upon us.

With the proximity of the other there is a pure communication, a meaningfulness established by the immediacy of the other. Levinas wishes to talk about the primacy of this meaningfulness or signifyingness which is prior to language; which calls language forth as a witness of what has passed. 'We have called face the auto-signifyingness par excellence', he writes (*Collected Philosophical Papers*, p. 120). 'The neighbour is precisely what has a meaning *immediately*, before one ascribes one to him' (*ibid.*, p. 119). For Levinas, subsequent representation of this 'epiphany' (*ibid.*, p. 121) is necessary in order for there to be knowledge of it at all. Subsequent representation is demanded by the more primordial call itself since signifyingness is both what systems of signification aim at and what systems of signification issue from. The subject, then, and its relation to objects, the signifier and its relation to the signified – the very bases for representation as act and expression – is a product of the signifyingness of proximity. Levinas distinguishes between the immediate sign, meaningfulness, language or communication which comes with the relation of proximity and the subsequent representation of this signifyingness with the terms the saying (*le dire*) and the said (*le dit*). The saying is akin to Bultmann's *kerygma*. It is prior to consciousness, will and intention. However, just as the I realizes its selfhood lies in substituting itself for the other, seeing itself as responsible for the other, saying is caught up in the endless chain of substituting signs which make up any particular language. Here Levinas draws his transcendental Word into the economy of signification outlined by Saussure. For 'Words do not refer to contents which they would designate, but first, laterally, to other words' (*ibid.*, p. 77). Words are caught up within a system of differences, but meaning is not endlessly deferred (as with Derrida); the trace of a signifying prior to signification circulates within the endless chains of signs. As Levinas insists, although representation is necessary, 'in representation presence is already past' (*ibid.*, p. 120) or betrayed. The chains of signs substitute for an ultimate Word which informs but cannot be embraced by them.

Buber and Rosenzweig, as philosophers of dialogue would have concurred with Levinas that sociality is established through language; in language responsibility for the other manifests itself. Where Levinas would differ from such dialogical philosophers would be in the diachrony, the rupture in time, he would demand between the saying and the said. The said always does violence to the transcendental saying, so that only a trace of the pure communication remains. 'Trace' is another important term for Levinas as we saw it was also for Derrida and for the Annales School.[42] But for Levinas the trace is the suggestiveness of the infinite or the unthinkable that remains in the totality of the said. This infinity, the unsaid, the unthinkable places a 'question mark in this said' which is 'the very pivot of revelation' (*Otherwise than Being or Beyond Essence*, p. 154). It is a revelation constituted as and through asymmetrical difference. The difference is between ourselves and another, the difference between the saying and the said. It is asymmetrical because the other always has priority and therefore we are *for* it, not simply *with* it.

Illeity

The infinite (and God) enters Levinas' work because the saying which arrives with the face of the other person bears witness to an elsewhere, a transcendence which is totally other (*autre* – translated with a lower case to distinguish it from *autrui* which is translated 'Other'). Here we move beyond being, essence and ontology, as Levinas interprets them, towards that which is otherwise than being. This is the Good beyond being, testified to in Plato. It is from this transcendental Good that the command, the saying, the call to and of responsibility issues. If being consists of that about which we can speak, the totality of that which is present in the world – that which appears, that which is phenomenal – then the other is a null-site outside the totality of this being or what Levinas terms the *there is* [*il y a*]. The good is that which is *disinterested*.

The final chapter of Levinas' masterwork *Otherwise than Being or Beyond Essence* is entitled 'Outside'. Here Levinas 'ventures beyond phenomenology' (*Otherwise than Being or Beyond Essence*, p. 183) to describe the 'signification of saying without the said'. What Saying testifies to is an eternal Word which comes to us *in* the one-for-the-other relationship of the face-to-face. Quoting the Jewish thinker Joshua Halévy, Levinas states that with this eternal Word 'God speaks to each man in particular' (*ibid.*, p. 184). Elsewhere, this significance of saying, the good beyond being, is termed *illeity*. *Illeity* is beyond being. It is what Levinas calls the *third person* which is not definable by the oneself, by ipseity' (*Collected Philosophical Papers*, p. 103). This third person breaks up the face-to-face relation of the I and the other, interrupts even proximity. Prior to ipseity, to the split self, to the bipolarity of immanence and transcendence, it designates that which is totally other. The *il* is the French 'He' and the

> pronoun 'He' expresses its inexpressible irreversibility, already escaping every relation as well as every dissimulation, and in this sense absolutely unencompassable or absolute, a transcendence in an absolute past. (*Ibid.*, p. 104)

Rupture as revelation bears the trace of this third; in the trace of *illeity* being has a sense, a signification, a meaningfulness. This is the glory of the Infinite which inspires and commands the witness of 'Here I am' (*me voici*) and prophecy that then ensues. 'It is by the voice of the witness that the glory of the Infinite is glorified' (*Otherwise than Being or Beyond Essence*, p. 146). Levinas frequently frames discussion of *illeity* with references to the Jewish God (see *Collected Philosophical Papers*, pp. 106–7 and *Otherwise than Being or Beyond Essence*, pp. 147–52).

Like Kristeva, there is an endless movement or work involved here. The new notion of selfhood as constituted in the ecstasy of interiority or consciousness and governed by the proximity of the other, emerges from an economy of desire. Ethics, for Levinas (as for Kristeva) is inseparable from desire for the other which was analyzed in his early work in terms of a phenomenology of eros (see Section IVB of *Totality and Infinity*). 'The desire for the other, which we live in the most ordinary social experience, is the fundamental movement', he writes (*Collected Philosophical Papers*, p. 94). It is linked to the nature of time,[43] and the disclosure of the other in and through desire has a trinodal economy. Levinas has likened this economy to a family in which *illeity* is paternal, *ipseity* filial and the power whereby the other is birthed in the same maternal (see *Otherwise than Being or Beyond Essence*, pp. 75–6, 108).[44]

Desire is the very dynamic for personhood, for both these thinkers. For Levinas this is because the enigma of the infinite haunts each one's finitude. In this he owes something to Descartes' analysis of our inborn idea of the infinite. But then Descartes received this from Augustine and Plato. 'The idea of the Infinite is a desire' (*Collected Philosophical Papers*, p. 98), and in this way the other is always part of us. So, again like Kristeva, it is the divided self which becomes the desirous self. Levinas will speak of being 'obsessed' by the other, of the 'fecundity' (in terms of significance) of the caress, of the 'excess' which issues from this infinity, of *jouissance* and the ambiguity of love. We are both commanded by, and attracted to, the other which draws us ever beyond – beyond ourselves, beyond the given, beyond history, beyond Being itself. We submit as servants, as suffering servants, both to the command and the attraction. That is our responsibility and it is a duty which exceeds human rights and humanism as conceived by the Enlightenment project.[45] It is these rights which have become for us 'the measure of all law and, no doubt, its ethics' (*Outside the Subject*, p. 116).

In this sense, Levinas presents us with an ethic of ethics. But it is a transcendental null-site for ethics, the good, which challenges any natural or conventional 'rights of man'. The transcendence of the good transports us beyond the concern with being and beings which is the sphere for the operations of such 'rights'; rights founded upon Enlightenment notions of subjective autonomy and personal freedom. Linguistically, metaphor is emblematic of this transportation towards the excess of significance.

This, again, has similarities with Kristeva's position. Where they would differ is on exactly what characterizes this desire. For despite her Catholic illustrations and intimations, for Kristeva desire is a psychic economy. Transcendence, as such, can only be self-transcendence. The goal of psychoanalysis is adulthood and self-integration which constantly provides room for self-adjustment and development through accepting inevitable separation and alienation.[46] Psychoanalysis, therefore, differs from faith – although they share similar structures and elements. Kristeva's economy of desire is also trinodal and illustrated through the family – with the subject as child, desiring maternal gratification which intrinsically recognizes the role of an imaginary, loving father. 'To the analyst, however, the representations on which the Credo is based are fantasies', Kristeva concludes (*In the Beginning Was Love*, p. 43). For Levinas, as a Talmudic scholar (see his *Quatre lectures talmudiques* (1968), *Du sacre au saint* (1977) and his translated 'Messianic Texts' in *Difficult Freedom*) the *'credo* is closed to history ... but open to the high virtues and most mysterious secrets of Proximity' (*Outside the Subject*, p. 127). Levinas' concern is with a transcendence *(illeity)* beyond self-transcendence *(ipseity)*, an externality far more radical than Kristeva's and the rewriting of a transcendental desire which fissures human intentionality. The philosophical coherence of such a project (which actually wishes to reject the possibility of a natural theology, an analogical correlation between self, Other and other) has been criticized, as we have said. Derrida, among others, has pointed to the Messianic theology which underpins Levinas' work and compromises, the coherence of that work as philosophy.

Our concern here is with the themes and emphases of this work, rather than the impeccability of its logic. Perhaps the difference between Kristeva and Levinas can be summed up in terms of their presuppositions, what Lyotard would call their metanarratives or explanatory principles – psychoanalysis, on the one hand, Judaism's God who is 'always being mediated by one's neighbour' (*Outside the Subject*, p. 131) on the other. What both articulate is an ethics on the far side of modernity's universal moral laws which gives preference to the marginalized and alien. To this extent they offer a postmodern ethics.

Jean-Luc Nancy[47]

With Levinas and Kristeva, ethics are no longer tied to acts of will or moral decision-making on behalf of autonomous subjects. Subjects are always in relation, subjectivity is constantly undergoing transformation, and an economy of love or desire ties each into bonds of responsibility. Early in its self-representations, Christianity figured this reciprocity (as Plato had done before Christianity) in terms of what I have called elsewhere 'transcorporeality'.[48] That is, the physical body of any one person does not end at its finger-tips or toes. It is always a part of and extends into larger bodies than itself: the social body, the civic body, the ecclesial body and the body of Christ, for example. In this way, ethics is indissociable from politics, the doing of the good inseparable from social justice: what I do to (or refuse to do for) my neighbour effects these wider circles in which any action has implications. To return to the parable of the Good Samaritan, for example – the act of kindness by one man is politically freighted because this man is a Samaritan and his act on behalf of a man who is maybe a semite or a gentile (the wounded man is simply 'a man') is contrasted with the indifference of the priest and the Levite. This inter-relatedness of all actions, and the consequent co-implication of ethics with politics, runs counter to the private and public distinctions that arose in the early modern period. What is done in private will also have manifestations in public. There are not two discrete realms. As such the ethical project has always culminated in the political. In Plato, the pursuit of the Good is most particularly the task of the philosopher king who will regulate the workings of the Republic. Kant's moral philosophy ends with his account of the ethical commonwealth; in Hegel, men (*sic.*!) enter the ethical life by leaving the family for the wider public sphere wherein is developed the civil society, the cultivation of which will bring about the ethical Idea itself, the national-state. With Kant and Hegel, the ethico–political project is wedded to an historical teleology – the movement in time towards the goal of the community as corporation. Both also announce that the greatest individual freedom pertains to the establishment of such communities. The work of Jean-Luc Nancy sets itself against the hegemony of such localized and substantial notions of community while promoting a sense of the ultimate value of freedom.

Born in the French province of Gironde, Jean-Luc Nancy has been a Professor of Philosophy at the University of Strasbourg for over thirty years. The past history of this city – batted between Germany and France – and its present position on the border between the two countries, has no doubt been influential on a philosopher concerned with mapping and boundaries, belonging, excluding and embracing difference. His early work displays a close association with Germany: he translated Nietzsche and Jean Paul and was profoundly interested in German romanticism. The work of Hegel, Heidegger and Derrida can all be traced within his writing: Hegel's concern with history, community and the positive work of what is other; Heidegger's concern with time and *mitandersein* (being-with-one-another); and Derrida's concern with writing and difference.

The importance of his thinking lies in the development of the Kristevan ethics of subjects-in-process and the Levinasian ethics of subjects-in-relation in terms of the political. He envisages a new form of 'community'. Like other French thinkers, such as Nancy's close friend and collaborator Philippe Lacoue-Labarthe, Nancy distinguishes between 'politics' (*la politique*) which names specific struggles between local, defined positions and 'the political' (*le politique*) which names the play of forces from which 'politics' emerges. Nancy's work describes a step-back from 'politics' to an examination of 'the political'. Returning to the Greek and Christian metaphorics of the body as an anatomical, a social and even theological entity, Nancy attempts to depict the relation of individual bodies to what he calls 'the community of bodies' (*The Birth to Presence*, p. 197). He is concerned then with the material, the corporeal, rather than the working out of the Kantian moral law or the Hegelian Idea. Furthermore, what is fundamentally different about Nancy's work is the lack of an historical teleology and a new understanding of freedom which develops out of this. History is finite:

> The possibility of saying 'our time' and the possibility of this making sense (if it does) is given by a reciprocity between 'our' and 'time'. This does not imply a collective property, as if first we exist, and then we possess a certain time. On the contrary, time gives us, by its spacing, of the possibility of being we, or at least the possibility of saying 'we' and 'our'. In order to say 'we', we have to be in a certain common space of time ... '[O]ur time' can be the history of one single day. This is finite *history* – and there is perhaps no other kind. It is a matter of the space of time, of spacing time and/or of spaced time, which gives to 'us' the possibility of saying 'we' – that is, the possibility of being *in common*, and of presenting or representing ourselves as a community – a community which shares or which partakes of the same space of time, for community itself is this space. ('Finite History', pp. 156–7)

History is no longer a process here; there is no grand narrative in which we, now, constitute one more drama. Furthermore community is no longer a substantive; it does not have a here or a there, a specific location on a map with its boundaries drawn and outsiders positioned. Nancy's community is without determinative shape. It is not based upon territory or exclusion. It is not a community contracted into. It exists before all contracts; it exists to resist all such exclusive, self-legitimating communities. It is radically heterogenous and inclusive. In this is its freedom. Time is primary, as the quotation above indicates; freedom is the community's continual exposure to time.

Concomitant with this commitment to time is a commitment to writing, to mimesis. Like Derrida, Nancy recognizes that the metaphysics of presence have to be deconstructed. Neither subjects nor things are present to themselves as discrete and self-founding entities, they make their appearance *as* this person or *as* that thing in and through representation. This has two important consequences, one for Nancy's understanding of subjectivity and the other for Nancy's understanding of bodies *tout court*.

Subjectivity

Concerning subectivity, Nancy's position means that subjects are not origins of certainty. Like the other people we have been considering in this chapter then, Nancy offers a critique of Cartesian subjectivity – upon the basis of which Enlightenment certainties could be founded. Descartes overcomes the uncertainty, groundlessness and scepticism he posits by asserting the will of the I as immaterial thought, announcing this I as separate from the confusions of the body and able to attain clear and distinct ideas. Nancy troubles and disrupts the autonomous Cartesian I. Subjects are not present to themselves and so identity is always caught up in a temporal deferral. As Nancy puts it: 'I will never be able to speak from where you listen, nor will you be able to listen from where I speak, nor will I ever be able to listen from where I speak' (*The Birth to Presence*, pp. 189–90). It is not, as with Levinas, that the subject as ego is disrupted by the other person (*autrui*) who comes before me and places me in the accusative. Nancy's subject is always the subject as it represents itself to itself: the I which is always already the written or vocalised 'I'. His account of subjectivity is therefore more Derridean: the identity of the 'I' is caught up in an endless process of *différance*. So too is the 'you', the other. Difference is ineradicable and yet, framed by the participation in the one temporality, the now. Even though we cannot grasp the presence of this now, I and you are sharing this spacing. More like Kristeva, then, subjectivity for Nancy is always changing in and through the inscriptions it gives (by any action within the world) and any inscriptions it receives (by the action of the world upon it). Nancy, like Kristeva, has been profoundly influenced by Lacan. The I is born into a chain of endless signs which preceded and situate it, but which it must necessarily employ in order to grasp something of its self. The double-bind of signification is evident here: the I gives signs of itself and it is itself caught up, as itself a sign, within the intratextuality of all things. This does not mean there is not a real body involved in this process of signification. In fact, it is the presence of a real person, a particular material body, which allows for the ongoing nature of signification. For the subject as embodied person always exceeds the meaning it gives and receives in and through the endless exchange of signs. 'This is indeed what writing is: the body of a sense that will never tell the signification of bodies, nor ever reduce the body to its sign' (*ibid.*, p. 197).

Bodies

It is exactly at this point that Nancy recognizes the ethics and politics of this textualized embodiment. This takes up the second consequence pointed to above: that all bodies are complicit with the double formula of signification. '*Sign of itself* and *being-itself of the sign*: such is the double formula of the body in all its states, in all its possibilities', Nancy writes (*ibid.*, p. 194). So that where one body ends and another begins, where boundaries can be drawn, is undecidable. We do make decisions. This is inevitable because we cannot be still and, therefore, we cannot be silent, as Nancy sees. But such decision-making is a form of violence, a repression of freedom, unless the decision is for the ungrounded freedom and so resists the attempt to grasp and stabilize meaning. For what we have here

> is nothing other than the interlacing, the mixing of bodies with bodies, mixing everywhere, and everywhere manifesting this other absence of the name, named 'God', everywhere producing and reproducing and everywhere absorbing the sense of sense and of all senses, infinitely mixing the impenetratable with the impenetratable. (*Ibid.*, p. 195)

'God' is a figure here, for Nancy (as for Derrida) of the absolute identity, the *Logos*: where name and being coincide; the transcendental signifier which gathers all sense and meaning within its omnipotent omniscience. Sense is forever circulating, being interpreted, being passed on, without ever being finally grasped and so the *logos* is forever disseminated: 'destiny is nothing other than the announcement, and the passing out of the announcement of the *logos*' (*La partage des voix*, p. 82). We will return to this shortly when discussing the significance for Christian theology of Nancy's critical thinking.

All bodies exist, then, beyond themselves in 'an indefinitely ectopic corpus' (*The Birth to Presence*, p. 203). Because all bodies are caught up with the processes of representations, they communicate and this communication, or sense, though elusive, is constantly being read and reiterated by others. No one stands alone, because we are each bound by the circulation of sense, and it is this which constitutes us as, employing Nancy terms, an 'inoperative [*désoeuvrée*] community'. The word *désoeuvre* is difficult to translate. On the one hand, Nancy is defining community negatively – as one which does not work [*oeuvre*], does not produce anything. The communities which work are organized corporations, whose limits and limitations are policed. The community Nancy envisages is 'inoperative' because the community is not a substantial thing; it is not a stable, geographically or ethnically located entity. This is where Nancy differs radically from the thinking on the relationship between the physical, social and transcendental body of the seventeeth-century philosopher (who has been highly influential on contemporary French thinkers such as Deleuze and Lyotard), Benedict Spinoza. As we noted earlier, for Spinoza all that is constitutes one substance, so that everything (and every person) is a modification of this one substance. As such there is no real difference in the world; no real other: all discrete bodies are illusory positions within the one corporate communion.[49] But Nancy wishes to emphasize that though 'these singular beings are themselves constituted by sharing, they are distributed and placed, or rather *spaced*, by the sharing that makes them *others*' (*The Inoperative Community*, p. 25) so that in the ecstasy of sharing there is no communion, only the endless need for communication. 'These "places of communication" are no longer places of fusion, even though in them one *passes* from one to the other: they are defined and exposed by their dislocation' (*ibid.*, p. 25). But *désoeuvre* is more frequently understood as 'idle' or 'unoccupied', more favourably 'at leisure'.

Community

We need to elucidate this further, because it touches upon an important theme in Nancy's thinking, that of abandonment, a theme with a profound Christian past. In fact, Nancy's thoughts concerning community arise because the epoch we live in is one in which Christian understandings of 'communion', which expressed a desire for a place of community 'at once beyond social division and beyond subordination to technopolitical dominion', (*ibid.*, p. 9) are no longer tenable. Nancy accepts Zarathustra's announcement that God is dead. Other understandings of community:

> the community desired and pined for by Rousseau, Schlegel, Hegel, then Bak-ouine, Marx, Wagner, or Mallarmé [are] understood as communion, and communion takes place, in its principle as in its ends, at the heart of the mystical body of Christ. (*Ibid.*, p. 10)

The modern political *polis* is a Christian parody; a nostalgia for a community lost. The 'inoperative' community is an attempt to think of a communion (through communication) which, once more, transgresses all boundaries and locations, all homogenization, all racial, sexual or ideological hegemonies. Nancy's ek-static selves, in their resistence to the local and instrumental, live out their finitude in the infinity of an endless giving. They live continually exposing themselves to what is infinitely other and unobtainable (and therefore escapes all 'technopolitical domination'). This is Nancy's notion of 'abandonment' – which parallels Levinas' construal of kenosis. This living of the finite towards the infinite is also Nancy's understanding of love, a love which is continually shattered:

> As soon as there is love, the slightest act of love, the slightest spark, there is this ontological fissure that cuts across and that disconnects the elements of the subject-proper ... Transcendence will thus be better named the crossing of love. What love cuts across, and what it reveals by its crossing, is what is exposed to the crossing ... – and this is nothing other than finitude itself ... There are no parts, moments, types, or stages of love. There is only an infinity of shattering. (*The Inoperative Society*, pp. 96–101)

As such love is an action, not a substance; a transcending action, a movement which promises the eternal and the infinite through a profound recognition of the finite and the singular. Like love as Kristeva conceives it, it will never achieve its end, but yearn infinitely.

Nancy, like Kristeva's appeal to a *theologia crucis*, is indebted to Hegel here, who places the experience of Good Friday at the centre of his own understanding of community, though Nancy's community has no end or goal. But, more significantly for our study, Nancy's community of kenotic love is yet another parody of Christian construals of 'ecclesia' and 'communion'. In an important and influential essay 'Corpus', he acknowledges that Christian doctrine of incarnation which forms the metaphorical orientation for his writing: 'The *spirit* of Christianity is incorporated here in full. *Hoc est enim corpus meum*' ('Corpus', p. 22). Furthermore, 'there was a spirituality of Christ's wounds. But since then, a wound is just a wound' (*ibid.*). And it is as an open wound, the body 'turned into nothing but a wound' (*ibid.*, p. 30), that Nancy sums up his description of the community without communion. Critics have been quick to point out the Christian and Catholic imaginary at work here. Spivak asks if Nancy is 'performing an Augustine who cannot himself undo the metalepsis of the

Eucharist.'[50] For as Christ poured Himself out and, liturgically, the host is endlessly fractured and the communicants sent out to give themselves in love for the redemption of the world, so Nancy pictures joy as issuing from the acceptance of this total exposure of finitude to the infinite. He conceives a world without horizons in which difference is maintained and productive. A new globalism, extending itself endlessly is announced. The ethical is defined as participating in such a vision. As such, Nancy's thinking presents the sublime, the unnameable, as that in which community is consummated. I will say more about the sublime and the sacred in Chapter 4 with respect to Jean-François Lyotard, but for the moment it is significant that Nancy himself states:

> To celebrate transcendence beyond being, or the immanence of the divine, or else, like the German mystics whose heirs we all are, the 'sublimeness' of God (nowadays 'the sublime' has at times began to take on the role of a new negative theology), is not to pray, is no longer to pray. (*The Inoperative Community*, p. 121)

Although there is a continual performance of abandonment (a secularized version, like Heidegger's of Meister Eckhart's *gelassenheit*), there is no work as such, nothing is produced. The action is not orientated (as in prayer) or disciplined (as in prayer). It is in this sense that the community is 'at leisure', 'unoccupied'; it is made up of those who pour out (and in pouring out receive the recognition of) their finitude endlessly. Community is simply what happens, 'And so, Being "itself" comes to be defined as relational ... and, if you will ... *as community'* (*ibid.*, p. 6).' We neither construct nor constitute (through inter-subjectivity) this community. It is with this experience of the infinite openness of the finite-in-relation that Nancy speaks of freedom.

God

The sublime horizon is given names like the sacred, the divine, God – but these are names which collapse before the unpresentable, the impossible, the unnameable. Nancy plainly states:

> I do not know, however, whether this abandonment is still to gods, to another god which would be coming, or to 'no god'. But it has death as it generic name, and an infinite number of forms and occasions throughout our lives. (*The Inoperative Community*, p. 136)

As in Christianity the sacrifice demanded is a moral one, and constitutes the ethics of love. But the kenosis here leads not to resurrection, only death. The crucifixion is endless; Hegel's continuous Good Friday. In wishing to avoid the easy assimilationism of 'communion' and emphasize the importance of singularity and difference (singularity as difference), Nancy invokes a social atomism – which, ironically, is axiomatic for the social contractual communities, the technopolitical communities, Nancy inveighs against and wishes to resist. It is no longer the social atomism of neo-liberal individualism because it is not founded upon the self-determining Cartesian subject who asserts a choice by his or her will. Neither is it the Cartesian subject divided between a corporeal and an intellectual existence. The subject is situated and determined by that situation, it is the anonymity of Being – the way things are – which forces the subject to understand its finitude. Nevertheless, the singularity of this finitude as it faces its being-with and therefore being-in-relation-with the infinite number of other singularities is another form of atomism: the older, pagan, Heracletian form. Nancy's community of bodies 'call again for their creation' ('Corpus', p. 23). They are 'incarnate bodies, bodies which have the same structure as spirit' (*ibid.*, p. 26), participating in the infinite giving and receiving of love. But without the theological structure of the Christian faith, though existence 'is sacrificed, it is sacrificed by no one, and it is sacrificed to nothing' (*Une pensée finie*, p. 101). The nihilism is frank here, but theology has little to fear from such nihilism – for out of nothing God did and does create something. Without God, though, this corporeality will dissolve into what Nancy describes as 'millions of scattered places' (*The Inoperative Community*, p. 137).

Like other critical theorists, Nancy is concerned with uncovering and deconstructing the dualisms which characterize and, for the most part, have their origin in modernity – dualisms which are recognized as producing a certain metaphysics. The dualisms Nancy seeks to overcome are those concerned with the private and the public, the individual and the community, the subject and the object, the immanent and the transcendent. For these dualisms produced certain moral and political alternatives for modernity: an ethics based upon individual rights as opposed to an ethics based upon civic duties; progressive liberalism, on the one hand, and formalist conservatism, on the other. The kind of community Nancy seeks to describe – and in describing produce – displaces each of these dualisms. It is a 'communism' revisited, a communism which for all its emphasis upon sharing and participation is without communion, and a communism more primal than the laws of economics and proletariat development in Marxism. Like Levinas and Kristeva, Nancy calls us to be responsible and responsive to what is wholly other, not because this is a Kantian imperative founded on the possibility of a Supreme Being who is good, but because this is the way things are: what he calls, 'Being-*in*-common' (*ibid.*, p. xli). But unlike Levinas and Kristeva is it more difficult to see what constitutes response and responsibility and what facilitates it. For community 'happens' to us; my response to my neighbour is not demanded (as it is by Levinas' *autre* or Kristeva's psychological dependency upon that from which one has been primally separated). Like other critical theorists Nancy is announcing a non-foundational metaphysics or he is constructing what is sometimes termed a quasi-transcendental argument; Derrida will speak of *archi-différance* and the impossible, Lyotard of the sublime, Levinas of the ethics of ethics and Nancy of the politics of politics.

Theological implications

In an era where advanced communication systems and the operations of transnational corporations are producing the sense of a global village, Nancy's thinking through of the political offers another form of global community, another *ethos* than that created by hegemonic powers and the consumer choices of self-interested agents. It announces a politics of resistance towards a globalization which is in the hands of technopowers; resistance to what Alphonso Lingis has called the 'community of euphoria' that the image of the global village generates: 'the material euphoria of mass-produced consumer products, the immaterial euphoria of information not generating convictions, integrity, and resolve, but marketed as infotainment'.[51] The centrality of resistance means that his is a politics which requires and perpetuates violence. And it has been suggested that politically Nancy is proposing a community of free people in permanent revolution that resembles the Jacobin notions of freedom in the eighteenth century. But Nancy's concern with the specificity of bodies and Being-*in*-common calls for an ethical and political response which is not identical with the Enlightenment humanism of eighteenth-century French political thinkers like St Just. For the bodies involved in Nancy's resistance are not just human:

[T]here are five billion human bodies. Soon, there will be eight billion. Not to say anything of the other bodies ... Since we know that it is all for nothing, for no other purpose than to exist, and to be *those bodies*, what will we be able to do to celebrate their number? (*The Birth to Presence*, pp. 196–7)

The more profound danger with Nancy is that the endlessness of violence accepts an ontological violence and finds in that acceptance a fulfilment, a freedom. Nevertheless, the radical sense of one's finitude, the desire to write about (and in writing produce and perform) an all-inclusive community, the wish to celebrate the corporeal and our 'being-*in*-relation', the call for a new concept of freedom no longer based in the the rights of the autonomous individual to be happy, the emphasis upon love beyond self-interest – are all themes important for rethinking the theology of politics beyond Christian socialism and the Marxism of liberation theology. They are themes which despite Nancy's nihilism are dependent, as he has shown, upon a Christian symbolics. His critical thinking could help Christian theologians then to reconsider the nature and function of the ecclesial body – made up as it is of so many diversely located and temporally dislocated physical bodies, working in, through and beyond local, national and institutional bodies to figure forth the global body of Christ. Nancy can help theology to rethink bodies and corporeality, notions fundamental to Jewish and Christian forms of incarnationalism. Furthermore, Nancy's thinking (its insights and its dangers), which is ultimately monistic, requires theology to give an account of the analogy whereby difference is accepted, celebrated and allowed to stand within commonality such that the pluralizing of differences does not lead to indifference. This is the danger of Nancy thinking, for if 'we know that it is all for nothing, to no other purpose than to exist', the celebration of difference can become a celebration of indifference. A new construal of the analogy of being is required, based upon a new construal of presence as *both* communion and communication. Nancy points a way ahead but the Christian symbolics of his discourse need to be foregrounded and re-invested with a theological content.

To some extent, the importance of Kristeva's work and Levinas' for contemporary ethical discussion depends upon how we characterize the present moral climate. Since the late 1950s there has been a growing sense among some ethicists that the age we live in can resolve its moral dilemmas according to Enlightenment paradigms. The *ethos* of modernity no longer sustains an ethics. The complexities involved in any person attempting to assess the greatest happiness for the greatest number, and act in a way which contributes to a maximal goodness, the utilitarian approach, raises questions concerning being able to grasp a social totality and questions about the homogeneity of any social grouping such that the greatest good is manifest across the board. The Kantian development of duty – one ought do that which can become a universal law for others, a categorical imperative – requires a system of rewards and punishments demanding, for Kant, that we act *as if* God exists as the summation of goodness and the moral judge of all our actions. The social contractual notion of not taking certain actions because they contravene the social consensus, and the contract whereby the well-being of the community is preserved, demands greater and greater levels of policing, more legislative prohibitions and the increasing punishment of offences. It does not seek to develop moral reasoning, but rather curb moral turpitude. Each of these ethical paradigms, and others which depend upon strong, Cartesian notions of the individual (ethical egoism) may only be thought to function within certain forms of sociality. Furthermore, as Elizabeth Anscombe suggested, back in 1958, the sheer plurality of ethical paradigms and the incommensurate approaches they offer for any moral dilemma, militates against moral agreement.[52]

There are those ethicists like Alasdair MacIntyre who would describe modern Western society as already being engulfed by a new Dark Ages. The barbarians (not identified) are at the door, moral relativism or solipsism is endemic, moral casuistry appealing to a universal reason or common form of rationality is no longer possible in an age of conflicting incommensurate logics. So 'What matters at this stage is the construction of local forms of community within which civility and the intellectual and moral life can be sustained.'[53] For MacIntyre (or Martha Nussbaum[54]), we have to return to the classical pursuit of virtue or happiness (eudemonism) of Plato and Aristotle, in the face of Nietzsche. MacIntyre, like the sociologist Zygmunt Bauman – who describes contemporary society in terms of neo-tribalism – is working towards a postmodern ethics.[55] For MacIntyre, ethics which presuppose moral autonomy, attempts by ethicists to distinguish objective facts from subjective values and forms of analysis which align being ethical with being rational, are all understood as being part and parcel of modernity's project. The title of one of MacIntyre's most significant contributions to contemporary ethics asks *Whose Justice? Which Rationality?*[56] Furthermore, in the wake of work done in psychology and moral development, feminists have raised questions about the masculine values pertaining to certain forms of moral reasoning. There is a continuing exploration into feminist ethics or, as Irigaray puts it in the title of one of her books, *An Ethics of Sexual Difference*. The possibilities for a moral realism, founded upon an objective moral reality, are diminishing as a new pragmatism, irony and local rationality gains popularity with figures like Richard Rorty.[57]

Theological investigation has always been suspicious of founding any ethics on human capacities alone. To this extent, it must always remain critical of modernity's attempt to tear morality away from divine revelation, religious texts, ecclesial authority and practices of belief. Where the world has been desacrilized by the project of the Enlightenment – in which facts are made distinct from values, means are related to definable ends and reason made the ally of ethics – the projects of Kristeva, Levinas and Nancy (and the ethical projects too of Irigaray and Cixous) 're-enchant' the world.

Bauman, who recognizes the importance of this new departure for ethics, explores the characteristics of this 're-enchantment'.[58] Three characteristics in particular are observed. First, a dignity is restored to the emotional and experiential. It is no longer understood as contrary to a monolithic reason. We can see that both Kristeva, Levinas and Nancy are concerned with touch, the erotic, the experience of transcendence. Love is a religious experience for Kristeva and Levinas, and clothed in sacramental language for Nancy.[59] Secondly, there is a new respect for what cannot be explained, for that which remains mysterious and ambiguous. Because the other can never be possessed, for either Kristeva or Levinas, the other remains elusive and the ethical becomes irreducible – to rules, duties and prescriptions. It is irreducible too to subjects as culpable or responsible agents; for the ethical is constituted in the between, the asymmetrical *aporia* distinguishing self from other. Thirdly, morality is re-personalized and no longer abstract, supposedly objective and universal. In theological terms, ecclesiology is seen as central; the community within which love is to circulate is particular. The subject, for Levinas, is called to serve in that community – a person is elected – no one else can take their place.

These three characteristics of a 're-enchanted', re-sacrilized world begin to flesh out the implications of Krisetva's, Levinas' and Nancy's work with regard to theology's concern with ethics and politics as a social ethics. A new model of selfhood is brought to the forefront by Kristeva and Levinas. The self is now part of a much larger economy of desire. It is not simply self-defining, it is also defined. For both Kristeva and Levinas this is an economy of love which ruptures the economies of self-love. There is an ethics of servanthood, of kenosis, which bears close affinities to pre-modern models of God's love and the creation of persons.[60] Where liberal ethics investigates personal freedom, individual will and intention, Kristeva and Levinas investigate an obligation prior to will and intention. Selfhood is thus also constituted in being moral. We is not the plural of I, because there is a radical asymmetry between self and other. The other will always remain other. The we is constituted in the never-to-be-eradicated space created by I and Thou, which maintains desire.[61] Two implications of this self-as-process or the economic model of ethics follow. First, in mapping and investigating this space between its temporality, its rhythms of trust and strangeness, ethics is brought into the field of narratology. The self as an economy is the self as story, as character. Theological ethics is also a narrative ethics.[62] Secondly, as Derrida has pointed out, there is 'the necessity of thinking justice on the basis of the gift, that is, beyond right, calculation, and commerce' (*Specters of Marx*, p. 27). Gift, revelation – those notions that Enlightenment ethics wished to strip away – return to be theologically examined. The projects of phenomenology (closely associated with plotting and development) and theology interconnect.[63]

Furthermore, Kristeva's, Levinas' and Nancy's work issues from analyses of language. Derrida speaks of Levinas developing a form of analogy *sui generis* in which the saying is traced in the said. For Kristeva and Levinas, language emerges within this economy of love and the self-in-process. It is a form of analogy which refuses any symmetrical relation between God and beings or any synthesis. It disrupts classical understandings, then, of analogy. 'Yet the analogy once interrupted is again resumed as an analogy between absolute heterogeneity's by means of the enigma, the ambiguity of uncertain and precarious epiphany.'[64] Nancy, as I have said, suggests ways of developing a new construal of analogy. Theology is always dependent upon some form of analogy. What form should this take? Kierkegaard once noted that 'to love is to be changed into a likeness with the beloved'.[65] Christian theology has always read this transformation in terms of a complex relationship between discipleship, Christology, the Trinity, atonement and ecclesiology.[66] It is in these areas (inextricably involved with ethics) that the work of Kristeva, Levinas and Nancy might have its most profound implication. We move towards a new *analogia entis*, which would also be an *analogia fidei* (where faith is trust trusting through ambivalence) founded upon a divine economy of love, an *allegoria amoris*. However, it is an allegory of love which does not distinguish between agapaic and erotic love; rather it sees their inter-association. If the division between agapaic and erotic love fostered certain denunciations of the body, then Kristeva and Levinas would both reject such denunciations. They would emphasize that the economy of love could certainly be abused (narcissism is not only possible it is inevitable). However, theirs is an incarnate love, and therefore an incarnate transcendence through and in that love. We may need to think again about God's love for us as divine eros. It was Kierkegaard again who noted: 'A man who cannot seduce men cannot save them either.'[67]

4
Theology and Aesthetics: Religious Experience and the Textual Sublime

Introduction

The sacred word

Texts have always been recognized as having the power to transform their readers, for good or evil. In the early years of post-exilic Israel, when the Temple of Solomon and the walls of Jerusalem had been rebuilt, we find Ezra holding a public reading of the Mosaic Law. The effect of this reading is recorded in the *Book of Nehemiah*: 'all the people wept, when they heard the words of the law' (Nehemiah 8.9). Though Ezra bids them to change their response to one of celebration, the day is considered holy because it effects a change, a repentance, in the hearts of the people. Performed, the law communicates, and God's Word is disseminated.

In Luke's gospel we have a similar account of the power of reading. This time the reading comes not from the law but the prophets (the *Book of Isaiah*) and it takes place in a synagogue in Nazareth. Jesus reads, closes the book and 'the eyes of all them that were in the synagogue were fastened on him' (Luke 4.20). In the awe-filled silence, he announces the fulfilment of the Scriptures, and then, the tension caused by the reading breaks, violently: 'And all they in the synagogue, when they heard these things, were filled with wrath, and rose up, and thrust him out of the city' (Luke 4.28–9). Again, in the liturgical performance, the Word of God disrupts, provokes and initiates reaction.

The power of the sacred word to affect the lives of hearers and readers is a major characteristic of Judaism and Christianity. Reading or hearing the scriptures can become an occasion for revelation and/or judgement. We examined the textual aspect of this, the representation of revelation, in Chapter 1. We examined the ethics of representation in Chapter 3, pointing out how the new models of personhood gave renewed dignity to the affective side of human nature. Here we will examine the experiential aspect in terms of the reading or listening subject. For the experiential aspect has been fundamental in Christianity as one element in the mechanism of repentance and conversion (the means whereby the atonement wrought by Christ is personally appropriated through the spirit). The experience of reading or listening to the sacred text is a necessary part of any doctrine of Scripture. It also bears closely on the doctrine of God's calling, vocation, and the Church's commission to preach the Word elaborated in missiology.

Augustine, thrashing about in the guilt of his own lustful condition, wanders in solitude about his garden in Milan. In a dramatic gesture he flings himself beneath a fig-tree and from there he hears chanting from nearby: *'Tolle. Lege.'* [Take. Read.] He writes: 'I interpreted it solely as a divine command to me to open the book and read the first chapter I might find.' He does so, and a scripture so apt strikes him with such force that he can read no further. 'At once, with the last words of the sentence, it was as if a light of relief from all anxiety flooded into my heart.' The effect of this reading is Augustine's conversion and subsequent baptism.[1] The relationship between reading the Scriptures and receiving grace (reading as a sacramental process, as a liturgical performance) is more than evident in the lives of the medieval mystics. To take only one example, in *The Revelations of Divine Love* by Julian of Norwich, reading the Scripture becomes a vehicle for meditation, prayer, visionary exegesis and mystic rapture.[2]

In different circumstances, which lack Augustine's broad understanding of how to interpret Scripture, the effect of such reading-as-grace procedure can have devastating psychological effects. In the context of seventeenth-century Protestantism and the doctrines of the verbal inspiration of Scripture, reading the Bible for John Bunyan becomes a journey into the depths of paranoia:

> 'I was followed by this scripture, 'Simon, Simon, behold Satan hath desired to have you' (Luke xxii. 31). And sometimes it would sound so loud within me, yea, and as it were call so strongly after me, that once above all the rest, I turned my head over my shoulders, thinking verily that some man had, behind me, called to me.[3]

The public liturgical act, evident in the *Book of Nehemiah* and *Luke,* goes on in private here. The absence of authoritative interpretation, creates a cavernous space for the echo of one's own voice. Bunyan narrates the story, as he rehearses the hermeneutical problem haunting those who followed in the wake of Luther's and Calvin's *sola Scriptura.*

For Christianity, then, reading, hermeneutics and revelation are closely related to personhood (its intentions and the disciplining of its desires) – to a theological anthropology. It is, in this way, related to ethics, and ethics to narrative. For reading operates at a boundary between interiority and exteriority; it is the process of mediation itself in which we give to the text and we receive from it. Reading, as such, is a religious act. However, the power of what Kristeva would term 'transference' in and through reading is not restricted to the reading of Biblical texts. It is at this point that the character of religious experience and the character of aesthetic experience constitutes a profound question.

In the second circle of Dante's *Inferno*, a troop of lovers pass by the poet and his guide. The last of these are blown like doves through the whirlwind of their desire. They are identified as Francesca da Rimini and her lover Paolo. Weeping, Francesca narrates the story of her downfall. For it was while reading about Lancelot and Guinevere that she and Paolo felt the powers of mutual attraction. 'Many times that reading drew our eyes together and changed the colour in our faces.'[4] Reading turns to kissing, and kissing to adultery. The book becomes the pander who mediates between them and draws them down into the circles of hell. Reading here occasions a second Fall, another Adam and another Eve surrender to a desire greater than that sanctioned by the will of God. Reading is dangerous; for the powers it incarnates and releases are unforeseen. A butterfly spreading its wings in Osaka can have tidal effects off the coast of Portugal, according to popular accounts of what contemporary scientists define as 'chaos theory'. Reading or the appropriation or performance of a representation, similarly has indeterminate consequences.

With Keats' sonnet, 'On First Looking into Chapman's Homer', the experience of reading is one of self-transcending passion. Here it is an experience of the romantic sublime. Reading opens a space for infinite exploration and discovery: 'Then felt I like some watcher of the skies/ When a new planet swims into his ken.' It leads to the rapture of standing above the vast stretch of the Pacific ocean in speechless admiration: 'Silent, upon a peak in Darien.' Highly lifted up, to a point where there is no point any longer, and no horizon where the azure sea folds into the azure heavens, Cortez (and the reader) is frozen in the light of the eternal.

The experience of reading in these passages of Scripture and literature opens again the question of revelation and mediation. But the problem here (unlike our examination in Chapter 1) is with the nature of what is experienced in the performance itself. Recently, in an analysis of experience in Proust's *Remembrance of Things Past*, Martha Nussbaum has used the word 'catalepsis' to describe those accounts in Proust's narrative when a knowledge emerges which is more profound and prior to rationality. Catalepsis is characterized by surprise, vivid particularity, a qualitative intensity in which, with blinding certainty, we gain self-knowledge. As such, catalepsis shares these characteristics with mystical intuition (such as Augustine's).[5] With Keats (as with Proust) the experience has no religious overtones. Romanticism (and eighteenth-century Enlightenment thinkers like Boileau and Burke) had already begun to secularize and technologically colonize the terrain of the ineffable in their teachings on the sublime as an aesthetic mediation of the infinite. Philosophers of religion, examining the nature and certainties of religious experience, would wish to ask precisely where Keats' experience of the ineffable differs from St John the Divine's experience of the last degree of love:

> In this state the soul is like a crystal that is clear and pure; the more degrees of light it receives, the greater concentration of light there is in it, and the enlightenment continues to such a degree that at last it attains a point at which the light is centred in it with such copiousness that it comes to appear to be wholly light, and cannot be distinguished from the light ... and thus appears to be light itself.[6]

Religious experience examined philosophically, rather than psychologically (by Freud[7]) or theologically (by Nicholas Lash[8]), is concerned with its validity as grounds for rational belief in a transcendent deity. Various aspects of religious experience as an argument for the existence of God have been examined. Recently, this examination would include: an analysis of the relationship between knowledge, cognition and religious experience,[9] the relationship between religious experience and its representation,[10] the differences in the character of the religious experiences themselves.[11] Philosophically, the question is analyzed through notions of inference, deduction and probability; what constitutes and validates evidence and truth claims; what is the nature of perception, or the relationship between reality, subjective experience and interpretation. The analysis is part of larger questions in the philosophy of religion – questions concerning religious language and models of faith in their relationship to reason. In both the Keats and the St John the Divine passages, the experience itself is one where the self and the infinite (space in Keats, light in St John the Divine) blur; where distinctions become impossible; where participation, even union, necessitates silence. The experience can only be observed by others (Cortez' men with their 'wild surmise') or observed by ourselves after the event. The experience, then, requires representation in order for it to be. The representation re-enacts the moment of ultimate encounter. Several of the more analytical mystics, or the mystics with a pedagogical concern (Walter Hilton, St Teresa of Avila, St John of the Cross), take pains not to simply describe but examine different forms of religious experience. Nevertheless, when they recount their mystic ascents to the full union, representation faces a crisis because the distance required for observation collapses. We enter the realms of apophatic or negative theology. As the passage from *The Flame of Living Love* illustrates (see n. 6 above), in trying to explain representation attempts to persuade, to perform, to communicate something of the experience. In this how different is it from, and to what extent can it be distinguished from, aesthetic experiences? In both examples (the Keats and the St John the Divine), the world of the text confronts the world of the reader; an experience of transcendence offers the reader possibilities for trans-formation. Paul Ricoeur, whose work we examined in Chapter 2, has done much to expound and examine the relationship between the dynamics of reading and revelation, writes: '*Aisthesis* itself already reveals and transforms. Aesthetic experience draws this power from the contrast it establishes from the outset in relation to everyday experience' (*Time and Narrative*, 3, p. 176). He is discussing here 'aesthetic experience as it is invested in reading' (*ibid.*, p. 176) and much of his works bears out that

> the wholly original relation between knowledge and enjoyment [*Genuss*] that ensures the aesthetic quality of literary hermeneutics … parallels that between the call and promise, committing a whole life, characterizing theological understanding. (*Ibid.*, p. 174)

With Ricoeur, aesthetic experience is religious experience. Reading offers an encounter with the stranger, the other. As readers we are encouraged to welcome this other. Most recently, in his book *Oneself as Another*, Ricoeur concludes:

> the philosopher as philosopher has to admit that one does not know and cannot say whether this Other …, is another person …, or my ancestors …, or God – living God, absent God – or an empty place. With this *aporia* of the Other, philosophical discourse comes to an end. (*Oneself as Another*, p. 355)

The experience of reading is an experience of entering *aporia*.

The philosophical background to reader–response theory

At this point let us step back. Contemporary attention in critical theory to the experience of reading or, with Hélène Cixous, the mystical body of the text, has possibly not been so lavish since Augustine's *Confessions*. The attention paid to it issues from deeper currents in nineteenth- and twentieth-century philosophical speculation. Three currents in particular have been important. The first is existentialism. With its roots in the *Lebensphilosophie* of Kierkegaard and Nietzsche, existentialism becomes entwined with the phenomenological project in Heidegger's early work. Its concern, manifest in its prominent concepts of dread, care, anxiety and alienation, is the lived experience of the human condition. The second contributary current is the development of phenomenology, which attempted to analyze the contents of an experience of an object itself as consciousness grasps it and makes it meaningful. With its roots in Hegel's Subject, Husserl's phenomenology mapped out the intentional structure of consciousness – as we saw, briefly, in Chapter 3. The later phenomenological investigations of Heidegger, on the poetry of Hölderlin, George and Trackl[12] and the later work by the French phenomenologist, Merleau-Ponty, on perception and painting,[13] both encouraged examination into the aesthetic experience. To these names must be added those of the Polish philosopher, Roman Ingarden, whose influential work *The Literary Work of Art: An Investigation on the Borderlines of Ontology, Logic and the Theory of Literature*, was first published in Halle in 1931, and also the German philosopher, Hans Georg Gadamer, who worked within the traditions of Romantic hermeneutics. It is with Gadamer's pupil, Hans-Robert Jauss, and his colleague at the University of Constanz, Wolfgang Iser, that a strict methodology of aesthetic reception was sought.[14] They constituted a school of *Rezeptionstheorie* influential on figures like Ricoeur and Stanley Fish (whose work we will examine later).

The third of the currents behind the contemporary interest in reading and reception is the concept of the sublime. In the eighteenth century, the concept of the sublime underwent a revival which fed the streams of romanticism, both in England (through Joseph Addison and Edmund Burke) and Germany (through Kant, particularly his late work on aesthetics). The sublime came to be characterized by the experience of transcendence, awe and ineffablity. In Rudolf Otto's celebrated book *The Idea of the Holy* (published in 1913), analogies are drawn between the concept of the sublime and the concept of the numinous, the *mysterium tremendum et fascinens*. He observes:

> While the element of 'dread' is gradually overborne, the connexion of 'the sublime' and 'the holy' becomes firmly established as a legitimate schematization and is carried on into the highest forms of religious consciousness – a proof that there exists a hidden kinship between the numinous and the sublime which is something more than accidental analogy, and to which Kant's *Critique of Judgement* bears distant witness.[15]

Once more, with the concept of the sublime it becomes difficult to locate the point at which one can distinguish between an aesthetic experience and a religious experience.

Otto's predecessor here is Friedrich Schleiermacher, whose *On Religion: Speeches to its Cultured Despisers* (published in 1799 and deeply indebted to Kant's later work on aesthetic judgement) was the first to announce the synonymity between the 'feeling' [*Gefühl*] which constitutes religious piety and the 'feeling' which finds expression as culture. In the second of his 'Speeches', entitled 'On the Essence of Religion', he develops his thesis that religion is 'the sum of all higher feelings'. It bears witness to the endless energies of the eternal mind, creating unity in and through multiplicity. Culture, and the particular form of a religion is also a cultural expression, creates and represents for itself, in its finitude, the infinite giveness of the universe. It constantly expresses its absolute dependence. What is revelation, Schleiermacher asks? 'Every original and new intuition of the universe', he answers. What is inspiration? 'It is merely the religious name for freedom.'[16] God and human beings are involved in an endless mutual creativity that is both aesthetic and divine. Humanity is God's great work of art. The history humanity produces surrounds us with 'an endless gallery of the most sublime works of art' which humanity reproduces 'by a thousand brilliant mirrors'.[17] Hence, the inner affinity between religion and art, intuitions of the infinite and their endless cultural mediations in religious practices and aesthetic endeavours. Later, in *The Christian Faith*, Schleiermacher composed his systematic theology on the basis of the most profound religious experience, absolute dependence. Beyond the antithesis of pleasure and pain (which characterizes Burke's understanding of the sublime), lies the highest consciousness, a God consciousness. 'This state we speak of under the name of the Blessedness of the finite being as the highest summit of his perfection.'[18] Schleiermacher takes pains to emphasize that this feeling of absolute dependence is first awakened 'by communicative and stimulative power of expression or utterance'.[19] This emphasis will provide him with the rationale for the Protestant attention to preaching the Word.

Once more, mediation of this feeling is central; the mediation of blessedness here parallels the mediation of the sublime in Schleiermacher's earlier work. If Roland Barthes, in his essay *The Pleasure of the Text* draws attention to the 'bliss', the *jouissance*, which both transcends and yet plays within the material body of the text; if Barthes attempts to define this 'bliss' as sublime – then in what way does Barthes' concept differ from Schleiermacher's?

Co-extensive with the new models of selfhood, the ecstatic self of Kristeva and Levinas, among others, is a renewed interest in the experience of the mediated sublime. We will examine this through the work of Jean-François Lyotard, turning finally to the textual mysticism (and feminism) of Hélène Cixous' promotion of *écriture féminine* and the mystic voice in the work of Michel de Certeau. Uppermost in this theological evaluation of reading, the textual and the sublime is an understanding of incarnation. Roland Barthes remarks: 'What we are seeking to establish in various ways is a theory of the materialist subject.'[20] Irigaray, who shares this concern, will wish to speak of 'incarnation'.[21] The rarest materialists, Barthes notes, 'have all been overt eudaemonists'.[22] What we are uncovering here is a contemporary notion of incarnation, a sublimity indwelling the body of a text only constituted by its reader – a sublimity, then, indwelling our bodies.

Stanley Fish

New Criticism

Although trained in the American school of New Criticism,[23] Fish's work owes much to Barthes and Derrida and to a reaction against the position of New Criticism *vis-à-vis* the autonomy of the text. He encountered the French approach to textuality early in 1970, while on sabbatical in Paris. Although he had already shown an interest in the reading experience (see his first work *Surprised by Sin: The Reader in Paradise Lost*, 1967), he returned from France in the summer of 1970 to write his first essay on the phenomenology of reading which was appended to his acclaimed *Self-Consuming Artefacts: The Experience of Seventeenth Century Literature* (1972).

We came across the influence of New Criticism with respect to Stephen Greenblatt's work (see Chapter 2), now it is in evidence again with Stanley Fish. The focus of attention for New Criticism was the autonomy of the text – the organic unity of its form and content. To William Wimsatt and Monroe Beardsley the text was a verbal icon; neither its author's intentions nor its reader's response were important in elucidating the mechanisms whereby the integrated unity of the text was achieved. Formal techniques – such as analyses of grammar and numerical studies of certain images – were developed into the 'science' of stylistics. Fish's work began in dialogue and then in dispute with this perspective. 'In 1970 I was asking the question, "Is the reader or the text the source of meaning?"' (*Is There a Text in This Class?*, p. 1). For New Criticism, any attempt 'to derive the standards of criticism from the psychological effects of the poem' will result 'in impressionism and relativism'.[24] Beardsley and Wimsatt referred to this as the affective fallacy. Fish had to argue then on two counts: first, how critical interpretation could never divorce itself 'from the psychology effects' and, secondly, how the reader's response did not lead to relativism. Although his theoretical position has changed over the years, these two axioms of his thinking have remained important.

As Fish himself has stated, a dramatic development in his thinking took place with his development of 'interpretative communities' (around 1975). Prior to this date he was concerned with laying the foundations for a type of description prior to the descriptions of the formal composition of the texts constructed by new critics. He termed this an 'affective stylistics'. Attention was now paid to the temporal structure of the reading experience. The concern with textual form and its organic integrity (the priority of New Criticism) was spatial. The meaning of a text, Fish argued, arose from following the temporal unfolding of the text and the way the reader was surprised, cajoled, confused and called to account by it. The reader makes sense as s/he continually negotiates, projects and reassesses the text's intentions. The reader does not find sense as if the language were simply a container from which meaning could be extracted. The language and movement of sense in the text is an experience. Each reader undergoes the same experience (or so Fish thought in his early essays), whether they are conscious of doing so or not. 'The meaning of the utterance, I repeat, is its experience' (*Is There a Text in This Class?*, p. 65). The more the reader is informed – about the nature of the language, about the connotations of words, lexical unities, idioms and dialects, about literary discourses and genres – the more the reader can become conscious of the experience. This experience by the informed reader seemed to Fish to present a more objective description of the text than critical interpretation, in so far as it was prior to the selectivity and presuppositions of New Criticism. Literary criticism begins, he thought, when the reading experience is forgotten, or displaced. It is with literary criticism that opinions about texts begin to diverge. Fish frequently delineated the struggles among critics to define the exact meaning of a word or phrase in a text, and the histories of such struggles.

The text still remains central to Fish's work at this point, but contrary to the emphasis in critical stylistics, Fish downplays the referential function of language. This will have important repercussions, not least for Fish's characterization of theological discourse. For it will chime with the structural and post-structural debates about language in France (particularly the work of Barthes and Derrida). These critical theories too were emphasizing the temporality of language (on the basis of Saussure's diachronic and synchronic axes) and the materiality of the sign. In *S/Z*, *Writing Degree Zero* and *The Pleasure of the Text*, Barthes was engaged with describing 'a complex readability' (quoted in *Is There a Text in This Class?*, p. 183) which responded to the continuity, ruptures and abrasiveness of writing. Also countering scientific descriptions of the transparency and innocence of language, Barthes too announces that 'the book creates the meaning, the meaning creates life'.[25] Nothing is permanent. In the absolute flow of becoming 'the permanent exists only thanks to our coarse organs which reduce'.[26] Perceptively, Fish (trained in seventeenth-century literature) recognized this making of sense, this involvement in the viscera of the text, as a fundamental aspect of theological discourse and Baroque poetics. The role of the reader in such discourse is pivotal. For in the wake of a theology in which human subjects were fallen, and unable either to understand clearly or become the heroes of texts, readers of Baroque poetry and fiction frequently found themselves decentralized by the opacity of the text. They find themselves so even today, but without having the cultural context lend a logic to such obfuscation.

Fish developed this insight into the theological concerns of Baroque poetics. Rather than deciphering meaning, readers are 'merely creating new spaces into which the meaning that is already there expands' (*Is There a Text in This Class?*, p. 193). What is realized in the process, and constitutes redemption in these religious texts (Fish is discussing a sermon by Lancelot Andrewes)

> is the illusion of self-sufficiency and independence, the illusion of moving towards a truth rather than moving by virtue of it and within it, the illusion that destiny and meaning are what we seek rather than what had sought, and found, us. (*Ibid.* p. 195)

The faith we place in our ability to understand (and language as transparent in that understanding) is shown to be bad faith – the result of our fallen condition. The ideology of reference and the instrumental view of language it enjoins, is understood to be the product of sin and the belief in self-autonomy. Theological discourse seeks to undo the effects of this fallen condition by employing a radically different discourse in which the reader's experience of the text is both necessary and constitutive. The various strategies that a reader needs to employ establishes a new responsibility on behalf of the reader for the text produced and his or her relation to that text. The ethics of such a position, as well as the theology of the mediated Word, will become more apparent.

There remained the haunting question of relativism, more particularly as Fish intrepidly followed through some of the consequences of his own thoughts and eventually acknowledged that the experience of the informed reader was also an interpretation, not a more fundamental description of the text at all. The question of what controlled or contained the plurality if not the arbitrariness of interpretation, Fish attempts to deal with by three means. First, by an anthropology which claimed that the 'ability to interpret is not acquired; it is constitutive of being human' (*Is There a Text in This Class?*, p. 172). Secondly, by a sociology of knowledge which claimed that what is 'acquired are the ways of interpreting and those same ways can also be forgotten or supplanted or complicated or dropped from favour' (*ibid.*, p. 172). Thirdly, by an objectivity based in interpretive communities which 'are made up of those who share interpretive strategies not for reading (in the conventional sense) but for writing texts, for constituting their properties and assigning their intentions' (*ibid.*, p. 171). We are all, then, writers of texts and as such bound by conventions of how to write – conventions of genre, of what defines poetry as distinct from prose, literature as distinct from other discourses. The text as a stable entity out there disappears when examined from this perspective. Convention alone (always historically contingent) controls. Each reading creates a new text; and those who share similar readings belong to the same interpretive community. By 1975 this was the stage Fish had reached.

Interpretive communities

Following this date, Fish's essays begin to explore the social, political, epistemological and legal implications of his proposal that sense is made. In fact, the fixed points of both text and reader tend to disappear as Fish develops his view that there is no position possible which is either purely objective or subjective. His earlier notion of the 'informed reader', which helped to stake out boundaries between good, better and best readings, is now viewed as much more a product of a certain type of literary socialization. It is probably because of this that, though the reader's response is foundational for his or her insight into the contextuality of all meaning, Fish is no longer concerned to delineate that response. Rather, he wishes to defend how the instability of all meaning is stabilized through the particularity of a given context which limits the ambiguity of discourse. He wishes to defend himself against the charge of solipsism by emphasizing the conventions which fix the sense of something or the interpretative strategy for making sense of something. Conventions have to be socially agreed upon and accepted, and hence strategies for interpretation are already in place within the community which has sanctioned their use – sanctioned them to the point of forgetting they are convention-constructed and believing they are 'out there' as independent features of texts. In his idiosyncratic, witty and incisive way, Fish moves from the experience of textuality, from the making of sense, to analyzing how specific senses are made. Essays such as '*Is There a Text in This Class?*' illustrate this. He sketches out a structure for the evaluation of interpretations based upon the way a community appropriates and contextualizes any act of communication. He presents test-cases as evidence for the way a textual ambiguity is resolved by the modifications we make to our interpretive strategy as we transpose the text into another known context in which its sense is made out. He terms this 'code switching'. In this way Fish establishes a politics of reading and unmasks 'the unwritten rules of the literary, legal, and religious game' (*Is There a Text in This Class*, p. 343).

It is exactly at this point that he parts company with another significant proponent of reader–response theory, Wolfgang Iser. German born and educated, Iser's work owes much more to a philosophical tradition than Fish's – Romantic hermeneutics, German and British idealism and the phenomenological work of Husserl and Merleau-Ponty. What began, like Fish's work, as a phenomenological account of reading (see *The Implied Reader*, 1974, and *The Act of Reading*, 1978) has become an examination of the connections between literary structure, the nature and operation of human consciousness, particularly the imagination, and aesthetics (see *Prospecting: From Reader Response to Literary Anthropology*, 1989). Iser remains committed to the subject–object dialectic. The text always remains an objective fact. Our responses as readers are structured by the text and, to that extent, we create the text as an aesthetic object in the reading event. However, the text has an independence from its readership. In fact, it constitutes its readership, transforming us through the dialectic established between its objectivity and our subjectivity. The arbitrary suggestiveness of the subject is therefore controlled. The objectivity of the text is constituted alongside other objects in a world independent of socialized, intentional subjects. It is an empirical given. Signs mediate between this given and the individual. Therefore, aesthetics issue from the between, the oscillations back and forth between these two poles in the search for synthesis. In an interview, Iser speaks of 'the real world ... perceivable through the senses' and 'the literary text ... perceivable only through the imagination'. He concludes: 'the real world (uninterpreted) lives and functions independently of the individual observer, whereas the literary text does not'.[27] This presupposition of an ontological order (nature) locates him firmly within a foundationalism (even logocentrism) which Fish would reject. Iser is much closer to the fusion of two horizons made famous in the philosophical hermeneutics of Gadamer. As Fish writes towards the end of his own analysis of Iser's work, 'the world and the world of the text are differently interpreted – that is, made – objects' (*Doing What Comes Naturally*, p. 82).[28]

Fish's position since 1975 has become increasingly antifoundational. Unlike Derrida's notion of *différance*, meaning is not deferred in Fish's analysis of making sense, but meaning is always recreated anew. There is no movement towards a promise whose realization is forever forestalled. There is no dialectic between an outside and an inside. There is no examination of desire. Fish's work (like the work on the grammars of different cultures by Clifford Geertz[29]) might be used to suggest that given a specific community, the Christian community, the meaningfulness of theological discourse is assured. Such discourse will have meaning for those reading within that particular interpretive community, though it will not have meaning (or the same meaning) for those outside such a community. George Lindbeck, in his book *The Nature of Doctrine* develops such a notion in terms of ecclesiology.[30] However because there remains not even a trace of transcendence, a place above these interpretive communities from which to observe, speak and put into perspective, then Fish's work describes, at best, a pragmatics. We read like this in this situation because we can do no other. The value then of Fish's later work is reduced for the study of theology. He reminds us that meaning is sociologically mediated, and thus returns us to theology's problematic of revelation and its dependence upon representation. Because this mediation is not informed by even the quasi-transcendence of Derrida's trace or the sensible transcendental of Irigaray's utopic horizon it can be taken no further.[31] Fish is more radically a champion of antifoundationalism than some of the other critical theorists we have examined. In fact, ultimately, he is against theory. To go into Fish's later work (*Doing What Comes Naturally*, 1989 and *There's No Such Thing As Free Speech ... And It's A Good Thing Too*, 1994), though an entertaining and acerbic response to the cultural values of both American liberalism and neo-conservatism, would divert us from the experience of reading itself and its theological implications. It is with the work of Jean-François Lyotard that we take up again the experience of textuality, specifically here in relation to his interest in the sublime.

Jean-François Lyotard

If meaning can never be independent of its mediation, can never be extracted from its representation, then rhetoric can no longer simply be viewed as ornamentation, nor knowledge divorced from aesthetics. Fish characterizes our contemporary world as the world of *homo rhetoricus* (*Doing What Comes Naturally*, p. 482), the classroom as 'a performance occasion' and himself as 'a professional theatrical academic' (*There's No Such Thing As Free Speech*, p. 286). In Fish's earlier work on reader–response, making sense of a text became inseparable from the aesthetic reception of that text. It is that aesthetic reception which has interested so many French critical theorists. Roland Barthes wished to speak of the pleasure of the text, employing terms like bliss (*jouissance*), ecstasy, rapture, seduction and euphoria. The creative interchange between text, author and reader, with Barthes (Irigaray, Lyotard and Cixous), challenges those distinctions made between the aesthetic, psychological and theological interpretation of the experience itself.

Unlike several of the other French critical theorists, Jean-François Lyotard was born in France (just outside Paris at Versailles in 1924). He was not an exile – although he taught in the early 1950s in Algeria. He received his philosophical education at the Sorbonne and taught at the respectable University of Nanterre. His background and the institutions at which he trained and taught were not at the forefront of the *avant-garde*. What introduced him to the radical and subversive was his strong commitment to Marxism and his sensitivity to oppression. In a poignant essay entitled 'A Memorial for Marxism: for Pierre Souyri' (in *Peregrinations*), Lyotard recounts his struggles with and beyond Marxism. Through these struggles he came to see that 'there are several incommensurable genres of discourse in play in society' (*Peregrinations*, p. 73). Although, in 1954, he had published a work entitled *Phénoménologie*, it was only now, having left Marxism behind, that he devoted himself to a philosophical examination of those genres of discourse.

It is with Lyotard's work[32] on narrative, rhetoric, painting and the sublime, that the aesthetic experience is most thoroughly analyzed. The received experience is determinative. 'No longer "How does one make a work of art?", but "What is it to experience an effect proper to art?"' (*The Inhuman*, p. 97). The experience is not one of making sense so much as not making sense, as we will see. One of the most important terms in Lyotard's exploration into reading the textual surface is 'event'. We have seen with Foucault how 'event' is a theme in contemporary French critical theory. What characterizes an 'event' for Lyotard is that absolutely singular, punctuating moment. In his 1987 book *Que Peindre?*, he characterizes an event as 'Not a thing, but at least a caesura in space-time'.[33] He takes the notion from Kant [*Begebenheit*] and reads it through Heidegger's concept of *Ereignis*.[34] It is the irreducible given prior to will, desire or consciousness – the happening, the *that* which presences by presenting nothing. We will return to this, and the theological concepts of gift or revelation which 'event' calls forth, later.

The Kantian sublime

Before going on to outline Lyotard's own project, we need to examine the concept of the sublime in *The Critique of Judgement*, because it is on the basis of a critique and commentary upon Kant that Lyotard proceeds.[35] The reason for this attention to the last of Kant's trilogy – *Critique of Pure Reason, Critique of Practical Reason,* are Parts one and two, respectively – is that analysis of aesthetic judgement, for Kant, bridges the work done on the operation of transcendental reason, in its pure and ethical (practical) forms. For Kant, the operation of the aesthetic is more primordial than that of understanding, knowledge or ethics. For Lyotard, the sphere of the aesthetic constitutes 'a kind of transcendental pre-logic' (*Lessons on the Analytic of the Sublime,* p. 32) in which thought and sensation are complicit. The 'muteness of pure feeling' (*ibid.,* p. 46) which is the aesthetic judgement is prior to an orientation by the categories of the understanding which enable that feeling to be thought. Hence a new 'immediacy' emerges which Lyotard will call 'presence'. This 'presence' does not correspond with the ontological order of nature or things in themselves – the immediate apprehension of which Lyotard, like Kant, would see as impossible.

Kant, following Burke and Addison, distinguishes between the beautiful and the sublime. Lyotard's interest in the sublime, rather than the beautiful, issues from the way in which, for Kant, the sublime violates any affinity between nature and the harmony of the faculties. In the beautiful, for Kant, what is given to the faculty of the imagination conforms to the law of the faculty of the understanding. Intuition (in the faculty of the imagination) conforms to concept (in the faculty of the understanding). There arises from this a necessary delight, conformable to the teleological movement of reason towards a unity, and determined totality. The sublime, as Kant analysed it, creates a tension between faculties, fissuring the movement towards the universal and unconditioned. What awakens the 'intellectual feeling' (*Geistesgefühl*) is not nature or works of art that are compatible, in their determined form, to the law of understanding, but (as Lyotard puts it) 'rather magnitude, force, quantity in its purest state, a "presence" that exceeds what imaginative thought can grasp at once in a form' (*Lessons on the Analytic of the Sublime,* p. 53). Unpresentable 'presence' is the focus for the unconditional, and the focus of Lyotard's concern with the sublime and ours (as we examine the theological consequences of such a concern). This contra-nature and contra-representational character of the sublime Lyotard discovers most clearly expressed in the *avant-garde* and abstract.

The status of the sublime, for Kant, depends upon its relation to our practical or moral reasoning. It has two forms. In the first form (analyzed in sections 25–27 as the mathematical sublime), it emerges as a feeling when the faculty of the imagination is overwhelmed by the immensity of an object whose manifold sensibility cannot be synthetized into a single intuition. Hence there arises pain because of the imagination's incapacity to handle the object; but also pleasure because in this incapacity there arises the necessity of referring the feeling to an idea of the infinite which rules in the faculty of reason (theoretical and practical). This referral brings relief – though whether the relief is subsequent to or simultaneous with the pain depends upon whether you see the Kantian faculties operating hierarchically or in conflict with each other. Lyotard emphasizes the tensions between the faculties (*Lessons on the Analytic of the Sublime*, p. 24 and the abyss separating the faculties).[36] We need to point out here that this 'feeling' is not the immediate impress of nature upon the senses. It is a 'feeling' located in the mind itself caused by the tension and movement between two cognitive faculties (imagination and reasoning) which excites what Kant calls the 'mental faculties'.[37] It is a 'feeling', then, which is suprasensible. It gives us no knowledge of the object itself, only of the subject perceiving it. Lyotard calls it a 'quasi-perception' (*The Inhuman*, p. 137).

In the second form (analysed in sections 28–29 as the dynamically sublime), the sublime emerges as a feeling of fear in the face of a power able to destroy us. It is a fear which stimulates a courage in us to resist its domination. Hence, the dynamical mode of the sublime is more directly concerned with the laws governing our practical reason, whereas the mathematical sublime is more directly concerned with our pure reason. In either modes, what is significant about the sublime for Kant is that

> the idea of the suprasensible ... is awakened in us by an object the aesthetic estimating of which strains the imagination to its utmost, whether in respect of extension (mathematical), or its might over the mind (dynamical).[38]

This suprasensible cannot, Kant emphasizes, be determined further since the imagination in being overwhelmed is unable to create a concept of the manifold intuition and therefore no representation of the sublime is possible. Thus words freighted with negativity like 'infinity', 'abyss', 'unboundedness', 'incommensurate' and 'the unconditioned' are employed to describe its teleology and effect. For Kant, it is this awakening of the idea of the suprasensible grounded in the subjectivity of any reflective judgement upon the sublime, which ultimately relates the aesthetic feeling to the moral telos of all human nature. It is because of this accord with the faculty of practical (moral) reasoning that subjective aesthetic feelings can have universal significance. Since, for Kant, moral reasoning can only proceed on the pre-accepted understanding of the famous *as if* of God's existence, we can perhaps understand his statement in *The Critique of Judgement* that both

> the admiration for beauty and the emotion excited by the profuse variety of ends of nature, which a reflective mind is able to feel prior to any clear representation of an intelligent author of the world, have something about them akin to a religious feeling.[39]

The aesthetic, then, is analogous ('akin to') to the religious experience. Kant's views on aesthetics have had their critics,[40] but what is of interest here is how Lyotard has interpreted, extended and modified the Kantian perspective and what the theological implications engendered as a consequence are.

Lyotard's notion of the sublime

There are, in particular, two aspects of the Kantian perspective in which Lyotard is interested. The first concerns Kantian epistemology, where no object is directly presented and we only handle representations of objects (signs and *analogia*). The Kantian regulative ideas – freedom, God, immortality (the absolute) – all have no presentable object. The presentation of the sublime is, therefore, negative; for the sublime has 'no im-mediate communicability' (*The Inhuman*, p. 113) (see n. 32 above). It is, therefore, 'compatible with the formless' (*ibid.*, p. 113) – and hence is best depicted in *avant-garde* and abstract art. The second of Lyotard's concerns is consequent upon the first, the incommensurable, the unnameable – that which exceeds three of the Kantian faculties – imagination, understanding and reason. At the end of his programmatic essay, *The Postmodern Condition* (1979), Lyotard calls for a politics which 'would respect both the desire for justice and the desire for the unknown' (*The Postmodern Condition*, p. 67). In his later appendage to that essay, 'Answering the Question: What is Postmodernism?' (1983), he pursues and expands this 'desire for the unknown' specifically in terms of the aesthetics of the sublime which offers a phenomenological account of the 'unpresentable':

> The postmodern would be that which, in the modern, puts forward

the unpresentable in presentation itself; that which denies the solace of good forms … that which searches for new presentations, not in order to enjoy them, but in order to impart a stronger sense of the unpresentable. (*Ibid.*, p. 81)

He concludes with the exhortation, 'Let us wage war on totality; let us be witnesses to the unpresentable' (*ibid.*, p. 82).

The war on totality is a familiar battlecry – we heard it with Derrida (on logocentrism), with Foucault (on history), with Levinas (on Being). We will hear it again in the work of Michel de Certeau. With Lyotard it develops into a struggle against the rule of truth, metanarratives, or grand narratives – plots which seem to comprehensively explain all phenomena. Liberal humanism, Marxism and Freudianism, are all examples of grand narratives for Lyotard. From quite early in his work – developing out of his analysis of representation in *Discours, figure* (1971) – Lyotard turned to art and aesthetics as a means of challenging metanarratives.[41] Art perpetually gives rise to little narratives; it concerns invention not prescription. Since the early 1980s this aesthetic direction has specifically focused upon the concept of the sublime, culminating in his *Lessons on the Analytic of the Sublime* (first published in France in 1991). Several other important essays – which detail the profound impression made upon him by the American painter, Barnett Baruch Newman, who wrote an essay entitled 'The Sublime is Now' – are found in his earlier volume *The Inhuman* (1988).

Lyotard's attention, like Newman's, is upon the sublime as an experience of the instant, the event, the here. In the sublime what is presented is nothing but the presentation, the performance itself. That is, nothing is referred to, represented or configured by the colours, the paints, the lines, the materials itself of the presentation. This occurrence is prior to consciousness, signification and meaning: 'That it happens "precedes", so to speak, the question pertaining to what happens' (*The Inhuman*, p. 90). The presentation of the unpresentable has the paradoxical structure of the pain/pleasure experience of the aesthetic sublime. Lyotard relates this to Kant's notion of 'negative presentation'. Feeling, embodiment and a revised empiricism become crucial here because 'it is not a question of non-communication but of non-conceptual communication' (*ibid.*, p. 109). The arena in which this takes place, for Kant, is the imagination which, in association with the faculty of reason, furnishes us with a knowledge, after-the-event, of experience. For Lyotard also, the sublime is a *Geistesgefühl*, a 'sentiment of the mind' (*ibid.*, p. 137).

We are not passive in relation to this sentiment. Rather we are active receivers, what Lyotard terms 'passible' – intervening in this reception to modify and even enjoy what is addressed to us. We are constituted like this as human beings. Lyotard writes about 'an immediate community of feeling demanded across the singular aesthetic feeling' (*The Inhuman*, p. 117) – a universality. This is not a universality based on an external ontological order which finds form in artistic or natural creation. This is not the romantic sublime attempting to represent lost origins, ends or absolutes. This sublime evokes the absolute as unpresentable in the very 'matter of artistic work' (*ibid.*, p. 126). Transcendence is inseparable from the immanent and material. Irigaray calls this transcendent horizon of the body a 'sensible transcendental' and Lyotard, like Irigaray and Barthes, will speak of the experience as *jouissance*.

This model of corporeality is not based upon the dualism of matter and form upon which classical discussions of presence and mimesis are founded. This 'presence' is not a transcendental given re-presented in aesthetic form. This 'presence' occurs as an event, as the singular happening, the *that* of a thing given prior to will and understanding, desire and representation.[42] It challenges notions of incarnation based upon human–divine oppositions. It institutes a new form of incarnation; in which the givenness of a thing, its sublimity, its unnamable and unpresentable nature is its carnality itself. The material particularity escapes the *a priori* rules governing their possibility for us. There is that about corporeality which itself is sublime. It is itself incommensurate. The incommensurability of all else, our notion of the incommensurate itself, is given here in what Lyotard describes as 'the event of passion, a passibility for which the mind will not have been prepared, which will have unsettled it, and of which it conserves only the feeling – anguish and jubilation – of an obscure debt' (*The Inhuman*, p. 143). It is incommensurate because it is singular, 'as if it were something that appeared everytime for the first time' (*Lessons on the Analytic of the Sublime*, pp. 19–20). As such, it cannot constitute a universal, an objective predicate of any number of given objects.

What is of theological value is this thinking of the absolute without relation. When Lyotard asks 'How can the without-relation be "present" to relation?' (*Lessons on the Analytic of the Sublime*, p. 56), the structure of such a thought is as theological as it is aesthetic. We are returned again to theological questions concerning revelation and the economy of grace. We are also returned to the ethics consequent upon what Nussbaum terms catalepsis. The same observations hold true when we learn Lyotard's answer: the without-relation 'can only be "present" as disavowal (as metaphysical entity), forbidden (as illusion)' (*ibid.*, p. 56). To argue that this absolute without-relation is constitutive of critical thought itself is to suggest grace is the presupposition of thinking, faith of reason. On this model revelation of the absolute (the divine or God, theologically speaking) is not interventionist in itself, only in relation to our sensibility and judgement of it. Revelation as such adheres to the giveness of corporeality itself; we become aware that a thing's very thatness is the condition and animator for all our thinking and knowing. Revelation is donation itself.[43] There remains a question concerning the location of this 'presence'. If it is not in nature, is it in the mind? As Lyotard writes: 'There are no sublime objects, but only sublime feelings' (*Lessons on the Analytic of the Sublime*, p. 182). In the sublime we are offered a sensory glimpse of absolute power and freedom which, for Kant, are pure reason's analogues for practical reasoning's God. This is a God which is not conceived. It is a God whose presence is felt, albeit indirectly. The sheer giveness, donation or grace rests upon our disinterestedness. It is not a product of will, but prior to it, an animator of it. It is a grace which 'hides and offers itself in every atom ... perhaps' (*The Inhuman*, p. 164). There emerges a sense of respect and therefore a sense of justice and the Good.

Lyotard's concern with the corporeal, the body, its singularity and its desires, has been constant throughout his work. It parallels similar concerns in most of the key people whose work we have been examining (notably Derrida, Irigaray and Kristeva). Lyotard's analysis and application of the concept of the sublime develops his earlier notion of 'figure', which is also unpresentable and infects (whilst being heterogenous to) representation.[44] With his analysis of the sublime, Lyotard sketches a form of corporeal transcendence. Lyotard explains that this transcendent

> horizon is 'present' everywhere. What we are calling 'presence' in contradistinction to presentation is the effect of this transcendence, its sign, on theoretical, practical and aesthetic thought. (*Lessons on the Analytic of the Sublime*, p. 214)

This is not simply an anthropological horizon which is open to the incommensurate (as in Heidegger and Karl Rahner), but a phenomenology the possibility for which lies in that which is incommensurate; an incommensurability to which it is indebted, on which it is dependent, absolutely dependent. Perhaps we need to re-examine again the theological roots of Schleiermacher's work, with which we began this chapter. It is the aesthetic feeling, for both Lyotard and Schleiermacher (and Kant) which gives 'virtual direct access to the idea of this [suprasensible] substrate' (*ibid.*, p. 217). The question is raised, then, as to the relationship between aesthetic and religious experience. Kant raises it first, as we have seen, and suggests there is a kinship, but what kind of kinship? Both share a similar, paradoxical structure: 'a singular feeling claiming universal validity' (*ibid.*, p. 217). How do we assess the degree of similarity? The enigma of the sublime lies in keeping that question in play; the sublime remains inexplicable (Kant's *unerklärlich*).

In Lyotard's vocabulary, the 'sublime feeling is a differend' (*ibid.*, p. 234). Although, in his recent collection of essays, the sublime is used to analyze the unpresentable embodied in painting and music, Lyotard's concept of the differend arose through an examination of language (particularly naming, the referent and narrative). 'The differend is the unstable state and instant of language wherein something which must be able to be put into phrases cannot yet be' (*The Differend*, p. 13).[45] For Kant, as Lyotard emphasizes, communicatability is compelled, as a duty (see *The Critique of Judgement*, Sections 40 and 41). Making and communicating judgements of taste are necessary, 'just as if it were part of an original compact dictated by humanity itself'.[46] The body of the text, textuality as tissue, is the necessary locus for the 'instant' and it is in this way that the sublime is, therefore, a differend.

Lyotard's analysis of the sublime concentrates upon the body of the configured, an economy of representation which he earlier delineated as governed by erotic desire. We have encountered this position before – with Irigaray (in Chapter 1) and Kristeva (in Chapter 3). These feminists have seen the commitment to the corporeal, the thinking of the flesh, as being a characteristic of speaking as woman (*parler-femme*). As a feminist coda to this final chapter we will look briefly at the experience of 'textual mysticism' as it is evident in the work of Hélène Cixous.

Hélène Cixous

Like Derrida, Cixous was born in Algeria. This was in 1937, on the eve of the Second World War. Like Derrida also, Cixous has Jewish roots (her mother had fled Nazi Germany in 1933 and her father was of old

Mediterranean Jewish stock). Like several other French critical theorists, then, Cixous came to France (in 1955) as an outsider, and exile, with an ear for other languages. Her first full-length study was of the work of another exile, James Joyce. Loss, bereavement, the other and the work of language in recovering, healing and maintaining these themes has been an abiding concern, as it has also been one of the key concerns of Derrida and Kristeva.

'I write life', Cixous states ('*Coming to Writing*', p. 5),[47] comparing writing to blood and the act of writing as touching 'with letters, with lips, with breath, to caress with the tongue, to lick with the soul, to taste the blood of the beloved body, of life in its remoteness' (*ibid.*, p. 4). *Écriture féminine* sets itself the task of establishing woman as writer where writing has been dominated by the phallus (that is, the symbolic, the conceptual, the analytical as well as the masculinity of many of its practitioners). 'Inscribe the breath of the whole woman', Cixous advocates in one of her most forceful and programmatic essays 'The Laugh of the Medusa' (p. 250). The 'whole' woman means her drives, her imaginary, her sexed body.

To some extent, her work parallels other French feminists. Like Irigaray she believes their language is never neuter. It always expresses and incarnates a libidinal economy and women can therefore only challenge the imperialism of male thinking through writing (Irigaray would have 'speaking') as woman. Like Kristeva, Cixous associates the feminine in writing with the rhythmic and the material; that which allows the semiotic (Kristeva's word) body to manifest itself. Like Irigaray, Cixous is concerned with articulating a new incarnation. In her essay 'Clarice Lispector: An Approach', she writes:

> The soul is the magic of attention. And the body of the soul is made from a fine, fine ultrasensual substance, so finely sensitive that it can pick up the murmur of every hatching, the infinitesimal music of particles calling to one another to compose themselves in fragrance. ('*Coming to Writing*', pp. 70–1)

Spirituality here is inseparable from feeling, from bodily experience. Transcendence issues from and in the tissue of textuality, writing. 'Writing: touching the mystery, delicately, with the tips of the words, trying not to crush it, in order to un-lie' (*ibid.*, p. 134). However, writing and reading are not distinct activities for Cixous, whose own writing issues from readings of other texts. The axiom of intertextuality is that 'there is a manner of reading comparable to the act of writing' (*Three Steps on the Ladder of Writing*, p. 19). 'A real reader is a writer' (*ibid.*, p. 21). 'Mystery', 'enigma', 'unknown', 'inexplicable', 'unavowable' – these are the words Cixous employs in her descriptions of the process of reading as writing, writing as reading in which there emerges a 'transfiguration of the self'; the attainment of a proper distance (a distance which prevents incorporation of the other) 'through a relentless process of de-selfing, de-egoization' (*'Coming to Writing'*, p. 156). This is similar to the call for an 'inhuman' in Lyotard and Levinas, Foucault and Derrida. Like Lyotard and Fish, her attention is fastened to the process, the movement of writing/reading – the aesthetic experience of the language (or the paint or the sound). Like Lyotard, the telos of such an experience is the 'instant,' the 'event,' the 'miracle' or the 'surprise'. 'My life burns to rise above itself toward my secret ... At the heart of it lies a soft gleaming pearl like the flash of eternity at the heart of a moment' (*ibid.*, pp. 90–1). Cixous continues, with an allusion to the fourteenth-century English mystic, Julian of Norwich, 'My secret is no bigger than a hazelnut of eternity.' Like Julian (and like Kristeva), this 'epiphany' occurs only in an economy of love which demands a radical ethics of kenosis. 'It's at the end, at the moment one has attained the period of relinquishing, of adoration ..., that miracles happen' (*ibid.*, p. 117). The love is an adoration for the other, which is desired, which is lacked. Cixous calls for a positive reading of such a lack – a recognition of the necessity of lack which prevents, by forestalling, possession. Only the humility and the discipline of recognizing such a lack, only love as not having, can enable the other to be other and the gift to be received without being owned. The gift can then circulate freely in an exchange founded upon an economy of love.

If, with Lyotard, the aesthetics of the sublime suggests an upward movement (though not 'beyond' the concrete), with Cixous we have to descend through the materiality of language (whether as writer or reader) towards what she terms 'the truth' (*Three Steps on the Ladder of Writing*, pp. 5–6). In statements that recall the concerns of Levinas, this 'truth' (Cixous is conscious of its logocentric overtones) is the unveiling of the face of 'God', 'the staggering vision of the construction we are' (*ibid.*, p. 63). This descent is partly related to Cixous' feminism. By writing, women are to return to their bodies – bodies which have been confiscated from them and turned into the uncanny and the strange ('The Laugh of the Medusa', p. 251). The liberation that will follow, the truth that will emerge, issues from being able to release the immense resources of the unconscious. To this extent, the experience of self-transcendence through the materiality of writing, for Cixous, is the transcendence by women of a self, an identity, which has been culturally constructed for them by men. The other is therefore within woman. Cixous seeks the constitution of a new subject, the subject-as-woman who, like the mother, has 'hidden and always ready in woman the source: the locus for the other' (*ibid.*, p. 252). Writing inscribes this new body, and so woman inscribes from within herself the textual drives which break up and exceed the phallocentric and symbolic. Again this is similar to Kristeva's appreciation of the semiotic *chora*. It is similar also to Derrida's notion of the economy of *différance*. It could well be said that woman, as Cixous conceives her, embodies the *différance* which operates within 'the false theatre of phallocentric representationalism' (*ibid.*, p. 254).

The descent to the 'truth' in not simply an interior one. In her lectures, *Three Steps on the Ladder of Writing* (1993), given at the Critical Theory Institute in Irvine, we are uncertain whether the movement on the ladder is up or down. For the other is not just inside ourselves, it is also outside and beyond. Writing, like the body, moves between and confiscates the dualities of inside/outside, up and down. Again, this is a familar Derridean theme. Ultimately, the abyss we creep towards or the mystery we explore through writing/reading, with Cixous, is that which is unthinkable and unknown in the human condition, that which cannot be reduced to consciousness, subjectivity or agency. This mystery, in turn, makes a question of what it is to be human. It is in the shadow of such a question that a theological anthropology lies. It is for this reason – that any limits of what it is to be human, any limits of what is understood by 'body', are simply social constructions – that Cixous' language continually writes with theological resonance. 'We need to lose the world, to lose a world, and to discover that there is more than one world and that the world isn't what we think it is. Without that, we know nothing about the mortality and immortality we carry' (*Three Steps on the Ladder of Writing*, p. 10). Writing/reading allows us to experience 'a little of what we are unable to say' (*ibid.*, p. 53); allows us to 'look straight at God, look him in the eye. This is a metaphor' (*ibid.*, p. 61). Cixous, in clearing away the foundations of human subjectivity, in journeying towards some indefinable edge where humanity ends and the other begins (*ibid.*, p. 71), leaves herself no place from which to make a claim that this is a metaphor. The space for the encounter with and passing of the other is wide open. What is the relation of the other to that which tradition calls God, when the experience of this other so closely parallels the experience of those who have ascribed to this other a divinity? In fact, we could suggest that in these phrases 'look straight at God, look him in the eye', 'God' is not the metaphor but 'looking'. In this way, we return to the centre of the philosophical problem in analyzing mystical experiences. For the status of Cixous' 'looking' (like the status of Kant's 'feeling' and Lyotard's 'presence') is exactly parallel to the question of the 'spiritual senses' as they are employed by writers of the mystical tradition. St John the Divine wants to speak of experiencing the 'touch' of God; John of Ruysbroeck wants to speak of 'tasting' the sweetness of God; Angela of Foligno wants to speak of 'seeing' God with the eyes of the soul; Teresa of Avila wants to speak of the soul 'smelling' the sweet perfumes of the divine; Julian of Norwich frequently 'hears' God speaking to her.[48] What Cixous' (and Lyotard's) project affirms is an ineluctable concern with transcendence generic to the human condition. The concern manifests itself because the compulsion to transcendence is of the nature of desire itself. Desire requires the other, outside or inside. For Cixous, writing embodies (materially) this desire and therefore the journey towards the unutterable other. In writing and reading we experience this transcendence which is, fundamentally, a deconstruction of subjectivity; in writing and reading we live the economy of *différance*.

With Cixous, then, we appear to rehearse many of the major themes which have preoccupied this study – the questions of representation, ethics, aesthetics. These are questions which have theological implications and applications that many of these critical theorists are conscious of. This is not because Cixous' work is more comprehensive than, say, Derrida's or Kristeva's. This arises, as we said in the Introduction to this book, because several of these writers have a similar cultural perspective. We might have used Foucault's work in the chapter on representation, or Levinas' or Lyotard's. We might have used Derrida's perennial interest in painting in the chapter on aesthetics, or Kristeva's. We might have used Fish's concern with community and responsibility for the ethics chapter, or Ricoeur's, or Irigaray's. Each of these writers work within the milieu of postmodernity and their comments on representation, history, ethics and aesthetics inscribe the concerns of society at the end of modernity. Theology, which is also a discourse issuing from a certain cultural specificity, must take account of the cultural sea change at the end of modernity because it has implications for its own thematics. It must also take account of those who are both its products and purveyors.

Michel de Certeau

In an prose poem composed three years before his death, entitled 'White Ecstasy', Michel de Certeau pictured two men meeting in the mountains: Simeon the monk and a visitor from the distant land of Panoptie. Simeon speaks of the 'exorbitant goal of the millennial march ... of travellers who have set out to see God' ('White Ecstasy', p.155). The distant land of Panoptie sees everything and nothing; it is a shadowless plain. The visitor seeks to see God. Simeon describes the mystic journeying into 'the final bedazzlement' in which there is

> an absorption of objects and subjects in the act of seeing. No violence, only the unfolding of presence. Neither fold nor hole. Nothing hidden and thus nothing visible. A light without limits, without difference; neuter, in a sense, and continuous. (*Ibid.*, p. 157)

In the account the visitor recognizes the experience of 'this silent ecstasy' as the experience of living in Panoptie: 'I have known this in my country ... The experience you speak of is commonplace there' (*ibid.*, p. 158). He returns home. Luce Giard, the editor of a collection of Certeau's essays on theology, comments that when she first read the piece she believed it announced the immanent arrival of the angel of death. If so it is an angel which haunts Certeau's work from his first investigations into the mysticism of the seventeenth century Jesuit, Jean-Joseph Surin, published in the early 1960s, to his analysis of seventeenth-century religious wanderings of Jean de Labadie who 'passes through, one by one: Jesuit, Jansenist, Calvinist, Pietist, Chiliast or Millenarian' (*The Mystic Fable*, p. 271), published in 1982 in his last book *The Mystic Fable*. With Certeau, as with Cixous, the pre-occupation with the experience of the sublime takes on a distinctive theological colouring.[49]

Certeau was himself a Jesuit. Born in Chambéry in 1925 of an old Savoyard family, he studied classics and philosophy in Grenoble, Lyons and Paris. Having grown up through, and never forgotten, the Vichy years, he entered the Society of Jesus in 1950 and was ordained priest in Lyons six years later. He began work on the origins of Jesuit order, taking a doctorate in religious studies at the Sorbonne in 1960, but his interests considerably broadened. He became one of the found-ing members of Lacan's *Ecole freudienne* in 1964, for example, and following the riots of 1968 became known for his penetrating analyses of contemporary culture. Viewing himself increasingly as a 'traveller', both intellectually and physically, his work now began to cross through and over the frontiers of many disciplines: history, theology, social theory, ethnography, politics, philosophy and psychoanalysis. We might well have introduced his work in earlier sections on theology and representation or theology and history, for he has been concerned to show how history is written and how theology is inextricably bound up with systems of representation. But it is with respect to his concern with writing as wandering, as desire always exceeding itself, as 'seduced by an impregnable origin or end called God' (*The Mystic Fable*, p. 299), that his work is significant in this chapter. Mimesis – what Certeau called 'fables' or 'scriptural economies' or '*poiesis*' – always bears the trace of something which escapes it, the voice of an other and an elsewhere. It is a movement of perpetual departure towards that horizon of white ecstasy, the sublime. With Certeau we return to the concerns of Chapter 1 of this book on theology and representation, to Derrida's supplementation now figured as an Abrahamic journeying into exile. It is an exile which, as Certeau wrote in the final lines of *The Mystic Fable*, becomes 'voiceless, more solitary and lost than before, or less protected and more radical, ever seeking a body or poetic locus. It goes on walking, then, tracing itself out in silence, in writing' (*ibid.*, p. 299).

In this openness and literary walking three elements of Certeau's thinking become important loci for our present theological concerns: his examination of believing; his work on the voice or speech act, particularly the ecstatic cry; and his thinking about the body.

Believing

The cultural climate of 1968 became a personal and academic landmark for Certeau, revealing networks of subversive action which constantly destabilize and draw attention to the dominant ideologies of any society. In a small collection of essay entitled *La prise de parole* (translated as *The Capture of Speech*), he wrote breathlessly about what he saw as the vital significance of the events in May that year:

> The irruption of speech then created or uncovered irreducible differences that splintered the continuous network of sentences and ideas. Writing seems to respond to the will to fill or surmount these gaps. (*The Capture of Speech*, p. 42)

That France recovered its political equilibrium, that it was able again to arrest (another connotation of *prise*) and police the irruption of protesting speech, did not, for Certeau, weaken the force of what had taken place. In fact, the capture again of speech, the disciplining of anarchic utterance and the reweaving of revolutionary talk back into the dominant cultural and political matrix, only served to emphasize the power of 'the continuous network of sentences and ideas' which masks the plurality of operations or 'irreducible differences'.

In a way, given his Lacanian background, what the May 1968 rioting manifested was a certain pathology and a certain trauma. In Lacanian terms, through the networks of the symbolic the anarchic Real announced its irrepressible nonconformity. The riots were a symptom that required analysis. The flood of books following the event bore witness to the need to understand what had occurred, the need to write to fill the gap in authority, legitimation and the cultural order. In the light of analysis a new cultural order might appear. Certeau's journeying towards a utopic site now began.

He started to ask what makes us believe in the stability of the symbolic order or what makes any belief credible? In doing this he began to develop what he termed 'an anthropology of credibility' (*Culture in the Plural*, p. viii). That is, that it is impossible for we human beings to live without believing; to believe is an anthropological *a priori*. We believe because we desire and we desire because we lack the fulfilment, the *jouissance*, for which we are forever searching. What follows is an investigation, philosophical, psychological, sociological and semiotic, into what we believe in and how that belief is produced; the production, maintenance and mutation of beliefs.

For the events of May 1968 announced a specific disbelief in the social frames of reference that structured French society at that time. In a series of essays analyzing cultural plurality in the early 1970s, Certeau explored this question in relation to the new secular space which had opened up following the collapse of two major belief systems: the religious and the political, Christianity and Marxism. What each of these belief systems had effected was a solidarity, a network of values that were shared. A form of participation and social cohesion was possible. This collapsed because people were unable to believe in these systems any more. Certeau asks why this could come about. His verdict is that with the breakdown of ecclesial power, Christianity became privatized and this withdrew Christianity from politics leaving a vacuum that the political as such filled:

> Christianity had opened a gap in the interconnection of the visible
> objects of belief (the political authorities) and its invisible objects

(the gods, spirits, etc.) ... Christianity finally compromised the believability of the religiousness that it detached from the political. (*The Practice of Everyday Life*, pp. 181–2)

he writes. Political organizations became pseudo-ecclesias, often being invested with liturgies lifted from the religiousness they parodied. But then the social atomism that individualism and privatization of beliefs fostered brings about the collapse of political authority also. What we have today is what he calls a 'recited society':

> Our society has become a recited society, in three senses; it is defined by *stories* (*récits*, the fables constituted by our advertising and informational media), by *citations* of stories, and by the interminable *recitation* of stories. (*Ibid.*, p. 186)

In a recited society people believe what they see and what they see is produced for them, hence simulacra-created belief. '[T]he spectator-observer *knows* that they are merely "semblances" ... *but all the same* he assumes that these simulations are real' (*ibid.*, pp. 187–8). This 'objectless credibility' is based upon citing the authority of others. Thus the production of simulacrum involves making people believe that others believe in it, but without providing any believable object. In a recited society there is a 'multiplication of pseudo-believers' (*On Signs*, p. 202) promoted by a culture of deferral and credit; a culture which has affinities with Derrida's analysis of the economics of *différance* in *Given Time*.[50]

In his account of our contemporary believing, Certeau emphasizes an aesthetics of absence. We are brought to believe in that which in itself is a representation of an object, not the object of belief itself. We defer the truth about the object to other experts whom we have never met nor can substantiate. These hidden experts in whom we put our trust enable us to accept as credible that which *we are told* is true. The space we as believers inhabit then is a space of 'consumable fictions' (*Culture in the Plural*, p. 25). Caught up in the endless traffic and exchange of signs – from billboards, through television, in newspapers, on film – we construct from this seductive public rhetoric versions of 'reality' to which we give allegiance or in which we place our faith. These productions and exchanges organize what we take as our social reality. But since the flow of signs is constantly changing in the practices which make up everyday living, since ideas are constantly being modified, disseminated, re-experienced, re-expressed and transplanted, what is believable changes also. What is constant is the gap between

> what authorities *articulate* and what is *understood* by them, between the communication they allow and the legitimacy they presuppose, between what they make possible and what makes them credible. (*Ibid.*, p. 15)

It is this gap, negotiated and veiled by writing that facilitates an aesthetics of absence.

In both an early article published in French in 1971, entitled 'How is Christianity Thinkable Today?' and later, in his 1982 book *The Mystic Fable*, Certeau maps this aesthetics of absence upon Christian believing. For what is absent is the body of Jesus Christ. And yet it is that very absence which makes possible the Scriptures, the Church and the organization of a space for Christian practices of faith. As Certeau puts it:

> The Christian language begins with the disappearance of the 'author'. That is to say that Jesus *effaces himself* to give faithful witness to the Father who authorizes him, and to 'give rise' to different but faithful communities, which he makes possible. There is a close bond between the absence of Jesus (dead and not present) and the birth of the Christian language (objective and faithful testimony of his survival). ('How is Christianity Thinkable Today?', p. 145)

We will return to this understanding of Christianity and its implications later. For the moment it is the paradigm of the relationship between acts of writing and speaking (the Scriptures, testimonies, confessions of faith etc.) and the lost, irrecoverable, in fact, effaced body which has permitted there to be a believing, that is significant. For in the aesthetics of absence, where 'the empty tomb is the condition for a spiritual knowledge' (*ibid.*, p. 145), representation is both an act of mourning and an attempt to create a body, a textual body to replace an always already erased embodiment. There is, then, both a looking back and a moving forward. In this activity, this writing, new spaces are opened; and in this endless opening up, breaking up what is past, lies the spirituality of Certeau's aesthetics: 'He or she is a mystic who cannot stop walking and, with the certainty of what is lacking, knows every place and object that it is *not that*' (*The Mystic Fable*, p. 299).

The ecstatic voice

Walking and writing are correlational, for Certeau; they are both practices of everyday life, embodied expressions of a certain agency. Certeau, whose concerns with enthnography focus upon the politics of how other races are represented by the colonizer, is also concerned with the way the colonized, as other, escapes or fails to coincide with that representation. The other is always excessive to the way it is represented. So in his essay on the sixteenth-century writer Jean de Léry, who left an account of his voyage to Brazil and his encounter with the Tupi indians in *The Writing of History*, he examines what is effaced in the account. This encounter, for Léry, is the discovery of a new world in which there is celebration and festival, dancing and elaborate ornamentation, pleasure and social cohesion. But Certeau concentrates on the way the speech of the Tupis is lost in the account of the encounter, and how the figure of the other (in the representation of the Tupis) offers Léry a glimpse of the primitive as paradisial. By means of this glimpse of the primitive, Léry is able to understand and identify with his own civilized perspective. The other as other escapes Léry. It is this speech of the other, which, in its excess, offers a transcendent horizon which leaves its traces in writing. '[T]he *voice* can create an *aparte*, opening a breach in the text and restoring a contact of body to body' (*The Writing of History*, p. 235). It restores a contact because its communication of an insurmountable alterity invokes the subject's (in this case, Jean de Léry's) desire. The writing embodies this desire – the desire to possess the naked forms which so attract Léry.

The voice offers a different spacing, for Certeau, that forever incites the writing; just as, in Christian theology (particularly that marked by the Jesuit charism) vocation leads to mission, and to a spiritual walking. The ecclesia as those who are called out following the divine speech act in Christ. But the voice *as such* – suggestive of some utopic site – is irrecoverable. The aesthetics of absence then are, nevertheless, resonant with a certain transcendental excess.

Certeau's construal of the voice of the other receives its most detailed examination in two major works: *La Possession de Loudon*, published in 1970, which analyses the diabolic voice of a group of possessed Ursuline nuns in France, and *The Mystic Fable*, which analyzes the development of a science he terms 'mystics'. Both books are historical explorations of the seventeenth century, at the dawn of modernity when the technologies of secularism were organizing the world in order to facilitate maximal exploitation. This is significant, for in early modernity printing and publishing made increasingly available the written, galvanizing what Certeau terms the 'scriptural economy'. The world no longer can be perceived as *spoken* by God, 'it has become opacified, objectified, and detached from its supposed speaker' (*The Mystic Fable*, p. 188). Before modernity, Certeau suggests, there was another way of seeing the world, a sacramental way, whereby creation was interpreted as correlational to the eucharist as the *corpus mysticium*. With modernity, with the onset of the scriptural economy, the scientific world-view arises, which Certeau associates with the colonization of knowledge and the spread of capitalist production. The ecstatic cries – of the demonically possessed or the mystically inspired – manifest themselves as one world order gives way to a second. In *La Possession de Loudon*, the voice expresses the social inquietude following the religious wars, plague and the emergence of the modern State. In *The Mystic Fable* the new orderings of space in terms of cities, the map drawing of states, Republics and continents, parallels 'the task of founding places in which to hear the spoken Word that had become inaudible within corrupt institutions' (*ibid.*, p. 154). The voice of the possessed Ursuline sisters 'witnesses to a hole' (*La Possession de Loudon*, p. 8) that no writing, no one discourse, can broach. The voice of the mystic expounds 'the Silence of the ineffable One' (*The Mystic Fable*, p. 150). In both, a speech act, substitutes for a trancendent Name which cannot be named.

In *La Possession de Loudon*, Certeau carefully draws out the complex network within which the town of Loudon, the Ursuline convent, the Church (Catholic and Protestant) and its relations to the King, the practitioners of medicine, discourses on sorcery and its affective treatment, seventeenth-century spirituality and the emergence of modernity are all enmeshed. Like a cartographer, he plots the various institutional positions in terms of the town's own geography, spatializing what we have learnt Foucault call the 'grids of intelligibility'. Several sets of authoritative discourses seek to interpret and thereby constrain the diabolical events. Foucault's archaeological strategies have been influential here, for Certeau too is concerned with the movement of power. Where he differs from Foucault's attention to the architecture of control and the practices of discursive power is in his exposure of the way the diabolic speech act, the event and cry of the possessed, evades all attempts to structure and discipline it. Again, like the events of May 1968, what is revealed here is deviance and tactical subversion. His attention is not, as with Foucault, on the production and employment of a anonymous power, but on the wily resourcefulness of the peasant, the worker, the nuns in this case. In his historiography, then, he is not attempting to explain what happened at Loudon among those Ursuline sisters, which led to the execution of the so-called sorcerer, Urbain Grandier, by the very hands of those sisters, but he is attempting to point to the cry beneath the writing of history, the rupturing event itself. Here he points to the birth of a new language, a language which subverts all the other discourses attempting to explain and manipulate what is going on. In this respect 'the mystical and the possession often are drawn from the same areas of society in which language grows dense, losing its spiritual porosity itself and becoming impermeable to the divine' (*La Possession de Loudon*, p. 13). It is ultimately the divine that is being appealed to, a universal, pure and translucent speaking. The possessed one's speech act is like the mystic's speech act or the language of negative theology: it testifies to a performance, a tactic in which the dominating discourse is undermined, confused, or played against itself so that another voice can be heard. On one level, it is the voice of 'social inquietude', on another it is the voice of the erased Other, the inaudible voice of God. 'It is one of the definitions of possession that one is in this moment unstable and one symbolizes that in a language which furnishes an expression for it which is simultaneously archaic and innovative' (*ibid.*, p. 43). Similarly, mystic discourses 'effect displacements, they attract words and change them' (*The Mystic Fable*, p. 119). In fact, the very adjective 'mystic' when used before a substantive makes the thing signified disappear in favour of the signifier.

For this reason Certeau's attention to the voice, and therefore the agency of speakers, does not fall victim to Derrida's charges against logocentrism and phonocentrism (outlined in Chapter 1). For the voice is never fully present; speech never has the immediacy and directness of being self-transparent. The voice only speaks in and through and beyond a certain practice, a certain tactics, a certain writing (if the writing is only with one's body as gesture), a certain style of living. It is heard in the abrasions and the excesses of such writing, where desire is at its densest.

The body of God

What is distinctive about Certeau's work as a critical theorist is the way in which theology is explicit. That is a good reason for finishing this book with an account of his work. With our other critical theorists the theological, the religious, the transcendental is referred to and explored sometimes. But Michel de Certeau lived and died a Jesuit. As Luce Giard writes in the opening line of her collection of Certeau's theological writings, *La faiblesse de croire*, 'The question of God, faith and Christianity never ceased to preoccupy Michel de Certeau' (*La faiblesse de croire*, p. 1). As we saw earlier, it is the loss of the body of Christ which inaugurates the Church:

> The founder disappears; he is impossible to grasp and 'hold', to the extent that he is incorporated and takes on meaning in a plurality of 'Christian' experiences, operations, discoveries, and inventions. ('How is Christianity Thinkable Today?', pp. 145–6)

The effects of that rupturing event are disseminated in a thousand different directions and through a multiplicity of practices. No one can control either the direction or the nature of the 'incorporation'. That is why the word 'Christian' is placed between inverted commas; because it may not conform to 'the pronouncements of an individual (the pope) or [be limited] to an institutional body ... or to a body of doctrine' (*ibid.*, p. 149). The origin fast disappears into the past, the future is a continual risk-taking so that increasing sectarianism and heterodoxy are signs of continual life, for Certeau. In fact, Christian faith cannot exist without that which is other and not itself, that which continually reminds Christianity of what it does not have or what it lacks. This is what is essential for Christianity; for the death of Jesus opens up a distensive space for others. As this space grows exponentially, this expansive heterospatiality consuming secular and technological spaces from within, so Christianity itself, every Christian and every community 'is called on to be the *sign of that which is lacking*' (*ibid.*, p. 150).

Certeau affirms that in this essential covenant of Christianity with the unforeseeable or unknown spaces 'God opens'. Therefore, Certeau's theology refuses to speak about the death of God but rather 'the death of our [Christianity's] ideological reassurance of our missionary totalism' (*ibid.*). In and through a continual spiritual displacement and dissemination of the instaurational act, all things, occupying all space, take up their position within the one final, living body of God. It is the realization of this eschatological threshold as it adheres to each practice and speech act, each new walking and writing that gives textualities their theological watermark. And in this way the aesthetics of absence announce and foster a heterological plenitude. Early in *The Mystic Fable* Certeau examines Hieronymous Bosch's *The*

Garden of Delights, a space to get lost in, he says. It is a heterodox and scandalous paradise in which Certeau describes a calligraphy of bodies which write without speaking, refusing to be made symbolic of something, or turned into words meaning something. Rather the intermingling of the various bodies are 'silent graphemes', 'straight, slanted, reversible, and changeable, written without one knowing what one is writing. Lost to themselves, they describe instead a musicality of forms – glossography and calligraphy' (*The Mystic Fable*, p. 70). This is Certeau's 'Christainity', where the aesthetics of absence open a space of delight into which one can lose oneself.

Certeau's notion of body, in which the physiologies of individual bodies are already implicated in social, political, ecclesial and, with Christ, theological bodies, is similar to Jean-Luc Nancy's. Nancy, it will be recalled, employs the language of the eucharistic body endlessly fractured and sent out into the world. In *The Mystic Fable*, Certeau locates a change in the understanding of the eucharist at the origins of modernity's obsession with visibility. By the late thirteenth century *corpus mysticum* no longer referred to the body of Christ, but the body of Christ *as the visible Church* (*ibid.*, pp. 79–90). For Certeau, who had personal as well as confraternal relations with Henri de Lubac (who alongside Hans Urs von Balthasar and Teilhard de Chardin ranked as the leading postwar Jesuit theologian) and knew de Lubac's book *Corpus Mysticum*, a certain romanticism still adhered (as it did for de Lubac) to the early mediaeval eucharistic communities. Social atomism, the indeterminacy which was a cultural equivalent of Brownian motion, rapidly developed from the late thirteenth-century on. Theological construals of participation, focused upon the eucharist, collapsed.

Certeau's work suggests a new, post-1968 participation, a new poetics of the corporate body. It is a body without substance, which cannot be grasped because it cannot be made into an object for possession. It is animated and perpetually exceeds its location here or there by desire, the desire of all things for a primordial unity. In the restlessness of this desiring, Certeau imitates Augustine's understanding of God as what is truly desired, or Aquinas' understanding of God as the efficient, final, formal and material cause of all true loving. Certeau's emphasis upon the lack of closure avoids the possibly of monism. Certeau's construal of the body is not like Spinoza's. For Spinoza there is only one body and one substance, God's, and all else is a modification of that oneness. Certeau's body is endlessly pluralized and pluralizing; it diffuses rather than totalizes. But it is at this very point of its diffusion that significant theological and philosophical questions arise; and they arise in the same way they arise with respect to Nancy's work.

Certeau does not develop the theology of participation evident in Augustine or Aquinas. The danger here is a spiritualizing of homelessness, of destitution and exile. He alludes constantly to God but fails to develop the theology implicit in his work, as if either the work on practices of everyday life stands irrespective of the theology or the theology for such an understanding of the textualities of time, speech and action have already been developed elsewhere (in the work of the other Jesuits, de Lubac or Balthasar?) Does Certeau require the supplement of the work of his fellow Jesuit, Balthasar, to complete his project – Balthasar who writes in ether, in a stratospheric sphere that frequently seems too detached from everyday life? The philosophical (and political) danger of not having this supplement is that Certeau's heterology remains merely reactionary. Of course, as he tells us, it challenges the dominant ideologies and power configurations. But since these 'disciplines provide social life with an operative apparatus and an interpretation' (*Culture in the Plural*, p. 83), then they are necessary for there to be any cultural life at all. Tactical resistances, then, signify little more than a micro-politics all too easily absorbed by the dominant and necessary matrices of the status quo. Only as tactics of subversion in an alternative, divine ordering of creation, can tactics *per se* not simply react against the established order but promote a new and foreseeable order; an order in which belief has true content and is not simply believing in the need to believe.

Theological implications

With the interest of contemporary critical theories in aesthetic experience, our study returns to Chapter 1 on theology and representation. After Kant, philosophy has turned its attention to the relationship of experience to consciousness. Since Heidegger (and Wittgenstein) attention has been focused on perception's relationship with its representation. With the work of Fish, Lyotard, Cixous and Certeau, the aesthetics of experience and the aesthetic experience itself are involved in endless negotiation. There is no knowledge that is not caught up with its rhetoric, its mode of presentation, its aesthetics. Truth, for these people, as for Nietzsche, may be inseparable from the march of metaphors, but the death of God or the demise of theology is not necessarily the corollary of this claim. In fact, rather to the contrary, Fish, Lyotard, Cixous and Certeau, without developing their thinking theologically, depend heavily upon religious metaphors and models for the elucidation of their ideas. This arises because none of these thinkers are simply trying to create new aesthetic theories – theories concerning the form of the beautiful. Rather each is attempting to show how artistic representation problematizes and resists theorization, opening new and indeterminate spaces. Artistic representation propels us beyond strategies which would constitute boundaries for its value and meaning. 'The meaning of an utterance, I repeat, is its experience', Fish announces (*Is There A Text in This Class?*, p. 65). '[T]he speech act is at the same time a use *of* language and an operation performed *on* it', Certeau will claim (*The Practice of Everyday Life*, p. 33). Representation presences, performs something excessive to denotation, operates. It is this analysis of the experienced resistance in art, art as a question, which has these thinkers searching for analogues and metaphors with theological resonance.

We have already indicated how Certeau's project cries out for a more developed theological reading and how economies of salvation found in Augustine and Aquinas offer such a development. The same might be said of the work of Stanley Fish. In his early work on Milton, Stanley Fish was explicitly examining the relationship between the aesthetic experience of reading *Paradise Lost* and the theological notion of sin as it affects our understanding and ability to read a situation. He has been evidently influenced by Augustine's notion of the *regula fidei*, as it is propounded in *De doctrina christiana* (see *Is There A Text in This Class?*, p. 328) in his own notion of all reading being bound by previously learned conventions. Augustine advocates that interpretation of any single passage of scripture is bound by the general hermeneutic of God's love for us and the context of the rest of the scriptures. Fish develops his ideas in terms of the reading community, in a way which parallels Augustine's understanding of the Church as an interpretative community, reading by and through faith. The work, more recently, on narrative identity and ecclesiology by Stanley Hauerwas, John Milbank and Gerard Loughlin,[51] and the work on vocation and performance theory, relates to Fish's ideas. Fish himself made the distinction between plots operating according to the logic of narrative, where causality produces sequence according to 'the logic of human freedom and choice' and the Christian plot which is 'haphazard, random in its order, heedless of visible cause' (*ibid.*, p. 195). With the Christian plot, a person

reaches a point not because he chooses, but because he has been chosen, that is, redeemed. The price we pay for this redemption is the illusion of self-sufficiency and independence, the illusion of moving toward a truth rather than moving by virtue of it. (*Ibid.*, p. 195)

Waiting in the wings of this perception are more developed notions of narrative, personhood and the doctrine of the Trinity. For it is the Trinity which, for Augustine, relates artistic signs and their interpretation to the Church and the economy of its redemption. Analyses of faith, time and pneumatology in the light of Fish's work on the reading–experience are yet to be undertaken.

With Lyotard's and Cixous' examination of the 'present' or the 'event' we are brought again to the theology of the gift and the economy of mediated immediacy. The moment itself, for Lyotard, is without content. It is an encounter with nothingness (see *Peregrinations*, p. 17) consequent upon a certain personal ascesis: 'No event is at all accessible if the self does not renounce the glamour of its culture, its wealth, health, knowledge, and memory' (*ibid.*, p. 18). Karl Barth consistently emphasized that revelation was a mediated immediacy in which the hidden face of God was revealed. In his *Göttingen Dogmatics*, he wrote: 'We can seriously raise and treat the problem of the possibility of revelation only when we know its reality. Fundamentally, we can only construct it *a posteriori*.'[52] He directly relates this mediated immediacy to the Christ himself as both *logos ensarkos* and *logos asarkos*, 'indirect communication means God's incarnation'.[53] Karl Barth also examined the way in which such an incarnation judges all our representations. In his early work he expressed this in terms of Jesus Christ as the question mark which places all our knowledge and knowing into crisis. Lyotard, likewise, is concerned with a certain crisis of representation, an iconoclasm in which the figured is caught up within a contradiction so that it continually effaces itself. Hence all artistic signs are expressive of differends. 'What is at stake in a literature, in a philosophy, in a politics perhaps, is to bear witness to differends by finding idioms for them' (*The Differend*, p. 13). Might not Lyotard's examination of the sublime and the differend be developed theologically, so that incarnation and theological discourse itself are understood as expressive of differends? Religious experience, paralleling Lyotard's analysis of aesthetic experience, would then issue from an encounter with God as differend. The encounter would be Lyotard's 'event'. Once more, this would have Trinitarian implications. In *Peregrinations*, Lyotard's most autobiographical of texts, his early desire to be a (Dominican) monk plays an important part in drawing attention to the ethics and theology of his thought – the self-renunciation and the obedience to a law that can never be grasped. 'The desire to explore is the duty we are committed to by the law ... In that effort we are guided only by our feelings' (*Peregrinations*, p. 12).

With Cixous we have a developed understanding of incarnation – an anthropology which returns to language about the soul and the other to the Enlightenment subject. The incarnate self is compelled towards a transcendence, by its own unfathomable depths and by its need in love to surrender itself to the other. It is not simply an ethics which issues from this new model of personhood. Rather there emerges a spirituality of the body in which 'body' is no longer merely material, a collection of the carbon molecules. Exceeding the subjects of biological science, the meaning of corporeality is expanded, the flesh is dignified in a way that demands that we rethink Christology beyond dualism. In rethinking Christology, we have to rethink ourselves as sexual souls whose sexuality is no longer identified with our biological selves. That, in turn, demands a rethinking of what it means to be redeemed.

With all four thinkers (Fish, Lyotard, Cixous and Certeau), the body (the text as tissue) is prior to and constitutive of knowledge yet only available to us through representations of it. The indivisible relationship of experience and expression requires that all knowledge is bound to aesthetics. Religious knowing, religious experience as such cannot, therefore, be distinguished from aesthetic experience. The form for the mediation of the immediate may seem more or less specifically religious (the Bible rather than a novel or a sonata), and the form may govern our interpretation of the experience (the reader's experience of sin in *Paradise Lost*, of desire in *The Remembrance of Things Past*), but the experience as it emerges in and through the expression is of the unpresentable, is of an *aporia*. The invisible stretches along all the edges of the visible. Theology names this infinite giveness 'grace', the grace of God, and its unveiling 'revelation'. Theology then seeks to understand the economy of this primary donation in terms of the scriptures and tradition.

Lyotard draws three personae into conversation – the monk, the painter and the historian. Each represents talk on ethics (and theology), aesthetics and politics. They are the three figures which dominate his thinking. He writes: 'All three entities are active, unavoidable, in the three fields with the same force, even if not present in the same way' (*Peregrinations*, p. 5).

Conclusion:
Theology and the Re-enchantment of the World

As we have already noted, it is the sociologist Zygmunt Bauman who describes postmodernity in terms of 're-enchantment'. 'Postmodernity, one may as well say, brings "re-enchantment" of the world after the protracted and earnest, though in the end inconclusive, modern struggle to dis-enchant it.'[1] It was the sociologist Max Weber who declared the world conjured by technology was a dis-enchanted world. Many people are now familiar with this story in which science, the spirit of *techne*, empiricism, positivism and materialism all offered to explain the world and as a consequence expunged its mystery.

Lyotard, quite rightly, has always insisted that postmodernism is not a period concept. Postmodernity can be a term for sociologists and historians, descriptive of a culture in which certain kinds of emphases are dominant. But postmodernism, for Lyotard, is an aspect of modernism itself. His own examination of Kant's respect for ambiguity and *aporia* is an example, for him, of postmodernism at work in the Enlightenment project. It is a postmodernism that the Enlightenment wished to erase. Other philosophers, like Jean-Luc Marion, have re-explored Descartes with similar results.[2] Descartes is not simply the creator of the autonomous ego; the cogito is not simply the central focus for understanding the world. Cartesian epistemology operates within an 'ambivalent ontology [*ontologie grise*]'; the cogito moves within a 'blank theology [*théologie blanche*]'. Sometimes it appears that the mind in which the cogito can assert itself exists within the mind of God. There are other philosophical figures also who do not 'fit the account': Hamann, Jacobi and Kierkegaard, most notably. In the work of Marx, Nietzsche and Freud the self-determining consciousness, the rational subject, is already being displaced. Even modernity possessed moments when ambiguity was delighted in. In fact, this has recently led one philosopher and historian of science to ask, and this is the title of his book, *We Have Never Been Modern At All*[3] We will come back to this question.

It is the re-evaluation of ambivalence, mystery, excess and *aporia* as they adhere to, are constituted by and disrupt the rational, that lies behind the re-enchantment of the contemporary world. A culture is appearing in the West and North America suddenly full of angels, vampires, cyborgs and aliens. Observe the final scenes of the box-office sensation of the century, *Titanic*. Resurrection is high on Hollywood agendas. Reality is no longer tabulated and evaluated in terms of empirical fact. Existence is not simply chemical combinations on the basis of the periodic table. The world is now multiple worlds; and worlds are created by, and shift within, nets of signs and symbols pointing beyond themselves towards other nets of signs and symbols. Worlds can be composed of electronic data transmitted from one cyberspace to another. All these worlds are constantly in process. They are protean and transitional. Temporality rather than spatiality, economies rather than places, narratives rather than nouns are the vehicles for weaker, softer forms of identity and meaning. This subsequent re-enchantment is fostered and explored by contemporary critical theory. Though the project of the Enlightenment could be read in terms of an ongoing attempt to erase metaphysics, culminating in the work of the Vienna School and some contemporary philosophies of mind by Parfit and McDowell[4] – metaphysical assumptions simply masquerade behind empiricism, historicism, discourses of truth, explanation and validation. Critical theory not only unveils these forgotten metaphysics (in the name of logocentrism, phallocentrism or grand-narratives); it reinstates them. However, it is no longer metaphysics as that study of 'higher' things, that speculation on things higher than, which create the possibility for, the phenomenal. Critical theory is, quite simply, rewriting what we have come to call, in modernity, the Natural. Space, time and materiality become destabilized, open to other interpretations, installing an ineradicable law of quest-as-questioning that thwarts attempts at terriorialization.

But more than this is at stake. For in this rewriting what becomes of modernity itself; modernity as a sociological and historical concept? What does the current re-enchantment of the world say about the world in which all things were frozen and dominated by death, if we are to accept some contemporary readings of 'modernity'?[5] Furthermore, if modernity, like C.S. Lewis' Narnia, was the land where it was always winter and never Christmas, a land in which the theological voice was silent and silenced, what of that land now? What of that theological voice now? One recent critical theorist, from Slovenia, who comes out of a deep schooling in Lacanian teaching and whose cultural analyses are attracting much attention, may offer us one way of answering these questions, and one way also of reading the phenomenon of contemporary critical theory *tout court*.

Slavoj Žižek: a coda

In an interview given to a journalist writing about him for *The Times Higher Educational Supplement*, Žižek quite emphatically announces both an atheism and a profound antipathy towards the Catholic Church.[6] For a Lacanian philosopher who would submit various cultural phenomena from the films of Hitchcock to the writings of Schelling to a radical form of ideology critique, this profession of his religious views is interesting and significant. For, as we will observe, his work is continually drawing towards aspects of the Christian religion and Christian theology, the reality of which he – like Freud and Lacan before him – believes is illusory. What then is the future of this illusion for Žižek? What are the consequences of his confessed atheism given his preoccupation with theological fantasies of, dominantly, a Christian nature? What are the consequences, that is, not only for Žižek, but for his analyses of contemporary culture and the mapping of its ineradicable ideologies? To begin to answer these questions we shall look mainly at Žižek's 1997 book *The Plague of Fantasies*, because it is with reference to what he terms 'Fantasy's transcendental schematism' that the theological becomes clearly voiced.[7]

The Plague of Fantasies is an eclectic book, even for Žižek. He traverses myriad sites of contemporary commodity fetishism – from the work of Mother Teresa, to Spielberg's *Star Wars* trilogy, from the *X-Files* to cyberspace and the songs of Robert Schumann. In what has become a trade-mark of his method, he weaves a scintillating narrative in which all these sites are interpreted through a Lacanian reading of Hegel and Marx and, in doing this, he produces a politico–psychoanalytical analysis of present ideologies. It is the production of these narratives that are of interest to theologians, just as it is the production of the commodity fetishes which interest Žižek. As he states, 'fantasy is the primordial form of narrative' (*The Plague of Fantasies*, p. 10), for the narrative itself emerges to resolve (and therefore mask) a more fundamental antagonism. Lacan is, therefore, 'radically anti-narrativist' for the *réel* remains forever excessive and anarchic to the symbolic order.

What then of Žižek's narratives? Are they not, with their constant appeal to popular culture marketing a new, North America-friendly, Eastern European (even Balkan) intellectualism? What fundamental antagonism produces Žižek's commodity narratives and is masked by them? To come at this in a slightly different way, though Žižek considers Lacan and Hegel to both escape Lyotard's proclaimed demise of the grand narrative – because they affirm 'the irreducible plurality of particular struggles' – is there not a narrative, a fantasy, operating beneath the work of both Lacan and Hegel that Žižek himself is continually having to wrestle with? The fantasy, it appears, is that found in the Christian narrative of the Fall, the coming of the Christ, and the move towards a redemption in which we return again to polymorphous pleasures of paradise.

If we turn to the text itself – that tissue of condensed and displaced symbols, drives and desires – the Christian metastory frames the hyperventilating movement from one cultural scene to another. The writing itself is a form of panic attack in which constant appeal is made to an impossible soteriology. For narrativization occludes a primary loss – the paradox of the Lacanian *objet petit à* – a loss conceived in terms of 'the problematic of the Fall' (*The Plague of Fantasies*, p. 13). Žižek, significantly, states: 'it is possible to elaborate a precise theory of the Fall via a reference to Milton's *Paradise Lost*' (*ibid.*, p. 15). And yet no quotation or further reference to Milton's epic is made. In fact, Žižek turns to an interpretation of the Genesis story (with quotations from Henry Staten's book *Eros in Mourning*)[8] and accounts of sex in Paradise by theologians (Aquinas is named). This is significant, because it is symptomatic of a certain denial, concealed by an appeal to a poem which never appears and a philosophical vocabulary ('theory' of the Fall) which in fact articulates or ventriloquizes a theology of the Fall. What kind of denial is this? What kind of wrestling does this denial express? The Christian mythos grounds Lacanian theory and is seriously investigated: 'in Paradise the impossible coincidence of knowledge and *jouissance* persists' (*ibid.*, p. 15) because sex in Paradise is both enjoyed and controlled. But one notes again, just as the theological analysis is underway, Žižek veers towards an argument through which he can make his startling and attention-seeking point that pre-lapsarian sex is perverse and 'fist-fucking is Edenic; it is the closest we can get to what sex was like before the Fall' (*ibid.*, p. 16).

The return to Eden is longed for and yet barred; the impossible is both sort and denied. But who is producing this denial? Textually, the shock-tactic sensationalism – found elsewhere in such statements as 'Nazism actually does carry out the "return of the repressed" of Christianity' (*ibid.*, p. 42) – is itself a symptom, the logic of which is escaping Žižek. So that, a certain irony emerges – again the textual manifestation of a struggle – when Žižek goes on to unmask an inherent transgression (his words, again theologically unglossed) evident because of the 'gap between an explicit texture and its phantasic support' (*ibid.*, p. 20). This transgression is examined with relation to the violent homophobia in the old Yugoslav People's Army, in which Žižek concludes that 'the discourse of the military community can operate only by censoring its own libidinal foundation' (*ibid.*, p. 25). The power edifice – manifest textually in assertions of the kind 'fist-fucking is Edenic' – is always split, that is its inherent trangression, its original sin: 'in order to reproduce itself and contain its Other, it has to rely on an inherent excess which grounds it' (*ibid.*, p. 26). Yes, but isn't this exactly what we observe in the production of Žižek's own 'explicit texture'?

Let us examine another example from the same book. Here he discusses the soteriological function of Jesus Christ with respect to an aspect of substitution he terms 'interpassivity'. Following Lacan, the Real cannot be encountered directly, the trauma of experiencing it is displaced by the freeze-framing of the imaginary. Displacement then is both original and constitutive, and it is this mechanism which results in the plague of fantasies (the title of the book) and Žižek's main thesis: that there is no non-ideologically free-zone. We continually trade and traffic in pathologies, hindered from 'any neutral representation of external referential reality' (*ibid.*, p. 214). In the move from the imaginary to the symbolic it is the act of substitution that becomes primordial. That is, signifiers are substituted to stand in for, and negotiate the identity of, the subject. The symbolic substitution mediates between the trauma of the Real and the fixity of the imaginary, for Žižek. Its plasticity enables us to 'adapt ourselves to ever new situations, radically change our self-perception' (*ibid.*, p. 94). It can do this because included in this symbolic universe are empty signifiers which can be filled by a new particular situation. What characterizes human existence, Žižek states, is 'the "irrational" fixation on some symbolic Cause, materialized as a Master-Signifier to whom we stick regardless of the consequences' (*ibid.*). This is the most empty of all signifers and therefore the most flexible in regard to every signified content. God is named by Žižek as such a Master-Signifier, following Lacan's own statement (reversing Dostoyevsky's) 'If there is no God, nothing at all is permitted.' Interpassivity, is the 'believing or enjoying through the other' (*ibid.*, p. 113); the externalization, made possible because of the primordial disposition towards substitution, of my feelings enacted by another.

It is at this point that Žižek introduces Christ. He asks:

> is not the ultimate example of interpassivity that 'absolute example' (Hegel) itself: that of Christ, who took upon himself the (deserved) suffering of humanity? Christ redeemed us all not by acting for us, but by assuming the burden of the ultimate passive experience. (*Ibid.*, p. 112)

The salvation wrought, then, by Christ is not achieved through some substitutional reading of the atonement (*à la Anselm*), but by fully subsuming within himself the human propensity for substituting, the suffering endemic to the sense of loss and mourning that makes passivity and substitution necessary. In this sense, Christ incarnates the mechanism of the symbolic order itself; incarnates the Law of the Father and mediates between the abyss of the real and the fixity of the imaginary. Now certainly, Žižek goes on to suggest ways in which this interpassivity can mollify and glaze the subject, particularly the bourgeois subject, the upper-middle-class academic who remains undisturbed by the political struggles and atrocities around him or her. It can involve an abnegation of involvement, a diremption of responsibility. But in his book *The Sublime Object of Ideology* he points out that this delegation to others does not involve a loss of sincerity (*The Sublime Object of Ideology*, p. 34). And in *The Plague of Fantasies* he will also suggest that 'perhaps the fundamental attitude which defines the subject is neither that of passivity nor that of autonomous activity, but precisely that of interpassivity' (*The Plague of Fantasies*, p. 115). Furthermore, 'Interpassivity is therefore to be conceived as the primordial form of the subject's *defence* against *jouissance*: I defer *joissance* to the Other who passively endures it (laughs, suffers, enjoys …) on my behalf' (*ibid.*). In this way I am radically decentred as a subject. And so, if Christ as the ultimate example of interpassivity He is the incarnation of that which is primordial to human identity, constantly enabling the renegotiation of identity by mediating between the Law of the father and the unspeakable and inaccessible truth of the Real. Christ negotiates, by mediating what Žižek calls 'the stumbling-block on account of which the symbolic system can never "become itself", achieve its self-identity' (*ibid.*, p. 217). And one has to note not just the content (and implications of Žižek's thinking concerning Christ) but its expression. For he moves from a rhetorical question implying the answer 'yes' ('is not the ultimate example of passivity?') which partly ventriloquizes Hegel, to a statement in which he employs the grammar of personal identification, albeit generally ('Christ redeemed *us* not by acting for *us*, but by assuming the burden of the ultimate passive experience'). What then are we to make of Žižek's treatment of the Christian doctrines of Fall and Redemption? In the mapping of imbricated ideologies which we cannot get beneath nor live without, is this not the soteriological metanarrative, as it was for Žižek's philosophical father, Hegel? Ultimately, for Hegel, we recall, the operation of the Trinity, God's prehistory, sustains all things while keeping them from final closure. In an article entitled, enticingly, 'How to Give Body to a Deadlock', Žižek rehearses the constitution of the subject's prehistory, its negotiation with external reality through rejection and the disruptive excess of the Real. He closes his article with these words and a reference to Schelling, 'This is the process that ... appears as the antagonism of God's prehistory, which is resolved when God speaks out his Word' ('How to Give Body to a Deadlock', p. 77). Why does Žižek rehearse the work of Christ (and here the doctrine of the Trinity) as the ultimate paradigm? It can only be because the truth of this paradigm is always excessive to its symbolization; but then the truth of any ideology is excessive to its social semiotics. A certain trauma, a certain irrationalism (symptomatic of trauma) surfaces. And so the Christian story, while designated as the primary fantasy, can be approached only obliquely, can be approached only pathologically through statements freighted with passionate outrage. 'Theologians are the true atheists', Lacan had said and Žižek cites. The structure of Christian belief (which interpassivity makes into an externalized social practice, not an internal conviction and, therefore, a primordial commitment prior to an act of conscious will) is paradoxical: it is both necessary and impossible. Which perhaps explains why Žižek's theological *confrères* are the Jansenists, Pascal and Kierkegaard. In *The Sublime Object of Ideology* his model for the operation of ideology is Pascal's wager which expresses the paradox of belief before belief because the external custom to which one commits oneself is finally understood to have always been the 'material support for the subject's unconscious' (*The Sublime Object of Ideology*, p. 40). 'Far from being limited to Catholicism', he writes, 'such a procedure for obtaining ideological conversion is universally applicable' (*ibid.*, p. 39). Christianity is the ultimate figuration of a primordial trauma, the logic of which haunts and yet eludes Žižek continually. A 'traumatic irrationality' (Žižek's words) or a 'traumatized rationality' (my words) remains.

But maybe we can say something more than this. For Žižek is not the only contemporary critical theorist, exposing the inviolability of ideology, to be haunted by the Christian imaginary. We have seen throughout this book that Kristeva, Irigaray, Certeau, Foucault, Fish, Ricoeur, Nancy, Lacan and Derrida re-employ aspects of the Christian mythos, its discourses on eschatology, ecclesiology, mysticism and sacramentalism, its language of love, to explicate their utopic or impossible or sublime horizons. Might not, then, Žižek's Lacanian interpretation of the cultural *Zeitgeist* of modernity and postmodernity suggest that modernity pathologized Christianity, sublimated its logic to constitute its own Enlightenment stabilities (the identities of the subject, the reifications of objects, the laws and schemas governing relationships between the two)? To adapt a phrase of Žižek's, Christianity is not the fantasy but the *'mise-en-scène* of the fantasy which is at work in the midst of [modernity's] social reality itself' (*The Sublime Object of Ideology*, p. 36). To adapt a second phrase:

> [Modernity's r]eality [its materiality, its metaphysics of presence, its empiricisms and positivisms] is a fantasy-construction which enables us to mask the Real of our desire. (*Ibid.*, p. 45)

And so now, in postmodernity, when attention turns to the construction, the production, the staging of modernity's fantasy (or ideologies) the trauma that modernity pathologized is being felt, is being heard – but heard as an hysteric's symptom: the panicking stutter of the necessarily impossible, the essential illusion, the impossibility of metalanguage.

To return to Žižek: he is a refusing a providence, structured in terms of a future anterior, which his work (as Lacan's) inscribes. But is he not also saying, through his adoption of Hegel (and Marx), that the history of modernity itself manifest a refusal of such a providence and that that is its pathology?

Rather than ending here, this is where we must begin. For what would it be for Žižek to pass through the transference involved in interpassivity, to accept the symbolization of the Christ event as a symbolization the excess of which constantly saturates the exchange and perpetuation of signs, all the narrativizations and repetitions of that event, with mystery? He informs us that to run with Lacan's *objet petit à*, the object of fantasy, the object causing our desire and at the same time – this is its paradox – posed retroactively by his desire; in 'going through the fantasy' we experience how this fantasy-object (the 'secret') only materializes the void of our desire. (*The Sublime Object of Ideology*, p. 65)

The trauma is the voiding, the kenosis, the diremption of 'our desire' – which must necessarily be, and will be, defended against and yet also must necessarily be, and will be, faced. But will he necessarily encounter the void of desire, why not the plenitude of desire as the illusion of our desiring is caught up in, but not obliterated by, a participation of a divine and cosmic desiring? Žižek continues:

the subject is confronted with some substantial Truth, a secret from which he is excluded, which evades him *ad infinitum* – the inaccessible heart of the Law ... the unattainable last answer ... And the solution ...: the subject has to grasp how, from the very start of the game, the door concealing the secret was meant only for him ... in short, how his external position *vis-à-vis* the Other ... is internal to the Other itself. (*Ibid.*, p. 66)

But why this recognition of our being 'internal to the Other itself' ultimately threatens nihilism and annihilation is that it is an economy still focused on the autonomy of the Cartesian subject, with its demand for substantial Truth; a subject which, with Hegel, is a desiring subject, but the desiring operates according to the logic of modernity's paradigm of 'reflexivity'. Let us think this in another way by presenting a Christian narrative of 'reflexivity'; a theological economy of desire. The account would go something like this: in the beginning there is no beginning because I desire because I am desired. What I have to learn, through the grace of time and the God's providence, is what it is that I desire, what it is that makes me happy. Only desiring the good will make me happy; satisfying my desire on any less than the good will not make me happy. What I come to understand, what God brings me to understand, in and through the spiralling of faith (which is desire seeking understanding), is that I desire God ... because God desires me. Now this too is a reflexivity (a continual confessing, for Augustine, praying, for Anselm, pedagogy, for Aquinas). But the Other is not immanent to the person – as the unconscious or the Real is immanent to Lacan's or Žižek's concept of the person. The person is immanent to the Other in a way that does not absorb the person into the Other (Žižek's void of desire). Rather, the identity of the person is established in recognizing and participating in the reciprocal desire which goes on within the Other. The logic of being able to become a distinct person within the immanence of the Other is the logic of the Trinity and our identification with the person of Christ, in his Trinitarian difference from the Father and the Spirit. It is also the logic of our redemption – being made one with Christ. One's desire is then perfected not voided. One's identity is constituted by the decentring not annihilated.

The significant point is, that Žižek's 'solution' could have a happy ending, a truly therapeutic conclusion. Or, rather, the future of the necessary illusion – which can never remain the same illusion because the retelling of the traumatic event of creation and redemption through the Word continues, so that foreclosure is impossible to conceive – can be a blessed one. If the soteriological story is told differently. But in being told differently modernity can no longer enjoy the symptoms of its own pathology.

Theological implications

With Žižek modernity is no longer just a sociological and historical concept; it is a psychological concept also. And in our present re-enchantment the theological voice may once more be heard. A landscape emerges in which it is no longer 'that the god is too far away but that he is too close, even if it is with his back turned as Hölderlin said' (Lyotard, *Peregrinations*, p. 15).

If the study of theology takes seriously the work of critical theory – if it also takes seriously its own status as a historically specific discourse (and therefore one among a number of cultural sciences) – then its emphases will change. We have pointed out some directions for this change with regard to theology's concern with ethics, history and interpretation. Other changes will follow. The philosophy of religion, for example, will neither be so phallocentric (and ethnocentric) nor so tied to Enlightenment texts (Descartes of *The Meditations*, Hume of *Dialogues Concerning Natural Religion*, Kant of the *Critique of Pure Reason*) and Enlightenment procedures (the law of non-contradiction, the logic of subject–predicate (*S–p*) relations, the law of causality). There is not one monolithic and pure reason, according to critical theorists. Rationalities are local, specific, and culturally and linguistically embedded. There are logics, some of which are incommensurate with each other. Neither is any subject self-identical. Identity issues within contextual differences and therefore is transitory. Critical theories advocate non-identical repetition which stands against the universalism (and essentialism) of Enlightenment notions of the 'identity' of any subject. Systematic theology will examine its own concerns (with the doctrines of God, creation and reconciliation and, therefore, Christology, ecclesiology, anthropology) in conjunction with not only the theological tradition, but also the current analyses of representation, history, ethics and aesthetics.

This would appear to be the direction postmodern theology is moving in – away from the atheologies of Mark C. Taylor and Don Cupitt, away from the 'death of God' theologies of Thomas Altizer and Charles Winquist, and towards a reappraisal and re-examination of the tradition (Augustine, Gregory of Nyssa, Pseudo-Dionysus, Meister Eckhart and Karl Barth, for example) in the light of critical theory.[9] Furthermore, the new gravitas given to desire, experience, theory as practice (rather than theory as over-against practice) and the sociology of knowledge will not only give precedence to the doctrines of pneumatology and ecclesiology, it will require a re-evaluation of the status of sociology of religion, psychology of religion and practical theology within our *curricula*. At present, these subjects are not regarded as important as courses on the Old and New Testaments, doctrine, philosophy and the history of religions.

As a consequence of the value given to personal experience there will also be a greater awareness of gender, of sexual difference, of our cultures as sexuate, diverse and complex fields of power relations. This will be of considerable assistance to feminist theologies which, at the moment, face something of an impasse. Four approaches are discernible. First, there is a retreat to a biological essentialism which cannot accept the maleness of Jesus Christ and therefore moves towards a post-Christianity (Mary Daly, Daphne Hampson). Secondly, there is a continuation of the liberal humanist project in which women are made socially equal and Jesus Christ becomes androgynous (Elizabeth Schüssler Fiorenza and Rosemary Radford Ruether). Thirdly, there is a pragmatics which attempts to rewrite patriarchal texts (Phyllis Trible) or localize the theological discourses of women. Fourthly there is a defence of orthodox Christianity which fights on several fronts (Sarah Coakley, Janet Soskice). Feminist critical theory offers sophisticated tools for discourse analysis and new roots for feminist theology (which should be understood as gendered theology) to explore. The work of Mieke Bal, Cheryl Exum and Mary McClintock Fulkerson points the way.[10] A more penetrating grasp of sexual difference will be paralleled by more profound recognitions of racial difference and the difficulties of representating such difference in a First-World language like English, French or Spanish. The work on ethnography by Certeau, social anthropology by Talal Asad and the subaltern studies group must challenge the way we approach comparative religion.

Overall, the theology of tomorrow, the theology working within a re-enchanted world, will be more aware of the place it occupies in discursive borderlands.[11] Theology is profoundly interdisciplinary – drawing upon the work done in all the other sciences (both natural and cultural). Aquinas recognized this, but the development of Protestant faculties of theology in the eighteenth and nineteenth centuries, and university programmes for the study of theology since, have frequently forgotten it. Theology traverses boundaries, like the cloud no bigger than a human's hand, rising over the sea in the west, bearing rains for a famished land.

Notes and References

Introduction

1. Derrida 'Living on: Border Lines', tr. James Hulbert in *The Derrida Reader: Between the Blinds*, ed. Peggy Kamuf (Hemel Hempstead: Harvester Wheatsheaf, 1991), pp. 256–7.
2. *Inferno*, tr. John D. Sinclair (Oxford: Oxford University Press, 1961), pp. 426–7.
3. See Victor Turner, *The Forest of Symbols* (Ithaca: Cornell University Press, 1967), particularly pp. 93–111; and *The Ritual Process* (London: Routledge & Kegan Paul, 1969).
4. Gerhard Ebeling, *The Study of Theology*, tr. Duane A. Priebe (London: Collins, 1979), p. ix.
5. See Raymond Williams, 'Marxism and Culture', in *Culture and Society 1780–1950* (London: Chatto & Windus, 1960), pp. 265–84.
6. For a translation of this essay and others by Horkheimer (such as his 1939 'The Social Function of Philosophy') see *Critical Theory: Selected Essays*, tr. Matthew J. O'Connell (New York: Herder & Herder, 1972), pp. 188–243. Two books have examined the connections and differences between the critical theory of the Frankfurt School and contemporary (particularly French) critical theory: Peter Dews, *The Logics of Disintegration: Post-Structuralist Thought and the Claims of Critical Theory* (London: Verso, 1987) and David Couzens Hoy and Thomas McCarthy, *Critical Theory* (Oxford: Blackwell, 1994).
7. Karl Mannheim, *Ideology and Utopia: An Introduction to the Sociology of Knowledge* (London: Routledge & Kegan Paul, 1936), pp. 237–80.
8. *The Dialectic of the Enlightenment*, tr. John Cumming (London: Verso, 1979), p. xv. Those aware of the work of the Frankfurt School will no doubt also be aware that their understanding of 'reification' is a considerable development upon Marx's.
9. Couzens Hoy and McCarthy, *Critical Theory*, p. 114.
10. *Language and Silence* (London: Faber & Faber, 1967) p. 340.
11. *Course in General Linguistics*, trs Roy Harris (London: Duckworth, 1983), p. 77.
12. *Ecrits*, tr. Alan Sheridan (London: Tavistock Publications, 1977), p. 147.
13. *The Feud of Language: A History of Structuralist Thought*, tr. Linda Jordan and Thomas Pavel (Oxford: Blackwell, 1989), pp. 4–5.
14. *Structural Anthropology*, 2 vols, tr. Claire Jacobson and Brooke Grundfest Schoepf (London: Penguin Press, 1977), 1, p. 34.
15. *Of Grammatology*, tr. Gayatri Spivak (Baltimore: Johns Hopkins University Press, 1976), pp. 158, 163.
16. 'Introduction' to his edited volume *The States of 'Theory': History, Art and Critical Discourse* (New York: Columbia University Press, 1990), p. 3.
17. See Terry Eagleton's *Literary Theory: An Introduction* (Oxford: Blackwell,

1983) and Stephen D. Moore's *Literary Criticism and the Gospels: The Theoretical Challenge* (New Haven and London: York University Press, 1989).
18. See T.R. Wright, *Theology and Literature* (Oxford: Blackwell, 1988 and the journal *Literature and Theology* (published quarterly by Oxford University Press).

1 Theology and representation

1. *The Crying of Lot 49* (London: Pan, 1979), p. 15.
2. For an introduction to the nature of revelation, see Avery Dulles, *Models of Revelation* (Dublin: Gill & Macmillan, 1983) and, more recently, Keith Ward, *Revelation and Reason* (Oxford: Oxford University Press, 1994).
3. *The Confessions*, tr. Henry Chadwick (Oxford: Oxford University Press, 1991), p. 3.
4. The last three books of the work are a meditation upon and exegesis of the first chapter of Genesis.
5. See Richard Southern, *Saint Anselm: A Portrait in a Landscape* (Cambridge: Cambridge University Press, 1990), pp. 197–227.
6. *Cur Deus Homo* in *St Anselm: Basic Writings*, tr. S.N. Deane (La Salle: Open Court Publishing, 1962), p. 193.
7. For the various forms intertextuality can take, see *Intertextuality: Theories and Practices*, eds Michael Worton and Judith Still (Manchester: Manchester University Press, 1990).
8. *Church Dogmatics*, II. 1, tr. T.H.L. Parker *et al.* (Edinburgh: T. & T. Clark, 1957), p. 236.
9. For a discussion of Aquinas' view of analogy, see David Burrell, *Aquinas: God and Action* (London: Routledge & Kegan Paul, 1979); and *Knowing the Unknowable God* (Notre Dame: University of Notre Dame Press, 1986). See also John F. Wippel, 'Metaphysics', in *The Cambridge Companion to Aquinas*, eds Norman Kretzmann and Eleonore Stump (Cambridge: Cambridge University Press, 1993).
10. *Church Dogmatics*, II. 1, p. 229.
11. For the most recent contributions to this debate see Henry Chavannes, *The Analogy between God and the World in St Thomas Aquinas and Karl Barth* (New York: Vantage Press, 1992); Bruce McCormack, *Karl Barth's Critically Realistic Dialectical Theology: Its Genesis and Development 1909–1936* (Oxford: Oxford University Press, 1995); Graham Ward, *Barth and Derrida: The Language of Theology* (Cambridge: Cambridge University Press, 1995); and Eugene F. Rogers, *Thomas Aquinas and Karl Barth: Sacred Doctrine and the Natural Knowledge of God* (Notre Dame: University of Notre Dame Press, 1995).
12. Sallie McFague, *Metaphorical Theology: Models of God in Religious Language* (London: Student Christian Movement, 1982), p. 13.
13. *Ibid.*, p. 15.
14. *Ibid.*, p. 18.
15. See here the work of David Tracy, most particularly *The Analogical Imagination* (London: Student Christian Movement, 1981), Chapters 3, 4 and 5.

16. *Interpretation Theory: Discourse and the Surplus of Meaning* (Texas: Texas Christian University Press, 1976), p. 64.
17. *Ibid.*, p. 68.
18. *Metaphor and Religious Language* (Oxford: Oxford University Press, 1985), p. 149.
19. *Ibid.*, p. 159.
20. See Timothy Jenkins' review article of her book in *Journal of Literature and Theology*, 3 (2)(July 1989).
21. *Church Dogmatics*, I. 1 (Edinburgh: T. & T. Clark, 1975), p. 11.
22. The interviewer was Catherine David of *Le nouvel observateur*. The interview took place in the Spring of 1983, it appeared on 9 September 1983, tr. David Allison. The translation is available in David Wood and Robert Bernasconi (eds), *Derrida and Différance* (Evanston: Northwestern University Press, 1988) pp. 71–82.
   The selection of texts referred to throughout this section on Derrida are as follows:
   Aporias, tr. Thomas Dutoit (Stanford: Stanford University Press, 1993).
   Limited Inc., tr. Samuel Weber (Evanston: Northwestern University Press, 1988).
   Margins of Philosophy, tr. Alan Bass (Chicago: University of Chicago Press, 1981).
   Mémoires: for Paul de Man, trs Cecile Lindsay *et al.* (New York: Columbia University Press, 1986).
   Of Grammatology, tr. Gayatri Chakravorty Spivak (Baltimore: Johns Hopkins University Press, 1976).
   Of Spirit: Heidegger and the Question, trs Geoff Bennington and Rachel Bowlby (Chicago: Chicago University Press, 1989).
   Psyché (Paris: Galilee, 1987).
   Specters of Marx, tr. Peggy Kamuf (London: Routledge, 1994).
   Speech and Phenomena and Other Essays on Husserl's Theory of Signs, tr. David Allison (Evanston: Northwestern University Press, 1973).
   Truth in Painting, trs. Geoff Bennington and Ian McLeod (Chicago: Chicago University Press, 1987).
   Writing and Difference, tr. Alan Bass (London: Routledge & Kegan Paul, 1978).
   For an excellent bibliography of Derrida's work (and the available English translations) until 1990 see Peggy Kamuf (ed.), *The Derrida Reader: Between the Blinds* (Hemel Hempstead: Harvester Wheatsheaf, 1991).
23. The secondary material on Derrida is already voluminous. Christopher Norris *Derrida* (London: Fontana, 1987) is readable, but needs updating. Rodolphe Gasché, *The Tain on the Mirror: Derrida and the Philosophy of Reflection* (Cambridge, Mass.: Harvard University Press, 1986) is an excellent discussion of Derrida's philosophical genealogy. Irene E. Harvey, *Derrida and the Economy of Difference* (Bloomington: Indiana University Press, 1986) is a thorough discussion of his early work, emphasizing the important place 'economy' has in Derrida's thinking. Two other books can be picked out as significant studies: Henry Staten, *Wittgenstein and Derrida* (Lincoln: University of Nebraska Press, 1984) and Herman Rapaport, *Heidegger and Derrida: Reflections on Time and Language* (Lincoln: Nebraska University Press, 1989).

24. *Course in General Linguistics*, tr. Roy Harris (London: Duckworth, 1983) p. 139.
25. *Ibid.*, p. 69.
26. *Ibid.*, p. 99.
27. *Ibid.*, p. 107.
28. 'Quest for the Essence of Language', in *Language in Literature*, eds Kystyna Pomorska and Stephen Rudy (Cambridge, Mass: Harvard University Press, 1987), pp. 413–27.
29. See R. Jakobson and M. Halle, *Fundamentals of Language* (Le Hague: Mouton, 1975).
30. See *Structural Anthropology* (London: Penguin, 1968), Chapter 2.
31. See Derrida's *Given Time: I, Counterfeit Money*, tr. Peggy Kamuf (Chicago: University of Chicago Press, 1992).
32. See *D'un ton apocalyptique adopté naguère en philosophie* (Paris: Galilee,1983) pp. 63–78; 'On a Newly Arisen Apocalyptic Tone in Philosophy', tr. John Leavy, Jr, in *Raising the Tone of Philosophy: Late Essay by Immanuel Kant, Transformative Critique by Jacques Derrida*, ed. Peter Fenves (Baltimore: Johns Hopkins University Press, 1993).
33. See Robert Bernasconi's article 'The Trace of Levinas in Derrida', in *Derrida and Différance*.
34. See *Philosophical Investigations*, tr. G.E.M. Anscombe (Oxford: Blackwell, 1953), Part II, section xi.
35. His clearest statements about theology and the economy of *différance* come in *Positions*, tr. Alan Bass (Chicago: University of Chicago Press, 1981); *Of Spirit: Heidegger and the Question*, trs Geoffrey Bennington and Rachel Bowlby (Chicago: University of Chicago Press, 1989); 'Comment ne pas parler: Denegations', in *Psyché*, tr. by Ken Frieden for *Languages of the Unsayable: The Play of Negativity in Literature and Literary Theory*, eds Sanford Budick and Wolfgang Iser (New York: Columbia University Press, 1989); *On the Name*, trs David Wood *et al.* (Stanford: Stanford University Press, 1995); 'Foi et Savoir: Les deux sources de la "religion" aux limites de la simple raison', in *La Religion: Seminaire de Capri sous la direction de Jacques Derrida and Gianni Vattimo* (Paris: Seuil, 1996), pp. 9–86.
36. Derrida's concern with the act of mourning and its relationship to the economy of the sign has parallels here with Kristeva's work on abjection and melancholy (see Chapter 3). For Derrida's more extensive analysis of the work of mourning see *Mémoires for Paul de Man* and *Memoirs of the Blind: The Self-Portrait and Other Ruins*, trs Pascale-Anne Brault and Michael Naas (Chicago: Chicago University Press, 1993).
37. For the positive and negative associations of Derrida's '*deconstruction*' see 'Letter to Japanese Friend', trs David Wood and Andrew Benjamin, in *Derrida and Differance*, pp. 1–5.
38. The selection of texts referred to throughout this section on Irigaray are as follows:
An Ethics of Sexual Difference, trs Carolyn Burke and Gillian C. Gill (London: Athlone Press, 1993).
The Irigaray Reader, ed. Margaret Whitford (Oxford: Blackwell, 1991).
Sexes and Genealogies, tr. Gillian C. Gill (New York: Columbia University Press, 1993).

Speculum of the Other Woman, tr. Gillian C. Gill (Ithaca: Cornell University Press, 1985).
Marine Lover: Of Friedrich Nietzche, trs Gillian C. Gill (New York: Columbia University Press, 1991).
This Sex Which Is Not One, trs Catherine Porter and Carolyn Burke (Ithaca: Cornell University Press, 1985).
The best systematic analysis of Irigaray's work at the moment is Margaret Whitford, *Luce Irigaray: Philosophy in the Feminine* (London: Routledge, 1991). The best bibliography of secondary literature, and an excellent collection of articles on Irigaray, can be found in *Engaging with Irigaray*, eds Carolyn Burke, Naomi Schor and Margaret Whitford (New York. Columbia University Press, 1994). A good, brief introduction to the significance of Irigaray's thinking can be found in Toril Moi, *Sexual/Textual Politics: Feminist Literary Theory* (London: Routledge, 1985), pp. 127–49.

39. There are parallel concerns here with representation and the feminine between Irigaray's feminist project and that of her contemporary, Hélène Cixous (see Chapter 4).

40. For an exhaustive, and highly readable, study of psychoanalysis in France and Lacan's work see Elizabeth Roudinesco, *Jacques Lacan & Co., A History of Psychoanalysis in France 1925–1985*, tr. Jeffrey Mehlman (London: Free Association Books, 1990). For the wider philosophical concern with desire, and the impact on France of Hegel's metaphysics of desire, see Judith Butler, *Subjects of Desire*.

41. *Ecrits: A Selection*, p. 147. *Lacan and Theological Discourse*, eds. Edith Wyschogrod, David Crownfield and Carl Raschke (New York: SUNY, 1989) offers several essays in which Lacan's thinking is employed in theological contexts.

42. *Ibid.*, p. 187.

43. *Ibid.*, p. 55.

44. *Ibid.*, p. 7.

45. *Ibid.*, pp. 5–6.

46. *Ibid.*, p. 285.

47. *The Title of the Letter*, trs Francois Raffoul and David Pettigrew (New York: State University of New York Press, 1992), pp. 114–15.

48. 'Women's Exile: Interview with Luce Irigaray', tr. Couze Venn, in Deborah Cameron (ed.), *The Feminist Critique of Language* (London: Routledge, 1990), p. 81.

49. *Ibid.*, p. 82.

50. For the relevant texts and something of the debate involved here, see *Feminine Sexuality: Jacques Lacan and the Ecole freudienne*, eds. Juliet Mitchell and Jacqueline Rose (London: Macmillan, 1982).

51. See her highly accessible *Je, Tu, Nous: Towards a Culture of Difference*, tr. Alison Martin (London: Routledge, 1993).

52. *Op. cit.*, p. 181.

53. See here an interesting account of the relationship between hysteria, mimetic performance and Irigaray's textual strategies in Elizabeth Grosz, *Sexual Subversions: Three French Feminists* (Sydney: Allen & Unwin, 1989), pp. 132–9.

54. See *Thinking the Difference: For a Peaceful Revolution*, tr. Karin Montin

(London: Athlone Press, 1994). Hélène Cixous, in her own exploration of the male and the female, wishes to propose the possibility of a bi-sexual culture. See her essays 'The Laugh of the Medusa', in *New French Feminisms*, eds Elaine Marks and Isabelle de Courtivron (Brighton: Harvester Press, 1981) and 'Tancredi Continues', in her *'Coming to Writing' and Other Essays*, ed. Deborah Jenson (Cambridge, Mass.: Harvard University Press, 1991).

55. See her books *Elemental Passions*, trs Joanna Collie and Judith Still (London: Athlone, 1992) and *Marine Lover: Of Friedrich Nietzsche*, tr. Gillian C. Gill (New York: Columbus University Press, 1991).

56. As an example of a philosopher who has developed Irigaray's suggestions, see Grace Jantzen, *Becoming Divine* (Manchester: Manchester University Press, 1998).

57. Tr. in Graham Ward (ed.), *The Postmodern God* (Oxford: Blackwell, 1997), pp. 198–213.

58. See my article 'Divinity and Sexuality: Luce Irigaray and Christology', *Modern Theology*, 12(2) (April 1996), pp. 221–37.

59. Perhaps a warning here issues from reading the rather forced parallelisms of Serene Jones, 'This God Which Is Not One: Irigaray and Barth on the Divine', in *Transfigurations: Theology and French Feminists*, eds C.W. Maggie Kim, Susan M. St Ville and Susan M. Simonaitis (Minneapolis: Augsburg Fortress, 1993). See the much better essay in the same volume by Elizabeth Grosz, 'Irigaray and the Divine'.

60. The major work by Gayatri Chakravorty Spivak on cultural politics is *In Other Worlds: Essays in Cultural Politics* (London: Routledge, 1988).

61. For Derrida, see *The Other Heading: Reflections upon Today's Europe*, trs Pascale-Anne Brault and Michael B. Naas (Bloomington: Indiana University Press, 1992) and *The Politics of Friendship*, tr. George Collins (London: Verso, 1997). See also Richard Beardsworth, *Derrida and the Political* (London: Routledge, 1996); Morag Patrick, *Derrida, Responsibility and Politics* (Aldershot: Ashgate, 1997); and Drucilla Cornell *et al.*, *Deconstruction and the Possibility of Justice* (London: Routledge, 1992). For Irigaray's more overtly political stance can be seen in her *I Love to You* and *Thinking the Difference*.

62. Spivak's attack on Kristeva's work is pronounced. She doubts her commitment to feminism, she is sceptical of what she sees as Kristeva's Western Eurocentrism, her Catholicism and psychoanalytical position. Some of this critique could be based upon a misreading of Kristeva. We do not have to read Kristeva as advocating a pre-originary space in which 'Christian *agape* can be seen to pre-date *Eros*' (*In Other Worlds*, p. 264). It is interesting that this is how she is perceived by one Marxist feminist.

63. The other contributors to *Subaltern Studies* include the Indian historians Ranajit Guha, Partha Chatterjee and Dipesh Chakrabarty. Their historiographical tools owe much to structuralism.

64. See Edward Said's work on cultural politics in *Orientalism* (London: Routledge, 1978) and *Culture and Imperialism* (London: Chatto & Windus, 1993) has affinities with subaltern studies. See also Homi Bhabha, *The Location of Culture* (London: Routledge, 1995).

65. The selection of texts referred to throughout this section on Judith Butler are as follows:

Bodies that Matter: On the Discursive Limits of 'Sex' (London: Routledge, 1993).

Gender Trouble: Feminism and the Subversion of Identity (London: Routledge, 1990).

The Psychic Life of Power (Stanford: Stanford University Press, 1997).

Subjects of Desire: Hegelian Reflections in Twentieth-Century France (New York: Columbia University Press, 1987).

66. The major voices in queer theory attempt to give queer readings to litera-ture and film. Butler engages in this kind of work in *Bodies that Matter*. Elsewhere there is the work of Eve Kosofsky Sedgwick, *Between Men: English Literature and Male Homosocial Desire* (New York: Columbia University Press, 1985); *Epistemology of the Closet* (Hemel Hempstead: Harvester Wheatsheaf, 1991); and *Tendencies* (Durham: Duke University Press, 1993). Kathryn Bond Stockton's work also belongs here, as does Bruce R. Smith, *Homosexual Desire in Shakespearean England: A Cultural Poetics* (Chicago: University of Chicago Press, 1991) and Michael Roche, *Forbidden Friendships: Homosexual and Male Culture in Renaissance Florence* (Oxford: Oxford University Press, 1996).

67. Louis Althusser was a French, Marxist philosopher who published much of his work in the 1960s. He lived and taught at the *Ecole Normale Supérieure* and had an influence over many of the French poststructuralists who came from there. In 1981 he was committed to hospital for murdering his wife.

68. See here Thomas Laqueur and Cartherine Gallagher (eds.), *The Making of the Modern Body; Sexuality and Society in the Nineteenth Century* (Berkeley: University of Califonia Press, 1987) and Thomas Laqueur, *Making Sex: Body and Gender from the Greeks to Freud* (Cambridge. Mass.: Harvard University Press, 1990).

69. More has been written on Derrida than Irigaray. The most important exam-inations of theological ideas in Derrida's work have been: Susan Handelman, *The Slayers of Moses: The Emergence of Rabbinic Interpretation in Modern Literary Theory* (Albany: State University of New York Press, 1982); Mark C. Taylor, *Deconstructing Theology* (New York: Crossroad Publishing Co., 1982); Kevin Hart, *Trespass of the Sign* (Cambridge: Cambridge University Press, 1989); Harold Coward and Toby Forshay (eds) *Derrida and Negative Theology* (New York: SUNY, 1992); Graham Ward, *Barth, Derrida and the Language of Theology* (Cambridge, Cambridge University Press, 1995); Isolde Andrews, *Deconstructing Barth: A Study of The Complementary Methods of Karl Barth and Jacques Derrida* (Berlin: Peter Laing, 1996); and John D. Caputo, *The Prayer and Tears of Jacques Derrida: Religion without Religion* (Bloomington: Indiana University Press, 1997). A number of other books have employed Derrida's work to develop a theological position – Jean-Luc Marion, *L'Idol et la distance* (Paris: Grasset, 1977) – or draw comparisons between Derrida's work and a particular theologian – Walter Lowe, *Theology and Difference: The Wound of Reason* (Bloomington: Indiana University Press, 1993).

On Irigaray no full-length study of Irigaray's philosophy of religion exists as yet. The nearest to it is the book by Tina Chanter, *Ethics of Eros* (London: Routledge, 1994). Besides the articles in *Transfigurations,* there is Philippa Berry, 'Woman and Space according to Kristeva and Irigaray', in Philippa

Berry and Andrew Wernick (eds.) *Shadow of Spirit* (London: Routledge, 1992). Margaret Whitford devotes pp. 140–7 in her book to outlining the central texts and thesis of Irigaray and the divine. Both Pamela Anderson in *Towards a Feminist Philosophy of Religion* (Oxford: Blackwell, 1997), and Grace Jantzen in *Becoming Divine* employ Irigaray's work for developing their own approach to a feminist philosophy of religion. One should also note Katheryn Bond Stockton, *God Between Their Lips: Desire between Women in Irigaray, Bronte and Eliot* (Stanford: Stanford University Press, 1994) which develops a number of queer readings of Victorian fiction on the basis of examining the divine in Irigaray's work.

70. I have attempted such work in 'Biblical Narrative and the Theology of Metonymy', *Modern Theology*, 7(4) (July 1991); Chapter 11 of *Barth, Derrida and the Language of Theology; 'Allegoria Amoris'*, in Paul Heelas (ed.), *Religion, Modernity and Postmodernity* (Oxford: Blackwell, 1997); 'Kenosis: Death, Discourse and Resurrection', in Luce Gardiner, David Moss, Ben Quash and Graham Ward, *Balthasar at the End of Modernity* (Edinburgh: T. & T. Clark, 1999).

71. *Typography: Mimesis, Philosophy, Politics* (Cambridge, Mass.: Harvard University Press, 1989), p. 118.

72. See Chapter 15 of *L'Idol et la distance* and *La Croisé de visible* (Paris: La Difference, 1991).

73. The term is described in Chapter 15 of *L'Idol et la distance*. The French Catholics working on the relationship between phenomenology and theology include: Jean-Luc Chretien, Michel Henry, Jean-François Courtine and Jean-Yves Lacoste. A collection of essays, *Phénoménologie et Théologie* (Paris: Criterion, 1992) is representative of this current theological enquiry.

74. Two theologians of the twentieth century, in particular, have attempted a theology of sexual difference: Barth and Hans Urs von Balthasar. For a critique of Barth's account see my article 'The Erotics of Redemption: After Karl Barth', *Theology and Sexuality* (March 1997); for a critique of Balthasar's account see Moss and Gardiner's essay in *Balthasar at the End of Modernity*, (n. 70 above).

75. For an attempt at constructing a gay theology in the light of queer theory see Malcolm Edward's contribution to Elizabeth Stuart and Adrian Thatcher (eds.) *Christian Perspectives on Sexuality and Gender* (Leominster: Gracewing, 1996).

76. See my article, 'In the Name of the Father and the Mother', *Literature and Theology*, 8(3) (September 1994).

77. On Patristic theology, see Gillian Cloke, *This Female Man of God: Women and Spiritual Power in the Patristic Age* (London: Routledge, 1995). On women in the Medieval period see the work of Caroline Walker Bynum, particularly *Jesus as Mother: Studies in the Spirituality of the High Middle Ages* (Berkeley: University of California Press, 1982).

78. The closest is perhaps the attempt at a feminist dogmatics (the doctrines of sin and atonement, in particular) in Mary Grey, *Redeeming the Dream: Feminism, Redemption and Christian Tradition* (London: SPCK, 1989). See also the essays by Janet Soskice and Sarah Coakley in Daphne Hampson (ed.), *Swallowing the Fishbone* (London: SPCK, 1997).

79. See here the work of Talal Asad in his *Genealogies of Religion: Discipline and*

Reasons of Power in Christianity and Islam (Baltimore: Johns Hopkins University Press, 1993).

2   Theology and history

1. *The Collected Works of Franz Kafka*, ed. Nahum N. Glatzer (London: Penguin Books, 1988), p. 449.
2. Introduction to Benjamin, *Illuminations*, tr. Harry Zohn (London: Fontana, 1973), p. 23.
3. *Ibid.*, p. 249.
4. *Ibid.*, p. 107 in Benjamin's essay 'The Storyteller'.
5. See J.N.D. Kelly, *Early Christian Creeds* (London: Longman, 1950), p. 149.
6. 'The Time of Revelation', *Church Dogmatics*, I. 2, trs G.T. Thomson and Harold Knight (Edinburgh: T. & T. Clark, 1956), p. 45.
7. See Hans-Georg Gadamer, *Truth and Method* (London: Sheed & Ward, 1975), pp. 153–214.
8. David Friedrich Strauss, *The Life of Jesus Critically Examined*, ed. Peter C. Hodgson (London: Student Christian Movement, 1973), p. 86.
9. *The Quest for the Historical Jesus* tr. W. Montgomery (London: Adam and Charles Black 1954), p. 396.
10. *Christology in the Making: An Inquiry into the Origins of the Doctrine of the Incarnation*, 2nd ed. (London: Student Christian Movement, 1989), p. xiv.
11. See E. Schillebeeckx, *Jesus: An Experiment In Christology*. tr. Hubert Hoskins (London: Collins, 1979). Earlier there had been the publication of W. Pannenberg, *Jesus: God and Man*, tr. Lewis L. Wilkins and Duane A. Priebe (Philadelphia: Westminister Press, 1977). More recently there has been E.P. Sanders, *The Historical Figure of Jesus* (London: Penguin, 1993).
12. *Church Dogmatics.*
13. *The Nature and Destiny of Man*, II, 'Human Destiny' (London: Nisbet & Co., 1943), p. 4.
14. *The Meaning of Revelation* (London: Macmillan, 1942), p. 80.
15. Rudolf Bultmann, *Existence and Faith* (London: Hodder & Stoughton, 1961), p. 284.
16. *Rudolf Bultmann: Interpreting Faith for the Modern Era*, Roger Johnson, ed. (London: Collins, 1987), p. 94.
17. Oscar Cullmann, *Christ and Time*, tr. F.V. Filson (London: Student Christian Movement, 1962).
18. See his essay 'History of Salvation and History', which is a review of Cullmann's thesis, in *Existence and Faith.*
19. *Systematic Theology*, 1, tr. Geoffrey W. Bromiley (Edinburgh: T. & T. Clark, 1991), p. 257.
20. *Ibid.*, p. 253.
21. Quoted in Gadamer, *Truth and Method*, p. 178.
22. David A. Pailin, 'The Supposedly Historical Basis of Theological Understanding', in Sarah Coakley and David A. Pailin (eds.), *The Making and Remaking of Christian Doctrine: Essays in Honour of Maurice Wiles* (Oxford: Oxford University Press, 1993), p. 216.
23. *Op. cit.*, p. 70.
24. This is why recent philosophers of discourse, from Heidegger and Ricoeur

to Derrida, have found it important to write about time, its representation and its trace. Derrida, like Kristeva and Cixous, has increasingly been drawn to examine writing in terms of memory and mourning.

25. *Systematic Theology*, p. 329.
26. The selection of texts referred to throughout this section on Ricoeur are as follows:
    Fallible Man, tr. Charles A. Kelbley (New York: Fordham University Press, 1986).
    Freedom and Nature: The Voluntary and the Involuntary, tr. Erazim V. Kohák (Evanston: Northwestern University Press, 1966).
    History and Truth, tr. Charles A. Kelbley (Evanston: Northwestern University Press, 1965).
    Oneself or Another, tr. Kathleen Blamey (Chicago: University of Chicago Press).
    The Rule of Metaphor, tr. Robert Czerny *et al.* (London: Routledge & Kegan Paul, 1986).
    Symbolism of Evil, tr. Emerson Buchanan (Boston: Beacon Press, 1969).
    Time and Narrative, vols 1, 2 and 3, trs Kathleen McLaughlin and David Pellauer (Chicago: University of Chicago Press, 1984, 1985, 1988).
    Of the many books now available introducing Ricoeur's work, the following are accessible and precise: Don Ihde, *Hermeneutic Phenomenology: The Philosophy of Paul Ricoeur* (Evanston: Northwestern University Press, 1971); David Klemm, *The Hermeneutical Theory of Paul Ricoeur* (London: Associated University Presses, 1983); S.H. Clark, *Paul Ricoeur* (London: Routledge, 1990); and John B. Thompson, *Critical Hermeneutics: A Study in the Thought of Paul Ricoeur and Jürgen Habermas* (Cambridge: Cambridge University Press, 1991).
27. *Nature and Destiny of Man*, II, p. 306.
28. For an analysis of Ricoeur's notion of 'fallibility' see his early essay in philosophical anthropology, *Fallible Man*.
29. Gadamer, *Truth and Method*, p. 180.
30. *Introduction to the Philosophy of History*, tr. G.J. Irwin (London: Weidenfeld & Nicolson, 1961), p. 118.
31. Marc Bloc, *The Historian's Craft* p. 84. For a wider analysis of the work of the Annales School see Jean-Pierre V.M. Herubel (ed.), *Annales Historiography and Theory: A Selective and Annotatied Bibliography* (London: Greenwood, 1994).
32. *Ibid.*, p. 159.
33. See Jean-François Lyotard, *The Postmodern Condition: A Report on Knowledge*, tr. Geoffrey Bennington (Manchester: Manchester University Press, 1984), pp. 18–37.
34. *Metahistory: The Historical Imagination in Nineteenth Century Europe* (Baltimore: Johns Hopkins University Press, 1973), p. ix.
35. See Frye's *The Anatomy of Criticism: Four Essays* (Princeton: Princeton University Press, 1957).
36. *Metahistory*, p. 11.
37. *Ibid.*, p. 14.
38. *Ibid.*, p. 24.
39. *Ibid.*, p. 31.
40. *Ibid.*, p. 430.

41. *Ibid.*, p. 5.
42. *Ibid.*, p. 38.
43. *Ibid.*, p. 160.
44. *Ibid.*, p. 433.
45. See Part III of Gianni Vattimo, *The End of Modernity*, tr. Jon R. Synder (Cambridge: Polity Press, 1988), pp. 113–80.
46. See Ricoeur's discussion of the work of W.B. Gallie in *Time and Narrative*, 1, pp. 149–55.
47. See Chapter 11 of Graham Ward, *Barth, Derrida and the Language of Theology* (Cambridge: Cambridge University Press, 1995), where the various forms of representation in Barth's theology are discussed.
48. L.P. Hartley *The Go-Between* (London: Penguin), p. 7.
49. The selection of texts referred to throughout this section on Foucault are as follows:
    The Archaeology of Knowledge, tr. A.M. Sheridan Smith (London: Tavistock, 1972).
    The Birth of the Clinic: An Archaeology of Medical Perception, tr. Alan Sheridan Smith (New York: Vintage, 1973).
    Discipline and Punish: The Birth of the Prison, tr. Alan Sheridan Smith (London: Penguin Books, 1991).
    History of Sexuality, vols 1, 2 and 3, tr. Robert Hurley (London: Penguin Books, 1981, 1987, 1990).
    Language, Counter-Memory, Practice: Selected Essays and Interviews, trs Donald F. Bouchard and Sherry Simon (Oxford: Blackwell, 1977).
    Madness and Civilization: A History of Insanity in the Age of Reason, tr. R. Howard (London: Tavistock, 1965).
50. For a detailed account of this background, see Gary Gutting, *Michel Foucault's Archaeology of Scientific Reason* (Cambridge: Cambridge University Press, 1989).
51. Quoted by his biographer, David Macey in *The Lives of Michel Foucault* (London: Vintage, 1993), p. 403.
52. *Daybreak*, tr. R.J. Hollingdale (Cambridge: Cambridge University Press, 1982), p. 307.
53. See Jean-François Lyotard's Introduction to his *The Inhuman* and 'The Crisis of Humanism', in Vattimo's *The End of Modernity*.
54. Macey, p. 367.
55. Foucault, 'The Subject and Power', in *Michel Foucault: Beyond Structuralism and Hermeneutics*, eds Hubert L. Dreyfus and Paul Rabinow (Hemel Hempstead: Harvester Wheatsheaf, 1982), p. 216.
56. *Ibid.*, p. 208.
57. This is the argument of Dreyfus and Rabinow. For a different perspective, see Gutting, pp. 271–2 (n. 50 above).
58. The concern for the body, particularly the concern with breaking down the metaphysical dualism of body/mind, was prevalent in France prior to Foucault. The work of Maurice Merleau-Ponty was concerned with developing a phenomenology of the body; the work of Georges Bataille and Maurice Blanchot, similarly, drew attention to the body and its libidinous economies.
59. See Jürgen Habermas, *The Philosophical Discourse of Modernity*, tr. Frederick

Lawrence (Cambridge: Polity Press, 1987), Lectures ix and x; Charles Taylor, 'Interpretation and the Sciences of Man', in *Interpretive Social Science*, eds, Paul Rabinow and William Sullivan (Berkeley: University of California Press, 1979), pp. 3–33.

60. *Power, Truth and Strategy*, tr. W. Suchting, p. 75.
61. The selection of texts referred to in this section on Greenblatt are as follows:
    Learning to Curse: Essays in Early Modern Culture (London: Routledge,1990).
    Marvelous Possessions: The Wonder in the New World (Oxford: Oxford University Press, 1991).
    Renaissance Self-Fashioning: From Marx to Shakespeare (Chicago: Chicago University Press, 1980).
    Shakespearean Negotiations (Oxford: Oxford University Press, 1988).
62. *The Interpretation of Cultures* (New York: Basic Books), p.10.
63. *Ibid.*
64. *Ibid.*, pp. 412–53.
65. *Ibid.*, p. 29.
66. For an excellent, critical account of Geertz's interpretive anthropological method, see Vincent P. Pecora, 'The Limits of Local Knowledge', in H. Aram Veeser (ed.), *The New Historicism* (London: Routledge, 1989), pp. 243–73, and Ricoeur, 'Geertz', in George H. Taylor (ed.), *Lectures on Ideology and Utopia* (New York: Columbia University Press, 1986).
67. See Veeser (ed.), *The New Historicism Reader* (London: Routledge, 1994) pp. 124–41.
68. *Ibid.*, pp. 206–28.
69. See Veeser (ed.), *The New Historicism*, p. 77.
70. *Ibid.*, p. 237.
71. *The Elizabethan World Picture* (London: Chatto & Windus, 1950).
72. *The Great Chain of Being* (New York: Harper Torchbooks, 1965).
73 See Veeser (ed.), *The New Historicism*.
74 See 'The History of the Anecdote: Fiction and Fiction' in Veeser (ed.), *The New Historicism*, pp. 49–76.
75. Interview with Stephen Greenblatt conducted by Jennifer Wallace in *The Times Higher Education Supplement* (1998).
76. Veeser (ed.), *The New Historicism*, p. 61.
77. Interview in *The Times Higher Education Supplement*.
78. *The New Historicism*, p. 272.
79. *The New Historicism*, p. 61.
80. *Ibid.*, p. 31.
81. *The New Historicism Reader*, p. 22.
82. *The New Historicism*, p. 270.
83. See *Violence and the Sacred*, tr. Patrick Gregory (Baltimore: Johns Hopkins University Press, 1977) for an account of generative violence and the victimage or scapegoat mechanism. For a brief introduction to Girard's work, see Girard in Graham Ward (ed.), *The Postmodern God* (Oxford: Blackwell, 1997).
84. Jana Sawicki, *Disciplining Foucault: Feminism, Power and the Body* (London: Routledge, 1991), p. 28.
85. The first three essays can be found in Lewis S. Mudge (ed.), *Essays in Biblical*

Interpretation (London: SPCK, 1981). The fourth essay can be found in *Phénoménologie et théologie: présentation de Jean-François Courtine* (Paris: Criterion, 1992), pp. 15–39.

86. Ricoeur himself has explicitly examined Biblical texts and others have commented upon his exegeses. See *Semeia*, 4 (1975), *Semeia* 13, (1978) and *Semeia*, 19 (1981). See also Anthony C. Thiselton, *New Horizons in Hermeneutics* (London: Harper/Collins, 1992) pp. 334–78. The most thorough analysis is found in Kevin J. Vanhoozer, *Biblical Narrative in the Philosophy of Paul Ricoeur: A Study in Hermeneutics and Theology* (Cambridge: Cambridge University Press, 1990). See also James Fodor, *Christian Hermeneutics: Paul Ricoeur and the Refiguring of Theology* (Oxford: Oxford University Press, 1995).

87. 'Trinity and Revelation', *Modern Theology*, 2(3) (1986), pp. 197–211. See also David Jasper, 'The Limits of Formalism and the Theology of Hope: Ricoeur, Moltmann and Dostoievsky', *Literature and Theology*, 1 (1987), pp. 1–10.

88. Foremost among such feminist readings of the New Testament is Elizabeth Schüssler Fiorenza and her ground-breaking book *In Memory of Her: A Feminist Reconstruction of Christian Origins* (London: Student Christian Movement, 1983).

89. See Talal Asad, *Genealogies of Religion: Discipline and Reasons of Power in Christianity and Islam*.

90. George Lindbeck, *The Nature of Doctrine* (London: SPCK, 1984).

91. For discussions of the relationship between Foucault and religion, see the work of Jeremy Carrette, *Foucault and Religion* (London: Routledge, 1998); and (ed. and sel. by Carrette), *Religion and Culture* by Michel Foucault (Manchester: Manchester University Press, 1999).

92. *Op.cit.*

93. See Kate Cooper, *The Virgin and the Bride: Idealized Womanhood in Late Antiquity* (Cambridge, Mass.: Harvard University Press, 1996); and Carolyn Walker Bynum (ed.), *Gender and Religion: On the Complexity of Symbols* (Boston: Beacon Press, 1986); *Fragments and Redemption: Essays on Gender and the Human Body in Mediaeval Religion* (New York: Zone Books,1991); and *The Resurrection of the Body in Western Christendom* (New York: Columbia University Press, 1995).

94. See Alan Bray, *Homosexuality of Renaissance England* (London: Gay Men's Press, 1982); for the work of Bruce Smith and Michael Roche see Chapter 1, n. 66 (p. 178).

95. See Daniel Boyarin, *Carnal Israel: Reading Sex in Talmudic Culture* (Berkeley: University of California Press, 1993) and *Unheroic Conduct: The Rise of Heterosexuality and the Invention of the Jewish Man* (Berkeley: University of California Press, 1997).

3   Theology and ethics

1. *De doctrina Christiana*, I. iii., tr. D.W. Robertson Jr (New York: Macmillan, 1958), p. 9.

2. See T.K. Abbott, *Kant's Theory of Ethics* (London, 1889), p. 47.

3. *Summa Theologicae*, II.

4. This final failure of appeal by Enlightenment and modern moral theorists at the bar of reason is examined profoundly by Alasdair MacIntyre in this

famous *After Virtue: A Study in Moral Theory* (London: Duckworth, 1981).
5. *Church Dogmatics*, IV. 1, tr. G. Bromiley (Edinburgh: T. & T. Clark, 1956), p. 216.
6. See Willi Marxsen, *New Testament Foundations for a Christian Ethics*, tr. O.C. Dean (Edinburgh: T. & T. Clark, 1993) pp. 243–5.
7. Jack T. Sanders, *Ethics in the New Testament: Change and Development* (Philadelphia: Fortress Press, 1975), p.28.
8. For the thematic approach, see J.L. Houlden, *Ethics of the New Testament* (London: Mowbray, 1973), pp. 70–100.
9. See G.H. Outka, *Agape: An Ethical Analysis* (New Haven: Yale University Press, 1972).
10. *Agape and Eros*, tr. Philip S. Watson (London: SPCK, 1953), p. 227.
11. *Ibid.*, p. 232.
12. *Sermon on the Song of Songs*, 20, 6, tr. William Walsh (Michigan: Cistercian Publications, 1981).
13. Donald MacKinnon, *The Problem of Metaphysics* (Cambridge: Cambridge University Press, 1972), pp. 136–45.
14. See O. Sydney Barr, *The Christian Morality: A Biblical Study of Situational Ethics* (New York: Oxford University Press, 1969).
15. *The Christian Faith*, trs H.R. MacKintosh and J.S. Steward (Edinburgh: T.& T. Clark, 1989), p. 736.
16. The selection of texts referred to throughout this section on Kristeva are as follows:
Black Sun: Depression and Melancholia, tr. Leon Roudiez (New York: Columbia University Press, 1989).
In the Beginning Was Love: Psychoanalysis and Faith, tr. Arthur Goldhammer (New York: Columbia University Press, 1988).
The Kristeva Reader, ed. Toril Moi (Oxford: Blackwell, 1986).
Nations Without Nationalism, tr. Leon Roudiez (New York: Columbia University Press, 1994).
The Powers of Horror: An Essay in Abjection, tr. Leon Roudiez (New York: Columbia University Press, 1982).
Revolution in Poetic Language, tr. Margaret Wailer (New York: Columbia University Press, 1984).
Strangers to Ourselves, tr. Leon Roudiez, (New York: Columbia University Press, 1991).
Tales of Love, tr. Leon Roudiez (New York: Columbia University Press, 1987).
To date there have been two full-length studies of Kristeva's work in English: John Lechte, *Julia Kristeva* (London: Routledge, 1990) and Kelly Oliver, *Reading Kristeva: Unveiling the Double-Bind* (Bloomington: Indiana University Press, 1993). There are also two excellent chapters outlining Kristeva's work in Elizabeth Grosz, *Sexual Subversions* (Sydney: Allen and Unwin, 1989) and a brief guide in Toril Moi, *Sexual/Textual Politics*.
17. See Leslie Hill's informative essay, 'Julia Kristeva: Theorizing the Avant-Garde', in *Abjection, Melancholia and Love: The Work of Julia Kristeva*, eds. John Fletcher and Andrew Benjamin (London: Routledge, 1990), pp. 137–56.
18. For a detailed account of this Hegelian background see Judith P. Butler,

Subjects of Desire: Hegelian Reflections in Twentieth-Century France and, for the French reception of Freud, Elizabeth Roudinesco, *Jacques Lacan & Co: A History of Psychoanalysis in France 1925–1985*, tr. Jeffrey Mehlman (London: Free Association Books, 1990).

19. *Phenomenology of Spirit*, tr. A.V. Miller (Oxford: Oxford University Press, 1977), p. 5.
20. *Ibid.*, p. 82.
21. *Ibid.*, p. 84.
22. *Ibid.*, p. 105.
23. *Ibid.*, p. 105.
24. See Butler, *Subjects of Desire*, pp. 61–99.
25. Both Irigaray and Derrida have also employed the concept of the *'chora'* (or *'khora'*) in their work. For Derrida see his essay 'Khora' in *On the Name*.
26. See Ludwig Feuerbach, *The Essence of Christianity*, tr. George Eliot (New York: Harper, 1957).
27. *Mysterium Paschale*, tr. Aidan Nichols OP (Edinburgh: T. & T. Clark, 1990), p. 79.
28. Oliver, p. 128. More recently, there have been critical examinations of the religious significance of Kristeva's thinking. Oliver would not be alone in criticizing Kristeva's 'religious' ruminations. A number of American feminists have attacked Kristeva (along with Irigaray and Cixous) for their metaphysical musings. See Alice Jardine, *Gynesis: Configurations of Woman and Modernity* (Ithaca: Cornell University Press, 1981). For essays which have explored Kristeva's religious themes more positively see Cleo McNelly Kearns, 'Kristeva and Feminist Theology' and Amy Hollywood, 'Violence and Subjectivity', in *Transfigurations*.
29. *Abjection, Melancholy and Love*, p. 154.
30. Kristeva in an interview quoted by Elizabeth Grosz, *Sexual Subversions*, p. 94.
31. For a summary of the criticism see Oliver, Chapters 5 and 6.
32. See here Simon Critchley, *The Ethics of Deconstruction* (Oxford: Blackwell, 1992) (particularly the last chapter) and Zygmunt Bauman, *Postmodern Ethics* (Oxford: Blackwell, 1993).
33. Critchley, p. 189.
34. Jean Hering had written the first French study of phenomenology, *Phénoménologie et philosophie religieuse* (Paris, 1925). For a biographical account of Levinas' life, see Marie-Anne Lescourret, *Emmanuel Levinas* (Paris: Flammarion, 1993).
35. The selection of texts referred to throughout this section on Emmanuel Levinas are as follows:
    Cartesian Meditations, tr. Dorian Cairns (Le Hague: Martinus Nijhoff, 1960).
    Collected Philosophical Papers, tr. Alphonso Lingis (Dordrecht: Martinus Nijhoff, 1987).
    Le Dieu qui vient a l'idée (Paris: Vrin, 1982).
    Difficult Freedom, tr. Séan Hand (London: Athlone, 1990).
    The Levinas Reader, ed. Séan Hand (Oxford: Blackwell, 1989).
    Otherwise than Being or Beyond Essence, tr. Alphonso Lingis (Le Hague: Martinus Nijhoff, 1981).
    Outside the Subject, tr. Michael B. Smith (London: Athlone, 1993).

Totality and Infinity, tr. A. Lingis (Pittsburgh: Duquesque University, 1969).

36. There are important differences between the thoughts of Buber, Rosenzweig, Marcel and Ebner, not the least of which is the fact the first two thinkers are Jewish and the second two Christian. For an excellent analysis of social ontology is Michael Theunissen, *The Other: Studies in the Social Ontology of Husserl, Heidegger, Sartre and Buber*, tr. Christopher Macann (Cambridge, Mass: MIT Press, 1986). See also Graham Ward's book, *Barth, Derrida and the Language of Theology* (Cambridge: Cambridge University Press, 1995) particularly Chapters 3 and 6.

37. *1 and Thou*, tr. Ronald Gregor Smith (Edinburgh: T. & T. Clark, 1958), pp. 18–19.

38. *Ibid.*, p. 149.

39. *Ibid.*, p. 143.

40. *Barth, Derrida and the Language of Theology*, Chapter 6.

41. See Derrida's two important essays on Levinas: 'Violence and Metaphysics', in *Writing and Difference* and 'At this Very Moment in this Work Here I am', tr. Simon Critchley in *Re-Reading Levinas*, eds Robert Bernasconi and Simon Critchley (London: Athlone, 1991), pp. 11–48. Besides Simon Critchley's *The Ethics of Deconstruction*, there have been three volumes of critical essays on Levinas' work: *Re-Reading Levinas; The Provocation of Levinas: Rethinking the Other*, eds Robert Bernasconi and David Wood (London: Routledge, 1988); and *Face to Face with Levinas*, ed. R. Cohen (Albany: State University of New York Press, 1986). There is also important discussion of Levinas' work in Bauman, *Postmodern Ethics*, and Paul Ricoeur's *Oneself as Another*, tr. Kathleen Blamey (Chicago: University of Chicago Press, 1992). John Llewellyn's excellent full-length study of Levinas' work, *The Genealogy of Ethics* (London: Routledge, 1995) also contains a bibliographical list of all the other major studies and Levinas.

42. For a 'historical' appreciation of the way 'trace' is used by Levinas and then by Derrida, see Robert Bernasconi's essay 'The Trace of Levinas in Derrida', in David Wood and Robert Bernasconi (eds), *Derrida and Différance* (Evanston: Northwestern University Press, 1988).

43. See here Levinas, *Time and the Other*, tr. R. Cohen (Pittsburg: Duquesne University Press, 1987), where he argues for a future which is constituted by and as the other. Desire creates time.

44. See my essay, 'The Revelation of the Holy Other as the Wholly Other', *Modern Theology*, 9(2) (April 1993), pp. 159–80.

45. See his essays, 'Humanism and Anarchy', in *Collected Philosophical Papers* and 'The Rights of Man and the Rights of the Other', in *Outside the Subject*.

46. See here the final chapter of Kristeva's *In the Beginning Was Love*, 'Children and Adults'.

47. The selection of texts referred to throughout this section on Jean-Luc Nancy are as follows:
The Birth to Presence, tr. Brian Holmes *et al.* (Stanford: Stanford University Press, 1993).
'Corpus', in *Thinking Bodies*, eds Juliet Flower *et al.* (Stanford: Stanford University Press, 1994).
The Experience of Freedom, tr. Bridget McDonald (Stanford: Stanford University Press, 1993).

'Finite History', in David Carroll (ed.), *The States of 'Theory': History, Art and Critical Discourse*.(New York: Columbia University Press, 1990). *The Inoperative Community*, tr. Peter Connor *et al.* (Minneapolis: University of Minnesota Press, 1991). *La partage des voix* (Paris: Seuil, 1982). *Une pensée finie* (Paris: Seuil, 1990). To date, besides brief essays comparing Nancy to Derrida *et al.* (see Critchley) there are only two studies in English on Nancy's work: a special edition of *Paragraph*, 16(2) (July 1995) and Simon Sparks *et al.* (eds.), *The Sense of Philosophy: On Jean-Luc Nancy* (London: Routledge, 1997).

48. See 'The Ontological Scandal: Transcorporeality', in Grace Jantzen (ed.), Special Edition of *The John Rylands Bulletin* (Spring 1999).

49. See *Ethics*, tr. Samuel Shirley (Indianapolis: Hachett Publishing, 1992), particularly Part I, 'Concerning God'.

50. See Spivak's discussion of 'Corpus', in *Thinking Bodies*.

51. See Alphonso Lingis' contribution to Sparks, *The Sense of Philosophy: On Jean-Luc Nancy*.

52. See Elizabeth Anscombe, *Intention* (Oxford: Blackwell, 1957).

53. Alasdair MacIntyre, *After Virtue: a Study in Moral Theory* (London: Duckworth, 1981), p. 263.

54. Martha Nussbaum, *The Fragility of Goodness: Luck and Ethics in Greek Tragedy and Philosophy* (Cambridge: Cambridge University Press, 1986); *Love's Knowledge: Essays in Philosophy and Literature* (Oxford: Oxford University Press, 1990); and *The Therapy of Desire: Theory and Practice in Hellenistic Ethics* (Princeton: Princeton University Press, 1994).

55. Zygmunt Bauman, *Intimations of Postmodernity* (London: Routledge, 1992) and *Postmodern Ethics* (Oxford: Blackwell, 1993).

56. Alasdair MacIntyre, *Whose Justice? Which Rationality?* (London: Duckworth, 1989).

57. See G. Sayre-MaCord (ed.), *Essays on Moral Realism* (Ithaca: Cornell University Press, 1988), particularly the essays by Bernard Williams and John McDowell.

58. See Bauman, *Postmodern Ethics*, pp. 33–6.

59. This reappraisal of the experience of transcendence becomes more important in the next section, concerning aesthetics and the sublime.

60. See John Milbank, The Face of Identity', in *The Word Made Strange* (Oxford: Blackwell, 1997) and Augustine's *De Trinitate*.

61. This is the central argument in Irigaray's book *An Ethics of Sexual Difference*. The analyses of Irigaray's and Kristeva's work might well have appeared the other way about in this book – Kristeva's notions of representation joining Derrida's, Irigaray's notions of love and ethics joining Levinas'. In fact, Irigaray has seen her work as answering Levinas' (for women). See her essays 'Fecundity of the Caress', tr. Carolyn Burke in R. Cohen (ed.), *Face to Face with Levinas* and 'Questions to Emmanuel Levinas', tr. Margaret Whitford, *The Irigaray Reader*. Such an order was decided against on the grounds that Irigaray also answers Derrida (for women).

62. For an examination of theological ethics as narrative ethics, see the work of Stanley Hauerwas and Gerard Loughlin, *Telling God's Story* (Cambridge: Cambridge University Press, 1995). The relationship between ethics and

story is explored in the work of Stanley Cavell, Martha C. Nussbaum and, more recently, Paul Ricoeur.

63. For the French work on phenomenology and theology see p.179 n. 73. Jean-Luc Marion, *Réduction et donation: recherches sur Husserl, Heidegger et la phénoménologie* (Paris: Presses Universitaires de France, 1989) and his essay 'Metaphysics & Phenomenology: A Summary for Theologians' in Graham Wood (ed.), *The Postmodern God*. See also Jean-Yves Lacoste, *Expérience et Absolu: questions disputées sur l'humanité de l'homme* (Paris: Presses Universitaires de France, 1994).

64. Derrida, 'At this Very Moment in this Work Here I am', *Re-reading Levinas*, pp. 44–5.

65. *The Last Years: Journals, 1853–1855*, tr. Ronald Gregor Smith (London: Collins, 1968), p. 186.

66. See here Robert P. Scharlemann's very interesting and pertinent book, *The Reason of Following: Christology and the Ecstatic I* (Chicago: University of Chicago Press, 1991); also the work of Judith Butler (in Chapter 1).

67. Quoted by Robert Bretall, in *A Kierkegaard Anthology* (Princeton: Princeton University Press, 1951), p. 19.

4 Theology and aesthetics: religious experience and the textual sublime

1. *The Confessions*, tr. Henry Chadwick (Oxford: Oxford University Press, 1991), pp. 152–3.

2. The first 10 of Julian of Norwich's revelations progress through the Passion narrative, from the crowning of Christ with thorns in the first revelation to the riven heart of Christ on the Cross in Revelation 10. Chapter 17 meditates upon the words of Christ on the Cross, 'I thirst'. These words are understood as expressing the more general condition of a suffering that nothing can alleviate. The pain of this suffering is then internalized by Julian in the move towards a self-transcendence in which she is brought to realize that she is suffering because she loves Christ more than she loves herself. This internalization – opening ourselves to be affected – is part of a purification process, a kenotic act of love which leads to new insights and new experiences of grace.

3. *Grace Abounding to the Chief of Sinners*, ed. Roger Sharrock (Oxford: Oxford University Press, 1960), p. 30. See also Graham Ward's article, 'To be a Reader: Bunyan's Struggle with the Language of Scripture in *Grace Abounding to the Chief of Sinners*', *Literature and Theology*, 4(1) (March 1990), pp. 29–49.

4. *Inferno*, tr. John D. Sinclair (Oxford: Oxford University Press, 1971), p. 79.

5. 'Love's Knowledge', in her collection of essays *Love's Knowledge: Essays on Philosophy and Literature* (New York: Oxford University Press. 1992).

6. Stanza I of *The Flame of Living Love*, tr. E. Allison Peers (New York: Doubleday & Company, 1962), p. 41.

7. The most famous text being *The Future of an Illusion*, tr. J. Strachey, in Penguin Freud Library, 12 (London: Penguin Books, 1985).

8. See *Easter in Ordinary: Reflections on Human Experience and the Knowledge of God* (London: SCM, 1988).

9. Keith Yandell, *The Epistemology of Religious Experience* (Cambridge: Cambridge University Press, 1993).
10. See here the two important volumes edited by Stephen Katz, *Mysticism and Philosophical Analysis* (London: Sheldon Press, 1978); *Mysticism and Language* (Oxford: Oxford University Press, 1992).
11. This comparative method was made famous by William James in his *Varieties of Religious Experience* (London: Penguin Books, 1982). More recently, an analytic approach to such a comparison has been argued for by Nelson Pike in *Mystic Union: An Essay in the Phenomenology of Mysticism* (Ithaca: Cornell University Press, 1992).
12. See particularly Heidegger's essays collected in *Poetry, Language, Thought*, tr. Albert Hofstadter (New York: Harper & Row, 1971) and *On the Way to Language*, tr. Peter D. Hertz (New York: Harper & Row, 1971).
13. A critical edition of the most important of these essays is available as *The Merleau-Ponty Aesthetics Reader: Philosophy and Painting*, ed. Galen Johnson (Evanston: Northwestern University Press, 1993).
14. Wolfgang Iser's two most influential books are *The Implied Reader: Patterns of Communication in Prose Fiction from Bunyan to Beckett* (Baltimore: Johns Hopkins University Press, 1974) *The Act of Reading: A Theory of Aesthetic Response* (Baltimore: Johns Hopkins University Press, 1978).

    Hans Robert Jauss's important works in English are: *Aesthetic Experience and Literary Hermeneutics*, tr. Michael Shaw (Minneapolis: University of Minnesota Press, 1982) and *Towards an Aesthetic of Reception*, tr. Timothy Bahti (Minneapolis: University of Minnesota Press, 1982).
15. *The Idea of the Holy*, tr. John W. Harvey (Oxford: Oxford University Press, 1923), p. 65.
16. *On Religion: Speeches to its Cultured Despisers*, tr. Richard Crouter (Cambridge: Cambridge University Press, 1988), p. 133.
17. *Ibid.*, p. 160.
18. *The Christian Faith*, trs and eds. H.R. Mackintosh and J.S. Stewart (Edinburgh: T. & T. Clark, 1989), p. 23.
19. *Ibid.*, p. 27.
20. *The Pleasure of the Text*, tr. Richard Miller (Oxford: Blackwell, 1990), p. 61.
21. See 'The crucified one: epistle to the last christians' in *Marine Lover: Of Friedrich Nietzsche*, where the textual refrain throughout is *et incarnatus est* and Irigaray asks, 'What does it mean that the word is made flesh?' (p. 179).
22. Barthes, *The Pleasure of the Text*, p. 64.
23. The selection of texts referred to throughout this section on Stanley Fish are as follows:
    Is There A Text in This Class? The Authority of Interpretative Communities (Cambridge, Mass.: Harvard University Press, 1980).
    Doing What Comes Naturally (Durham, NC: Duke University Press, 1989).
    Self-Consuming Artefacts: The Experience of Seventeenth Century Literature (Berkeley: University of California Press, 1972).
    Surprised by Sin: The Reader in Paradise Lost (Basingstoke: Macmillan, 1967).
    There's No Such Thing As Free Speech ... And It's A Good Thing Too (Oxford: Oxford University Press, 1994).
24. *The Verbal Icon* (Lexington: University of Kentucky Press, 1954), p. 21.
25. Barthes, *The Pleasure of the Text*, p. 31.

26. *Ibid.*, p. 61.
27. *Diacritics* (June 1980), p. 72.
28. For a more sympathetic, though still critical, reading of Iser's work see Ricoeur, *Time and Narrative*, 3, pp. 166–79.
29. Both Geertz and Fish are indebted to Wittgenstein on language-games.
30. See *The Nature of Doctrine*. In that book Lindbeck argues for theology as an intratextual description. A religion is to be understood only from within its own cultural–linguistic practices. Religion is therefore a semiotic system. 'Intratextual theology redescribes reality within the scriptural framework rather than translating Scripture into extrascriptural categories' (p. 118). This provides the basis for Lindbeck's post-liberalism. Lindbeck has also been highly influenced by Wittgenstein and Geertz. His theological position gives precedence to ecclesiology.
31. See *There's No Such Thing As Free Speech ... And It's A Good Thing Too*, pp. 290–1 for an interesting, if somewhat evasive, comparison between Fish and Derrida on rhetoric, as Fish perceives it.
32. The selection of texts referred to throughout this section on Jean-François Lyotard are as follows:
    The Differend, tr. George Van Den Abeele (Manchester: Manchester University Press, 1988).
    Discours, figure (Paris: Klinksieck, 1971).
    The Inhuman, trs Geoffrey Bennington and Rachel Bowlby (Cambridge: Polity Press, 1991).
    Lessons on the Analytic of the Sublime, tr. Elizabeth Rottenberg (Stanford: Stanford University Press, 1994).
    Libidinal Economy, tr. Iain Hamilton Grant (London: Athlone Press, 1993).
    Peregrinations: Law, Form, Event (New York: Columbia University Press, 1988).
    The Postmodern Condition: A Report on Knowledge, trs Geoffrey Bennington and Brian Massumi (Manchester: Manchester University Press, 1984).
    There have been, to date, two complete studies in English of Lyotard's work Geoffrey Bennington, *Lyotard: Writing the Event* (Manchester: Manchester University Press, 1988); Bill Readings, *Introducing Lyotard: Art and Politics* (London: Routledge, 1991). There is also a selection of essays on aspects of Lyotard's work, ed. Andrew Benjamin, *Judging Lyotard* (London: Routledge, 1992). David Carroll, *Paraesthetics* (New York: Methuen, 1987) has an incisive account of Lyotard's work on desire, the figure and the sublime. It is set alongside an examination of aesthetics in Foucault and Derrida. Unfortunately, it was published before Lyotard's extensive treatment of Kant's 'Analytic of the Sublime'. The best bibliography of work by and on Lyotard can be found appended to Lyotard's critical theory lectures for the Irvine Institute, *Peregrinations*, pp. 77–112.
33. *Que Peindre? Adami, Arakawa, Buren* (Paris: Editions de la Différence, 1987), 1, p. 11.
34. See *Beiträge zur Philosophie Vom Ereignis*, Band 65, Gesamtausgabe (Frankfurt: Klostermann, 1989).
35. Less prominent, though in the background, is the work of Edmund Burke and Pierre Boileau.
36. For a different account, in which the hierarchical superiority of reason

subsumes the imagination, see Paul Crowther, *The Kantian Sublime: From Morality to Art* (Oxford: Oxford University Press, 1989), pp. 100–3. Lyotard relates what he understands as a fundamental tension between the faculties to his own concept of the 'differend'. See n. 45 below. For a critical acount of the modern investment in the sublime, see John Milbank, 'Sublimity: The Modern Transcendent' in Paul Heelas (ed.), *Religion, Modernity and Postmodernity.*

37. See Kant's famous table of the faculties in their systemic unity and exactly where the feelings of pleasure and pain reside in *The Critique of Judgement,* tr. James Creed Meredith (Oxford: Oxford University Press, 1952), p. 39.

38. *The Critique of Judgement,* Part I, p. 120.

39. *Ibid.,* Part II, p. 159.

40. For recent evaluations see Paul Guyer, *Kant and the Claims of Taste* (Cambridge, Mass.: Harvard University Press, 1979); Paul de Man, 'Phenomenality and Materiality in Kant', in Gary Shapiro and Alan Sica (eds), *Hermeneutics: Questions and Prospects* (Amherst: University of Massachusetts Press, 1984); Mary McCloskey, *Kant's Aesthetics* (London: Macmillan, 1986); Paul Crowther, *The Kantian Sublime.*

41. This philosophical move towards aesthetics is also evident in Derrida (*Truth in Painting* and *Memoirs of the Blind*) and Kristeva's analysis in *Black Sun: Depression and Melancholia* of paintings by Hans Holbein the Younger and Jackson Pollock.

42. Earlier, Lyotard's work was governed by an analysis of desire. See his *Libidinal Economy,* tr. Iain Hamilton Grant (London: Athlone Press, 1993). For a critique of this analysis see Judith Butler, *Subjects of Desire: Hegelian Reflections on Twentieth-Century France.*

43. See the work of Jean-Luc Marion on donation and the gift here, particularly *Réduction et donation* (Paris: PUF, 1989), 'Le don d'une présence', in *Prolégomènes à la charité* (Paris: La Différence, 1986) and 'Ce que cela donne' in *La Croisée du visible* (Paris: La Différence, 1991). Lyotard, like Marion, is attempting a phenomenological reduction. See also John Milbank's essay, 'Can the Gift be Given? Prolegomena to a Future Trinitarian Metaphysic', in *Modern Theology,* 11(1) (January 1995).

44. See *Discours, figure* (Paris: Klinksieck, 1971).

45. The differend is used here to describe the complex relations between the moral and the aesthetic in the experience of the sublime. Unlike those readings of Kant which emphasize the moral as the final end of the aesthetic (both the beautiful and the sublime), Lyotard wishes to focus on the heterogeneity of the aesthetic and practical reasoning. One threatens the existence of the other. The experience of the sublime encapsulates this tension. (See the final paragraph of *Lessons on the Analytic of the Sublime.*) It constitutes what earlier he termed a 'tensor' – an intensity which necessitates and exceeds signification and unitary meaning.

46. *The Critique of Judgement,* Part I, p. 155.

47. The selection of texts referred to in this section by Hélène Cixous are as follows:

'Coming to Writing' and other essays, ed. Deborah Jenson (Cambridge, Mass.: Harvard University Press, 1991).

'The Laugh of the Medusa', trs Keith and Paula Cohen, in Elaine Marks and

Isabelle Courtivron (eds.), *New French Feminisms* (Brighton: Harvester Press, 1981) pp. 245–64.
Reading with Clarice Lispector, tr. Verna Andermatt Conley (Hemel Hempstead: Harvester, 1990).
Three Steps on the Ladder of Writing, trs Sarah Cornell and Susan Sellers (New York: Columbia University Press, 1993).
The only full-length study of Cixous to date is Verna Andermatt Conley, *Hélène Cixous* (Hemel Hempstead: Harvester, 1992). There is also a collection of essays edited by Helen Wilcox, Keith McWatters, Ann Thompson and Linda R. Williams, *The Body and the Text: Hélène Cixous, Reading and Teaching* (Hemel Hempstead: Harvester, 1990).Toril Moi has a good introductory chapter to Cixous' work and *Écriture féminine* in *Sexual/Textual Politics* (London, Routledge, 1985), pp. 102–26.

48. See Nelson Pike, *Mystic Onion*, Chapter 3, on spiritual perceptions.
49. The selection of texts referred to in this section on Michel de Certeau are as follows:
    The Capture of Speech, tr. Tom Conley (Minneapolis: University of Minnesota Press, 1997).
    Culture in the Plural, tr. Tom Conley (Minneapolis: University of Minnesota Press, 1997).
    La faiblesse de croire, ed. Luce Giard (Paris: Seuil, 1987).
    La Possession de Loudon (Paris: Gallimard, 1970).
    'How is Christianity Thinkable Today?', in Graham Ward (ed.), *The Postmodern God* (Oxford: Blackwell, 1997), pp. 142–55.
    The Mystic Fable, 1: *The Sixteenth and Seventeenth Centuries*, tr. Michael B. Smith (Chicago: University of Chicago Press, 1992).
    The Practice of Everyday Life, tr. Steven Rendall (Berkeley: University of California Press, 1984).
    The Writing of History, tr. Tom Conley (New York: Columbia University Press, 1988).
    'White Ecstasy', trs Frederick Christian Bauersmidt and Catriona Hanley, in Ward (ed.), *The Postmodern God*, pp. 155–8.
    To date, in English there has only been one full-length study of Michel de Certeau's work: Jeremy Ahearne, *Michel de Certeau: Interpretation and its Other* (Oxford: Polity Press, 1995). There have been two special editions of journals dedicated to his work *Social Semiotics* 6(1) (1996), ed. Ian Buchanan and *New Blackfriars* 77(909) (1996) ed. Graham Ward. A special edition of *South Atlantic Quarterly* is publishing the proceedings from the first International Conference on Certeau, some time in 1999. There is also Graham Ward (ed.), *The Certeau Reader* (Oxford: Blackwell, 1999), with introductions to various aspects of Certeau's work by leading scholars.
50. Certeau plays with the derivation of the term for both 'credit' and 'credence' – *credo*. To believe is to be caught up in the continual exchange of signs, representation. Revelation, the gift, for Derrida is always compromised because of this necessary involvement in exchange. But this seems to suggest, as much of Derrida's work suggests, an immediacy that we lack. Certeau explores another direction – mediation as revelatory, as not only caught up in the exchange of signs but making that exchange of signs possible and salvific (that is, of eschatological significance). See also Jean

Baudrillard, *Symbolic Exchange and Death* tr. Iain Hamilton Grant (London: Sage Publications, 1993).

51. For Milbank see the 'Polis' section of *The Word Made Strange* (Oxford: Blackwell, 1997); for Loughlin see *Telling God's Story* (Cambridge: Cambridge University Press, 1995).
52. *The Göttingen Dogmatics: Instruction in the Christian Religion*, 1, tr. Geoffrey Bromiley (Michigan: Eerdmans, 1991), p. 150.
53. *Ibid.*, p. 150.

Conclusion

1. *Postmodern Ethics*, p. 33. See also his introduction to Baudrillard, *Intimations of Postmodernity* (London: Routledge, 1992), pp. vii–xxviii.
2. His two major books on Descartes are: *Sur l'ontologie grise de Descartes* (Paris: Vrin, 1975) and *Sur la théologie blanche de Descartes* (Paris: Vrin, 1981).
3. Bruno Latour, *We Have Never Been Modern At All*, tr. Catherine Porter (London: Harvester Wheatsheaf, 1993).
4. See Derek Parfit, *Reason and Persons* (Oxford: Clarendon, 1984) and John McDowell, *Mind and World* (Cambridge Mass.: Harvard University Press, 1994).
5. See the work of: Edith Wyschogrod, *Spirit in Ashes: Hegel, Heidegger and Man-Made Mass Death* (New Haven: Yale University Press, 1985); Catherine Pickstock, *After Writing: The Liturgical Consummation of Philosophy* (Oxford: Blackwell, 1997); Grace Jantzen, *Becoming Divine*; and Graham Ward *et al. Balthasar at the End of Modernity*.
6. Interview in *The Times Higher Educational Supplement* (November 1998).
7. The selection of texts referred to in this section on Žižek are as follows:
   The Sublime Object of Ideology (London: Verso, 1989).
   The Plague of Fantasies (London: Verso, 1997).
   'How to Give a Body to a Deadlock', in *Thinking Bodies*, pp. 60–77.
8. *Eros in Mourning: Homer to Lacan* (Baltimore: Johns Hopkins University Press, 1995).
9. See John Milbank, Catherine Pickstock and Graham Ward (eds), *Radical Orthodoxy* (London: Routledge, 1998).
10. For Mieke Bal, see *Particularly Lethal Love: Feminist Literary Readings of Biblical Love Stories* (Bloomington: Indiana University Press, 1987); for Cheryl Exum, see *Tragedy and Biblical Narrative: Arrows of the Almighty* (Cambridge: Cambridge University Press, 1992) and *Fragmented Women: Feminist (Sub)versions of Biblical Narrative* (Sheffield: JSOT, 1993); for Mary McClintock Fulkerson, see *Changing the Subject: Women's Discourses and Feminist Theology* (Minneapolis: Fortress Press, 1994).
11. The work of Donald Mackinnon remains, yet again, relevant here. See *The Borderlands of Theology* (London: Lutterworth Press, 1968).

Index

200 *Index*